THE EARLY IONIANS

G. L. HUXLEY

THE
EARLY IONIANS

NEW YORK

HUMANITIES PRESS

1966

FIRST PUBLISHED
IN THE UNITED STATES IN 1966
BY
HUMANITIES PRESS INC.
303 PARK AVENUE SOUTH
NEW YORK, N.Y. 10010

LIBRARY OF CONGRESS CATALOG CARD NUMBER
66–19549

Printed in Great Britain

TO
NICOLAS COLDSTREAM

ACKNOWLEDGEMENTS

Mr Russell Meiggs read a draft of this book and made many helpful suggestions; Mr E. D. Phillips discussed several Ionian problems with me; and my wife patiently listened to a reading of the manuscript. I thank them all. The maps were drawn by Miss E. Duncan of the Department of Geography in the Queen's University, Belfast: they are based, though with some changes, on Kiepert's and preserve his spelling of place names.

CONTENTS

PREFACE

THIS BOOK IS ADDRESSED TO ANYONE WHO HAPPENS TO BE INTERESTED in the origins of classical Hellenic civilisation. I am more concerned here with political and intellectual history than with antiquities, and give, for example, more attention to poets and statesmen than to pots and statuary, but relevant archaeological evidence is not neglected.

In two respects the book may be thought quaint and old-fashioned: firstly, I give more emphasis to the thoughts and actions of great men, who are the true makers of history, than to social institutions or economic trends; and secondly, I treat the statements of all ancient writers with reverence, which must not be taken for credulity. I hold that it is bad practice to reject statements in late sources simply because they are late, and consider that scholars such as Callimachus and Apollodorus and those who made use of their work deserve a fair hearing, for they were not less intelligent, and were usually better informed, than ourselves. Only grim pedants will object to the inclusion, in the Herodotean manner, of a few amusing stories which, even if not true, help to show how the eastern Greeks lived when the Hellenic world was still young; and I hope that this book will enable its readers to share some of the happiness I have experienced in thinking about men and women whose wisdom and brilliance still instruct and delight, even after the passing of two and a half thousand years or more.

November 1965

CHAPTER I

The Forerunners of the Ionians

THE AIM OF THIS STUDY IS TO GIVE A CONCISE ACCOUNT OF IONIAN political and intellectual history from the end of the Mycenaean age to the defeat of the great revolt of the eastern Greeks from Persian domination at the beginning of the fifth century BC. We shall examine the history of the Asiatic Ionians, of the Ionians of the Aegean islands, and of the Aeolians of Lesbos and northwestern Asia Minor. The literary history of the period will also be studied, and we shall discuss the rise of natural philosophy and historical writing. Our method will be to fit together the fragmentary traditions, supplementing and checking them where possible with the material evidence from excavations and archaeological surveys. This is a valid procedure, but, apart from a few inscriptions, some allusions to Greeks in oriental records, and the fragments of early Greek poetry, none of the written evidence is contemporary with the events we shall be describing. Nor, for much of our period, is the archaeological record a very full one though it is much fuller now than it was a generation ago. So long as the limitations of the evidence are borne constantly in mind, there will be no temptation to fill gaps with vain conjecture, or to present hypotheses as though they were ascertained facts.

In the first half of the second millennium BC Minoan mariners from Crete established trading posts and founded colonies in many parts of the Aegean world and the Levant. Their activities in the Cycladic islands and on the western coast of Asia Minor are attested by many finds of Minoan pottery and by evidence of settlement by Cretans. By 1550 BC, in the Cyclades, pottery of Minoan type was in use in Delos[1] and in Ceos.[2] Further south Cretans had ties with Melos[3] and with Thera,[4] and in the eastern Aegean there were Minoan settlements at Miletus[5] on the Asiatic mainland, at Ialysus in Rhodes, and in Cos and Carpathus.[6] Minoan pottery made about 1600 BC has also been found in the island of Samos[7] and at Iasos[8] near Miletus.

The Greeks recalled the maritime ventures of the Cretans in the legends of the thalassocracy of Minos king of Knossos, whose navy suppressed piracy.[9] Minos, it was remembered, had kept Attica tributary to Crete;[10] he had visited the island of Ceos with his navy and left half his followers there before returning to Knossos;[11] and his brother Sarpedon had founded a colony at Miletus.[12] Cretans are also said to have settled in Samos.[13] Oenopion, a Cretan, was thought to have led settlers to Chios,[14] and legend recalled Cretan settlement on the Asiatic mainland opposite to that island;[15] but Minoan remains have yet to be found in Chios and nearby. In the Cyclades the places called Minoa in Amorgos and in Siphnos,[16] together with the spring named Minoe in Delos,[17] reminded the Greeks of the ancient naval power of the royal dynasty of Knossos.

In the fifteenth century BC Cretan rule declined and finally collapsed during the rise to dominance in the Aegean world of the kings of Mycenae, whose interests oversea, as the exports of Mycenaean pottery show, had been steadily increasing in the period from 1550 to 1400 BC. Mycenaean pottery of the fourteenth and thirteenth centuries BC has been found in many of the Cycladic islands, notably in Naxos,[18] and it is obvious that Mycenaean influence was strong here at that time. Whether this influence indicates political control is less certain. According to Homer the Cyclades were not part of the dominions over which Agamemnon of Mycenae was overlord, and it is possible that, after the fall of the Minoan thalassocracy, the Carians of the islands were independent of the Mycenaeans of the Greek mainland. We hear of a king of Delos, Anios, who was said to have been friendly with both sides at the time of the Trojan war.[19]

In western Asia Minor there is plenty of evidence for Mycenaean influence from the fourteenth to the twelfth century. Mycenaean pottery has been found at Troy, to which we return later; and there have been sporadic finds in the Aeolis and in the island of Lesbos south of Troy.[20] Mycenaean wares were imported to Chios[21] and to Samos,[22] and there have been finds of Mycenaean wares at Clazomenae,[23] Ephesus[24] and inland at Sardis.[25] In the southwest of Asia Minor, Mycenaean pottery reached the neighbourhood of Halicarnassus,[26] Mylasa in Caria[27] and Telmessus in Lycia,[28] but none of these sporadic finds suggests the presence of colonists from mainland Greece. There were Mycenaean colonists however in Rhodes[29] and Cos,[30] and also at Colophon, where a tholos tomb containing pottery of late Mycenaean type was found.[31]

At Miletus, where the archaeological record is clearer, the sequence of events was as follows. The Cretan colony had been abandoned by 1400 BC, and was replaced by a settlement having close ties with mainland Greece. This settlement, which like its Cretan predecessor was not fortified, was destroyed by fire, not earlier than about 1300 BC, to judge from the latest Mycenaean pottery found in it. A new settlement was then built, whose chief feature was a massive fortification wall of Hittite type;[32] this lasted until some time in the twelfth century BC, when it was destroyed, and a definite interruption of the inhabitation at Miletus occurred.

From the material remains alone we cannot tell what were the political relations between Miletus and mainland Greece throughout the period of Mycenaean influence, nor is it certain that any speakers of Greek had already settled at Miletus before the late Bronze Age ended, about 1100 BC.[33] However, some valuable contemporary evidence about Miletus is to be found in Hittite cuneiform texts. These documents date from the fourteenth and thirteenth centuries BC and were excavated at Ḫattušaš, the Hittite capital city, which lies far to the east in the arc of the Halys river in the middle of Asia Minor. A text of about 1300 BC refers to a place called Millawanda or Milawata.[34] This lay on the coast of western Asia Minor, and was approached by the Hittite emperor during one of his campaigns along a route which can be identified with the valley of the river Maeander. Millawanda, then, is the Hittite name of Miletus, which lay by the sea at the entrance to the Maeander valley.[35] The original Greek form of the name Miletus can be reconstructed as *Milwatos*, and this fits the Hittite name well.[36]

The emperor, whose name is unknown, entered Millawanda in pursuit of a freebooter called Piyamaraduš, only to find, much to his annoyance, that Piyamaraduš had made off across the sea, together with much booty claimed by the Hittites, to a place where they were unable to catch him. The Hittites had no fleet, and it seems that Piyamaraduš had put himself beyond their reach by fleeing to an island not far away, perhaps to Samos.

These facts about Miletus are found in a letter from the Hittite emperor to the king of a country called Aḫḫiyawā. The emperor apologises to his brother king for having entered Miletus, because the place was within territories over which the king of Aḫḫiyawā claimed authority. The Hittite texts do not by themselves give enough evidence to fix the position of Aḫḫiyawā or the seat of its king, but it is a tenable hypothesis that Aḫḫiyawā is the land of the Achaeans or Akhaiwoi, Mycenaean Greece, and the king of Aḫḫiyawā the lord of the most powerful Mycenaean state, namely Mycenae itself.[37] So we may perhaps infer from the Hittite emperor's letter that about 1300 BC Miletus was within the territories of the overlord of the Achaeans. It would not follow from this, however, that the place was already inhabited by speakers of Greek at that time. The people of Miletus may then have been Carians owing allegiance to the king of the Achaeans.

The Hittite emperor had no difficulty in entering Miletus during his pursuit of Piyamaraduš; it is likely therefore that the great fortification wall had not yet been built. Not long after the Piyamaraduš affair, however, the political status of Miletus changed. Sometime early in the thirteenth century BC the place ceased to be a dependency of the king of Aḫḫiyawā and became instead subordinate to the Hittites.[38] This change is perhaps to be associated with the building of the great fortification wall, which would have enabled the inhabitants to hold out against a Mycenaean naval attack, and to keep themselves outside the control of the king of Aḫḫiyawā.

By the beginning of the thirteenth century BC the Mycenaean world had achieved a remarkable degree of uniformity in its material culture. Everywhere, except in Crete, we see uniformity of architecture, and of dress, burial customs, and weapons. The uniformity is most striking in the pottery, in which the predominant influence of the Argolid is evident. Since Mycenae in the Argolid is by far the most imposing of the Achaean palace states, we are justified in placing the overlord of the Achaeans there, and in connecting the cultural uniformity of the Mycenaean world with the dominant position of the king of Mycenae; this agrees with Greek tradition preserved by Homer, who called Agamemnon, king of Mycenae, 'most princely' of the Achaean kings, that is, their overlord.[39]

The greatest military achievement of the Mycenaean age was the sack of Troy, after a long and exhausting war, by the united Achaeans under Agamemnon. Priam's Troy, Troy VIIa, as the excavations have shown, fell to fire and the sword in the middle of the thirteenth century BC. The date of the sack is shown by the latest pottery found in the settlement. The excavators found some pottery of Mycenaean IIIA type and some of early Mycenaean IIIB.[40] This suggests that the destruction happened well before c. 1200 BC when Mycenaean IIIB pottery ceased to be made, a conclusion which is strengthened by the fact that in the subsequent, and poorer, settlement Troy VIIb:1 some Mycenaean IIIB pottery was still in use.[41] The discovery of Mycenaean IIIA pottery in Priam's Troy, Troy VIIa, also shows that the sack should be dated well before 1200 BC, for it is clear from dated deposits in the near east and Egypt that Mycenaean IIIA pottery ceased to be made about 1300 BC.[42] Even allowing for a time lag, since Troy was on the periphery of the Mycenaean world and styles may have lasted longer there, the fall of Priam's citadel cannot be dated much later than c. 1250 BC. In view of this date it is significant that a Hittite text refers to a king of Aḫḫiyawā campaigning in northwestern Asia Minor in the middle of the thirteenth century BC.[43] We have here precious contemporary evidence of Achaean military action in the neighbourhood of Troy in the very epoch of the Trojan war.

It is not clear what the cause of the Trojan war was, unless there is truth in the story of Helen; but there are signs that the Hittites' grasp on western Asia Minor was weakening in the mid-thirteenth century, and the temptation to the Achaeans to intervene there for their own gain must have been great. The emperor Tudḫaliyaš IV put down an alliance of western states known as the confederacy of Aššuwa,[44] but after the middle of the century we hear of no further effective Hittite campaigning in the west, and the Achaeans may well have aimed at winning parts of the Asiatic coastlands of the Aegean, or at least to weaken them by persistent attacks. The Trojan war was, it seems, one such campaign, which became firmly fixed in Greek historical memory owing to its length and expense, but even in the Iliad we are told of marauding outside Troy. In a number of raids, which have aptly been named the Great Foray,[45] the Achaean hero Achilles attacked many places in northwestern Asia Minor–Thebe and Lyrnessus south of Mount Ida, Pedasus, and the islands of Lesbos and Tenedos. According to another tradition he attacked Miletus,[46] which, Homer says, was at the time of the Trojan war not within the confederacy of Agamemnon but allied with Priam and the Trojans.[47]

The last great emperor of the Hittites was Tudḫaliyaš IV, the last great overlord of the Achaeans, Agamemnon; and since Troy was taken about 1250 BC, they may well have been coevals. After their reigns internal strife, pestilence, and invasions from abroad brought ruin to the Achaean and Hittite dominions. When the exhausted Achaean army returned in disorder to Greece, the power of the Mycenaeans began to break-up.[48] According to tradition the great migrations of the Dorian Greeks had begun about two generations after the fall of Troy, and this is borne out by the evidence for widespread destruction in Peloponnese and elsewhere about 1200 BC. In the period of decay and collapse Dorians from northern Greece invaded Peloponnese, and moved to Crete and later to the islands of the southeastern Aegean; many Achaeans fled to Cyprus, and others took refuge in the mountains of Arcadia; and fugitives from the onslaught came from many parts of Greece to Attica, which, tradition recalled, was also attacked by Dorians from Peloponnese.[49] In this age of widespread unrest the Hittite empire also succumbed to invaders from outside, prominent amongst whom were Phrygians; they crossed the Hellespont from Thrace and struck into the Hittite heartland,[50] whilst other migrants advanced by land and sea from the coastlands of the eastern Aegean to Cyprus, Syria, Palestine, and the Nile Delta, where they were finally defeated by Rameses III about 1191 BC.[51]

In a last effort to withstand the migrants' attacks, the Hittites laid claim to Cyprus, and for the first time in their history commanded a navy.[52] But it was an idle gesture: in the first decade of the twelfth century BC Ḫattušaš fell and the Hittite empire was at an end. About the same time Pylos was burned[53] and the descendants of Nestor fled, many of them to Athens.[54] Mycenae held out for a few years more, but her Cyclopean walls were not impregnable, and she too yielded. By 1150 BC the glories of Hittite and Achaean imperialism had passed into history. Even Egypt was hard pressed to defend herself against the marauders, whose attacks had continued from the time of pharaoh Merneptah about 1225 BC until their final defeat on land and at sea in the eighth year of the reign of Rameses III. Amongst the invaders Egyptian texts name the Peleset,[55] who are the Philistines of the Old Testament.

These devastating migrations of the early twelfth century BC did not leave western Asia Minor unharmed. The records of Rameses III refer to the destruction of the kingdom known to the Hittites as Arzawa,[56] which lay to the west of the Hittite heartland, but has yet to be placed precisely on the map.[57] At Miletus the fortified settlement was destroyed when Mycenaean IIIC pottery was in use, that is to say during the twelfth century BC, and the stronghold may well have given in during the migrations of the Philistines and their allies. Greek tradition also recalled these movements, placing them correctly in the aftermath of the Trojan war.

It was remembered that shortly before the Trojan war the Cretan mariners settled at Colophon were joined by fugitives from Thebes in Greece, who had been driven out by the Argives. Manto, daughter of Teiresias the Theban, married Rhacius the Cretan leader and bore him a son Mopsus.[58] When Mopsus grew up, he led a motley band of Greeks and barbarians from Colophon through the Taurus mountains to Pamphylia and Cilicia.[59] As the tradition shows, Mopsus and his men took the land route also followed by some of the Philistines and their allies on the way from the Aegean to the Levant and to Egypt. The tradition may well recall here part of the Philistine migration, especially since it adds that part of Mopsus' force went on to Syria and Phoenicia, just as the Philistines and their allies did. Mopsus himself founded a barbarian kingdom in Cilicia, and the discovery of an intrusive late Mycenaean (Late Helladic IIIB to C) settlement dating from about 1200 BC at Tarsus[60] supports the tradition of a movement from the Aegean to those parts after the Trojan war. About 700 BC the name of Mopsus was still remembered there, for at Karatepe in the Pyramus valley two inscriptions, one in Phoenician and the other in Hittite Hieroglyphs, mentioning Mopsus were set up by a local dynast in his remote country palace.[61]

One tradition told of the coming of the Greek heroes Calchas, Leonteus, and Polypoetes to Colophon immediately after the Trojan war,[62] and another of the migration of Podalirius from Troy to Syrna in Caria at the same time.[63] The prominence of Colophon in these legends of the *Nostoi* or 'returns of the heroes from Troy' is remarkable in view of the Mycenaean remains found there. The stories may well, like the Mopsus legend, have a historical foundation. They refer in fact, or are assigned by tradition, to about 1200 BC and the break-up of the Mycenaean commonwealth.

Another movement of peoples in Asia Minor in this very disturbed period is recalled by Herodotus.[64] This concerns the Tyrsenoi or Etruscans of Italy, but we cannot discuss the vexed question of Etruscan origins here. It will be enough to point out that Herodotus reported that owing to a famine part of the population of Lydia was forced to emigrate; so they took ship at Smyrna and after many wanderings came to the land of the Umbrians in Italy. The historian implies that the emigration of the Lydians happened about 1200 BC and states that the migrants were called Tyrsenoi after their leader Tyrsenos. It is a remarkable fact that a late Hittite text does mention hunger in western Asia Minor shortly before the collapse of the Hittite empire about 1200 BC, and an Egyptian record from the time of the pharaoh Merneptah also refers to the sending of grain to the starving Hittites.[65] Amongst the allies of the Philistines Egyptian texts name a people called the Teresh. It may be that we have here a reference to the Tyrsenoi on the voyages that finally brought them to the western coast of Italy.[66] They were, it seems, not the only emigrants from Asia Minor to come to the west coast of central Italy in this period, for the legend of Aeneas' escape from the ruins of Troy implies that settlers came from the Troad to Italy after much wandering.

The Greeks knew that there were still Tyrsenoi in the Aegean long after the emigration from Lydia to Italy, for they called the barbarian inhabitants of the island of Lemnos Tyrsenoi.[67] Here a remarkable inscription of the seventh century BC, written in the Greek alphabet, but in a language not Greek, has been found.[68] Whatever the affinities of the Lemnian language may be—the Lemnian text is too short for any link with Etruscan to be proved—we may perhaps recognise in the Tyrsenoi of Lemnos a remnant of the emigrants from Lydia, who stayed in the Aegean when the others went to Italy.[69]

It is not certain when speakers of Greek first arrived in the eastern Aegean. There may have been Greek speakers in the Mycenaean colony in Rhodes from the fourteenth century onwards, and Homer places followers of Agamemnon in Rhodes, Cos, and the neighbouring islands.[70] The situation on the Asiatic mainland is unclear. Atpaš the agent of the king of Aḫḫiyawā in Miletus[71] does not have an obviously Greek name, and the use of Mycenaean pottery in the settlements there does not entail that Greek was being spoken. Homer implies that, at the time of the Trojan war at least, Miletus was inhabited by Carians. We also hear of Carians in the neighbourhood of Colophon, whence they were driven by Mopsus.[72] The Thebans at Colophon were perhaps Greek speakers. Of the Leleges who are often mentioned with the Carians as inhabitants of the coast and islands nothing certain is known.[73] There were said to be Lycians with the Carians on the coast north of Miletus in the Erythraea,[74] and these people may have spoken languages related to the Carian and Lycian tongues of historical times. Lycian is akin to Luwian, a language spoken in Arzawa in western Asia Minor in the second millennium BC,[75] and it is a reasonable hypothesis, but no more, that a language of Luwian type was being spoken on the Asiatic coast before the first Greek speakers arrived. The linguistic affinities of Carian are not clear, though a few Carian inscriptions of c. 650 to 550 BC scratched by mercenaries in Egypt have been found.[76] When the Greeks called the early inhabitants of the Cyclades, as well as the Anatolians of the coast at Miletus, Carians, they may well have known that the two groups of people were related;[77] but here, too, cogent evidence is lacking. At present it appears likely that little or no Greek was being spoken in the eastern Aegean, apart from Rhodes and the islands nearby, in the Mycenaean age. The arrival of numerous Greek speakers is best dated to the time of the eastward movements across the Aegean at the beginning of the Iron Age in Protogeometric times. To one of those movements, the Ionian migration, we now turn.

CHAPTER II

The Ionian Migration

AT THE END OF THE MYCENAEAN AGE, WHEN THE PALACE BUREAUC-
racies of Pylos and Mycenae had been overthrown and iron-working
was being introduced to the Aegean world, migrations of Greeks to the
eastern Aegean from mainland Greece began. In the north the Aeolians
sailed across to Lesbos and the Asiatic coast south of the Troad, and in
the south Dorians moved from Laconia and the Argolid to Crete and the
islands of the southeastern Aegean, while a few of them also settled on
the mainland in Caria.[1] The Ionian migrants passed through the Cycladic islands to the western coast of Asia Minor, and in the course of
time the whole of the coastland from the altar of Poseidon at Cape
Monodendri near Miletus northwards to Phocaea, together with the
islands of Chios and Samos offshore, came to be known as Ionia.[2] The
three Aegean migrations, Aeolian, Dorian, and Ionian, are not easily
dated, but finds of Protogeometric pottery in western Asia Minor suggest that movement thither had begun about the end of the twelfth
century BC. We still have much to learn about the first settlements and
about the time during which the migrations continued. Some of the
traditions suggest, as we shall see, that the first settlers in Ionia were
few, and had difficulty in securing a foothold on the coast, because they
were opposed by the native Carians.

Near Termera at the end of the promontory of Halicarnassus very early
Protogeometric pottery of Attic type was found in a cemetery,[3] but we
do not know how long the settlement lasted. At Miletus the Mycenaean
settlement was succeeded, after an interval, by one in which Submycenaean and Protogeometric wares were used.[4] Here the settlers may
well at first have had ties with Attica. In Geometric times the settlement
was prospering; it lay on a promontory projecting into the bay at the
mouth of the Maeander, which has now silted up completely. A short
distance from this harbour settlement is Hat Hill (Turkish Kalabaktepe)
on which the Ionians also established themselves by the eighth century
BC. Kalabaktepe was perhaps used as a place of refuge, for there was a
fortification wall.[5] The few Submycenaean sherds in the harbour
settlement, together with the literary tradition, suggest that the first
Ionians had settled at Miletus by about 1100 BC.

Protogeometric pottery has been discovered on a peninsula near

23

Kuşadasi;[6] and near Melie at the northern foot of Mount Mycale vases akin to Protogeometric were also found,[7] but it is not certain that these indicate the presence of Greeks rather than Carians using Greek pottery. South of the Mycale range the position of archaic Priene has yet to be determined, and Myus, which in archaic times lay on a peninsula near the head of the great bay into which the Maeander then flowed, has not yet yielded any early pottery.

The Cayster mouth, at which Ephesus stood, has also silted up. Here Mycenaean, but no Protogeometric, pottery has been found;[8] the earliest deposits have yet to be explored systematically. Protogeometric pottery is reported from Teos;[9] Lebedos awaits excavation. At Colophon the earliest pottery after the Mycenaean is Geometric, and there is a Geometric cremation cemetery with tumuli.[10] The literary tradition suggests, however, that there was continuous occupation from Mycenaean times onwards. Archaic Erythrae has yet to be explored, but Protogeometric pottery has been found at Mordoğan (perhaps ancient Boutheia)[11] on a peninsula in the northern extension of the Erythraean territory dominated by Mount Mimas. The literary tradition implies that Clazomenae on the south shore of the gulf of Smyrna was settled in the early Iron Age and perhaps earlier still;[12] but so far no Protogeometric pottery has been found here, though some Mycenaean and early Geometric is known.[13]

The Anatolian inhabitants of Old Smyrna used a little Mycenaean pottery,[14] and the first Aeolian Greeks appear to have arrived in Protogeometric times, as the pottery suggests.[15] The colonists used native grey wares too, as did their Aeolian neighbours to the north and in Lesbos; but Geometric pottery becomes abundant as Ionian influences from the south increased during the ninth and eighth centuries. The city lay on a promontory some way to the north of New Smyrna, a Hellenistic foundation, and had a causeway linking it to the mainland; this could be defended in the event of trouble with the Anatolian natives.

The ancient city of Chios lies under the present town and has not been explored. At Emborio[16] in the south of the island the Mycenaean settlement came to an end in the twelfth century BC after a brief existence. In the eighth century there was a settlement on a hill inland, but what happened in Protogeometric times is not clear. A similar gap exists at Phanai, where Mycenaean and Geometric pottery was found. The literary tradition reports that Carians held out for a long time in Chios,[17] but they have yet to be recognised in the material remains, and the archaeological history of the island in the eleventh, tenth and ninth centuries remains obscure.

The earliest temple in Samos may be of the ninth century BC, and the island was evidently prospering in the eighth, for there are abundant deposits of Geometric pottery over the Mycenaean at the Heraeum.[18] But apart from some late Protogeometric pottery, perhaps from a tomb, and a Protogeometric deposit at the Heraeum,[19] there is so far no archaeological support for the literary tradition which placed the arrival of the first Ionian colonists in the eleventh century.

At Phocaea Protogeometric pottery has been reported,[20] and monochrome Anatolian or Aeolian grey wares are also known from there. Like Smyrna to her south, Phocaea lay within an originally Aeolian area, but was later accounted part of Ionia owing to Ionian expansion northwards up the coast, as tradition, to which we now come, recalled.

The finds of Protogeometric pottery in Ionia show that migrants from mainland Greece arrived early in the Iron Age, and the discovery of Submycenaean pottery at Miletus suggests that the first Ionian colonists settled there early in the eleventh century at the latest. The archaeological evidence tells us more about the time of the arrival of the colonists than about their starting points. About their original homes in Greece the literary evidence is, however, explicit. Two factors stand out in the tradition: first, the large number of settlers who came to Ionia from or through Attica, and secondly, the prominent part taken by descendants of Neleus king of Pylos in the leadership of the colonists.

We shall now fit the evidence together, showing that it is coherent, and paying most heed to the earliest and least embellished accounts of the Ionian migration. Herodotus, whose uncle Panyassis had written an elegiac poem on the subject of the Ionian migrations,[21] stated that there had been Ionians in many parts of mainland Greece – in Attica,[22] in Boeotia,[23] in the Argolid where they 'had become Dorians in the course of time',[24] and in northern Peloponnese.[25] The Ionians of the twelve cities of northern Peloponnese were driven out to Attica by Tisamenus, a grandson of Agamemnon, who himself had been expelled from the Argolid by the Dorians.[26] After the victory of Tisamenus northern Peloponnese was henceforth called Achaea after his Achaean followers. The Ionians who gathered in Attica eventually took ship for the Cyclades and Asiatic Ionia. The memory of Ionians living in mainland Greece is found in Homer, who mentions them once only, but, significantly, with the Boeotians as though they were a people of central Greece;[27] Solon, writing in the sixth century BC, may have thought that the Ionians had originated in Old Greece, for he called Attica the senior land of Ionia.[28] Strictly interpreted this would mean that the first people to be called Ionians lived in Attica and moved from there to other parts of mainland Greece in very early times, but the true meaning of his words is unclear.

When the Dorians under the leadership of the Heraclidae invaded Peloponnese, the Neleidae who ruled after Nestor at Pylos were uprooted. Many of them, according to tradition,[29] came to Athens, where fugitives from other parts of Greece had also gathered. Amongst the Neleidae who fled to Athens was Melanthus, a descendant of Periclymenus, one of Nestor's brothers. Melanthus became king of Attica and threw back a Boeotian attack.[30] His son Codrus ruled in Athens; he died by the river Ilisus while repulsing a Dorian attack, made when the invaders were founding Megara on the western borders of Attica.[31] The Ionian migration from Athens began, so it was said, in the generation of the sons of Codrus. If we date the Trojan war in the middle of the thirteenth century BC, and accept Thucydides' statement that the Dorians occupied Peloponnese eighty years after the fall of Troy,[32] then Melanthus flourished about 1170 BC, and his grandsons began the Ionian migration towards the end of the twelfth century. There is no need to insist upon the veracity of these genealogies, but it is noteworthy that by genealogical reckoning Neleus or Neileos, a son of Codrus and the leader of the Ionians to Miletus, lived close in time to the Submycenaean reoccupation of Miletus.

The earliest surviving account of the Ionian migration was written by Pherecydes, an Athenian historian of about 500 BC,[33] whose remarks are summarised by Strabo.[34] They give the impression of a sober narrative, and the roles of the Neleidae and of Athens in the story do not seem to be exaggerated. A slightly different tradition is given by Pausanias, who unfortunately does not name his authority:[35] in this account the Neleidae are more prominent. We now consider the foundation legends of each of the Ionian cities in turn.

Miletus was founded by Neileos or Neleus, a Pylian by descent and a son of Codrus.[36] On the way eastwards he was held up at Naxos by contrary winds, and left some of his followers on the island.[37] He is also said to have given his sons Hegetor and Hippocles orders to conquer the Cyclades.[38] In this enterprise Hegetor prospered, but Hippocles was able to take Myconos only. The relative importance of Naxos in late Mycenaean and Protogeometric times is archaeologically well documented,[39] and is perhaps to be explained by the settlement of Ionians

26

there, who used it as a staging post on the journey eastwards. It was recalled that Carians were driven out of the Cyclades by the Ionians in the course of this movement.[40] At Miletus, Neleus and his men killed or drove out the natives, and took their women as wives.[41] Neleus set up an altar at Poseidon's cape,[42] and his follower Philistus established a shrine of Demeter of Eleusis on Mount Mycale.[43] In later times the tomb of Neleus was pointed out on the left of the road to Didyma.[44]

The founder of Ephesus was Androclus, a son of Codrus, and according to Pherecydes[45] he began the Ionian migration. At Ephesus he drove out the Leleges and Lydians from the upper city, but came to terms with the natives who lived by the shrine of the goddess whom the Greeks came to call Artemis–Diana of the Ephesians. He died in a war helping the Prienians against the Carians of Mycale, and was buried, so it was said, by the road which in later times led from the Artemisium to the Magnesian Gate of Ephesus.[46] During his Carian campaign Androclus had driven the Samians out of their island, charging them with taking the side of the Carians against the Greeks. The Samians spent ten years in a fort at Anaea on the coast south of Ephesus before they returned to their island and, led by their king Leogorus, expelled the Ephesians.[47]

Leogorus was said to be the son of Procles, who brought Ionians expelled by the Dorian invaders of the Argolid over from Epidaurus.[48] An earlier founder of a settlement in Samos was Tembrion,[49] about whom nothing is known, except that the Samian clan of the Tembrionidae took their name from him.[50] A doubtful story relates how Procles and Tembrion founded the colony together, joined forces with the native Carians, and divided the population into two tribes.[51]

The founder of Priene was Aepytus, a son of Neleus,[52] perhaps of that Neleus who founded Miletus. The Carians were driven out, and, later, Thebans led by Philotas arrived. The Theban element was strong in Priene and its neighbourhood, for the Prienians are sometimes called Cadmeians and a poetical name of the place was Cadme.[53] Not far away there was a Thebes on Mycale. From Myus the Carians were driven out by the settlers under Cydrelus;[54] it was said of him that he was a bastard of Codrus.[55]

North of Mycale the small town at Pygela, which never joined the Ionian League, was supposed to have been settled by troops of Agamemnon, a legend to which the name of its tribe Agamemnonis alluded.[56] The link with Agamemnon perhaps means that the settlers came from northeastern Peloponnese. Melie[57] at the northern foot of Mount Mycale was at first in control of the sanctuary and grove of Poseidon the

Heliconian before the Ionians took the cult from her;[58] Poseidon's epithet here points to Mount Helicon in Boeotia,[59] and it is likely that there were Boeotians and Thebans in Melie as well as in Priene nearby.

One of the founders of Colophon is called simply Andraemon a Pylian. Since he is not said to be a son of Codrus, he may have come straight to Colophon from Pylos, without passing through Athens. Mimnermus the Ionian elegist, who wrote about 600 BC, first tells us about Andraemon,[60] and a fragment of his verses implies that the poet's ancestors came straight from Pylos to Colophon and established themselves by force of arms.[61] Whether it was necessary for them to fight against their Theban forerunners at Colophon, as well as against the Anatolian natives, is not clear. After the Pylians there came to Colophon an Ionian contingent from Athens led by Promethus and Damasichthon, who were said to be sons of Codrus.[62] Later Promethus killed his brother in a dispute and had to flee to Naxos, where he died. His body was then brought back to Colophon and buried at a place called Polyteichides.[63]

According to Pherecydes, the founder of Lebedos was Andropompus.[64] He may well have been a Pylian, for the name is found in the Neleid genealogy.[65] Pausanias adds that the Carians were driven out of Lebedos by Andraemon, the founder of Colophon, whose tomb lay outside Colophon near the river Calaon.[66]

At Teos the settlers were a very mixed body. Athamas came first with Minyans from Orchomenus in Boeotia.[67] Greeks and Carians mingled, and later were joined by Ionians from Attica led by Poikes, Nauclus, and Damasus.[68] Boeotians too under Geres arrived in Teos to settle.[69] At Erythrae Cnopus, supposedly another Codrid, collected settlers from the rest of Ionia, who took land formerly held by the Anatolians and the Cretans.[70]

The people of Clazomenae were thought to be from Cleonae and Phlius in the Argolid.[71] They came first to Colophon and then attempted to found a settlement at the foot of Mount Ida. This did not prosper, or at least was soon abandoned, for the colonists under their leader Paralus[72] next moved to Scyppium in the territory of Colophon. After that they again moved house, this time to Clazomenae, which they built by the south coast of the gulf of Smyrna.[73] Much later, when the Persians took Ionia, the Clazomenians crossed to the island nearby.

Phocaea, the most northerly of the Ionian cities of the primary settlement, was occupied by Phocians from the neighbourhood of Mount Parnassus. They were brought over from Attica by Philogenes[74] and Damon, two Athenians, having put to sea at Thoricus, where they were joined by some Peloponnesians.[75] When they reached the Asiatic mainland at the mouth of the Hermus river they were opposed by Mennes, the king (τύραννος) of Kyme. The king's brother however, whose name was Ouatias, became friendly with the newcomers; helped by them and by the Kymaian populace, he overthrew Mennes. The Phocians were then able to establish themselves at Phocaea.[76] The city lay in Aeolian territory and was not allowed to join the Ionian League until princes of the Codrid line were brought in to rule; but when Periclus, Abarnus and Deoites came from Teos and Erythrae to govern, Phocaea was accounted an Ionian city.[77]

According to local Chian tradition reported by Ion of Chios in the fifth century BC, the island was settled by Carians and by Abantes from Euboea when Oenopion the Cretan was king.[78] Much later Amphiclus brought over from Histiaea in northern Euboea, an Aeolian neighbourhood, a body of colonists. His grandson, King Hector, attacked the Carians and Abantes in the island, killing some, and permitting others to leave under a truce. So peace came to Chios. King Hector was awarded a tripod by the Ionians for his bravery, and the Chians were allowed to join in the common sacrifices of the Ionian League at Panionion, to the consolidation work of which we return later. All these details come from Ion's *The Founding of Chios*.

The earliest reference to Ionians in the Cyclades is in the Homeric Hymn to Apollo,[79] in which a Chian poet, whom Thucydides thought to be Homer himself,[80] described them gathered at Delos for a festival in the god's honour. The islanders of the Cyclades, Herodotus remarks, were all Ionians from Athens,[81] and the historian specifically names Ceos, Naxos,[82] Siphnos, and Seriphos[83] as having settlers of Athenian origin. We have already seen how some of the party led by Neleus to Miletus remained behind in Naxos. Amongst them may have been Archetimus and Teuclus, whom an unique list of colonisers of the Cyclades calls the occupiers of Naxos.[84] The list records that Ceos was taken by Thersidamas, Siphnos by Alcenor, Amorgos by the Naxians, Andros by Cynaethus and Eurylochus, Cythnus by Cestor and Cephalenus, Paros by Clytius and Melas, Delos by Antiochus, Seriphos by Eteoclus, Rheneia by the Delians,[85] Syros by Hippomedon, and Myconos by Hippoclus. We are also told that many of the islands were subdued by Hegetor son of Neleus.[86] In Ceos part of the Cretan stock may have survived, for in the island there was a family, the Euxantidae, who claimed descent from Euxantius son of Minos.[87] We also hear of four distinct heroes of the four cities of the island: it was said that a

Megacles fortified Carthaea, Eupylus Iulis, Acaeus Poeessa, and Aphrastus Coresus.[88]

Amongst the many people who accompanied the Ionian migrants Herodotus names Dryopes.[89] This people had once lived by Mount Oeta, and were said to have been expelled by Herakles. Some of them moved to Asine and Hermione in the Argolid,[90] and others occupied southern Euboea, settling at Styra[91] and Carystus.[92] From there some of them spilled over to Cythnus,[93] and perhaps even as far as Cyprus, where there were colonists from Cythnus.[94] The Dryopians may well have been originally a barbarian, non-Greek, people, because many of the names attested in southern Euboea do not look Greek.[95]

In Euboea the Ionian element was strongest in Chalcis and Eretria. Both places were given legendary Attic founders in the epoch before the Trojan war;[96] Homer however refers to no Ionians in the island, but to Abantes instead;[97] it is likely that the Ionians of Euboea, whose speech is clearly related to that of the other Ionians, arrived at the time of the migration to the Cyclades and to Asiatic Ionia.[98] The western Ionians of Euboea had a share with the Ionians of Attica and the Aegean in the very ancient congress at Thermopylae, the Amphictyony of Anthela, the Ionian representation at which may well have begun even before the migration eastwards.[99]

Amongst other non-Ionian settlers in the Cyclades Lemnians are said to have settled in Sicinos,[100] and there may have been Magnesians in Seriphos, for two legendary kings of that island, Dictys and Polydectes, were sons of Magnes.[101] There is also a report of Locrians from Naupactus in Ceos,[102] and of Phoenicians in Oliaros.[103] These fragments of tradition show how little we know about the early history of the Cyclades from our sources. Genuine progress will come only from excavations such as those in Ceos and Naxos; but even now the finds of Protogeometric pottery of Attic type in the Cyclades do support the tradition's insistence upon the part taken by Athenians in their settlement. Continued work may enable us to estimate how long Carians held on in the islands after the Ionian settlement.[104]

Two other bodies of evidence confirm the close ties of Attica with the rest of the Ionians. The first is the existence of shared months in their calendars not found elsewhere in the Greek world, and the second is the distribution of the Old Ionian tribes. We take the calendars first. The names of Attic months are naturally commonest in the Cyclades and in southern Ionia, where Attic Ionian influences were stronger than in the originally Aeolian north. For instance, in Miletus we find the Attic month names Targelion (Thargelion in Athens), Metageitnion, Boedromion, Pyanepsion or Kyanepsion (with varying treatment of the original labio-velar k^w sound), Poseideon, and Anthesterion.[105] In Samos there were months called Kyanopsion, Poseideon, Anthesterion and Metageitnion[106] and in Paros Thargelion, Poseideon and Anthesterion.[107] Attic Maimakterion corresponds in time to the Ionian month Apatourion, which is attested in many Ionian cities.[108] This is the month in which the festival of kinsmen, the Apatouria, was celebrated. Now Herodotus remarks that the true Ionians are those who came from Athens and celebrated the Apatouria. The festival, he adds, was held in all the Ionian cities, but had fallen into disuse in Ephesus and Colophon owing to some bloodshed there.[109] At the Apatouria new members were admitted to the phratries, kinship groups within the Old Ionian tribes. The festival was also celebrated in Attica, to which it was perhaps introduced after the Ionian migration had begun, for not only does the Attic calendar lack the Ionian month Apatourion,[110] but also the form of the name Apatouria is most likely Ionic.[111] In Attica we perhaps would expect the form Apatoria to have developed, if the Apatouria had existed there before the Ionian migration. Thus though legend ascribed the institution of the Apatouria to the time of the defence of Attica by Codrus the Pylian,[112] this phratry festival may have been a creation of the epoch of the Ionian migration, later than the end of the Mycenaean age.

The phratries are an essential part of the tribal structure of the Ionians, and they may well, like the tribes, have been in existence before the Ionian migration. For the name phratry, whose root meaning is brotherhood, has analogies with kinship terms in other Indo-european languages.[113] It is true that there is no sign of phratries in the Mycenaean tablets, but this silence hardly proves that phratries did not exist in Mycenaean times. It may, rather, be the case that they were a very ancient unit of social structure amongst the Greeks which had no place in the bureaucratic organisation of Mycenaean society, but which re-emerged into importance when the bureaucracies collapsed. The purpose of the Apatouria would then have been to admit persons of non-Ionian descent to tribes and phratries in the disturbed period of the migrations. Amongst the first to be so admitted would have been the non-Ionian Neleidae of Pylian origin.

We have said that the phratries were parts of the tribes, and it is now time to consider the Old Ionian tribes themselves. The word *phyle* or *phylon* is conventionally translated 'tribe', but it may be that to the

Ionians the word 'tribe' is not apt. Some ancient theorists claimed that the four phylai–Aigikoreis, Hopletes, Argadeis, and Geleontes[114]–were castes formed according to their work. The Aigikoreis were thought to be the herdsmen, the Hopletes the guardsmen, the Geleontes the farmers, and the Argadeis the craftsmen.[115] We simply do not have enough evidence to judge this theory, but each caste would have supported the others and have had a specialised function if the ancient explanation is correct; and it is worth noting that the four phylai did not migrate separately, but rather, in mutual support, together. This can be inferred from the distribution of the phylai outside Attica.

In Attica itself the four Ionian phylai continued to be politically important until, in the reforms of Cleisthenes at the end of the sixth century BC, they were replaced by ten new tribes;[116] but even in Athens the Ionian tribes were still prominent in cult until the fourth century, as can be seen from an inscription mentioning the Geleontes and one of its *trittyes* (Thirds or Ridings).[117] In Miletus the four Ionian tribes ceased to have political significance after the middle of the fifth century during reforms imposed by Athens,[118] but it is clear that all four tribes had existed there earlier. In addition to the Geleontes, Argadeis, Hopletes and Aigikoreis, there were two tribes not found in Attica: these were the Oenopes and the Boreis. The Hopletes, Oenopes, and Boreis are found in an inscription of 450/449 BC from Miletus,[119] and the Argadeis in a slightly earlier inscription.[120] Cyzicus, a Milesian colony, had all six tribes,[121] and the tribal names are found in other Milesian colonies too: at Tomis the Oenopes, Argadeis, and Aigikoreis are attested,[122] and the Aigikoreis[123] appear with the Boreis at Istrus.[124] This evidence suggests that all six tribes had existed in Miletus from before the settlement of those colonies in the seventh century BC.[125]

Herodotus states that after the Ionians arrived from Attica, some of them had as their princes Lycians of the royal line of Glaucus and others Neleids from Pylos.[126] Since neither the family of Glaucus nor the Pylians were of true Ionian origin, we may infer that they were brought into the tribes of the Boreis and the Oenopes. The Neleids may have joined the Boreis, since Borus was the name of an ancestor of Neleus the founder of Miletus,[127] and the Lycian dynasts perhaps became members of the tribe Oenopes, for in Samos we find that the Oenopes became a subdivision of the local tribe Chesia, which contained the natives of the island.[128] The Oenopes in Miletus then may well have consisted of the Anatolians who could not be admitted to the four Old Ionian tribes, in which the immigrants from Attica were distributed.

In Samos we can infer the presence of the six Asiatic Ionian tribes from an inscription of the Samian colony Perinthus naming Boreis, Geleontes and Aigikoreis.[129] In Teos only the Geleontes are attested,[130] but in Ephesus the names Geleontes, Argadeis, Oenopes, and Boreis are found. Here they are attested as *chiliastyes* ('Thousands'), subdivisions of the tribe Ephesians.[131] It seems that the Ionian tribes had been converted to *chiliastyes* earlier than the fourth century, for by the time of the historian Ephorus who lived then, the citizen body of Ephesus was organised into five tribes–Ephesioi, Bennaioi or Bembinaioi, Teans, Euonymoi, and Carenians.[132] We can perhaps infer from this change that the six Ionian tribes of Ephesus had been reduced to the status of *chiliastyes* at a time when the citizenry of Ephesus had been greatly increased in numbers from outside. Ephorus dates the change to the time of the sons of the founder of Ephesus, Androclus, but the true occasion is unknown. Possibly the change happened during the tyranny of Pythagoras (*c.* 600 BC) when the powers of the Androclid dynasty were taken away. We can infer from the names of the five new tribes that the reformer, whoever he was, brought in new settlers from Teos and from Carene in the Aeolis, and weakened the Ionian element by gathering it into one single tribe of the five.[133]

We have seen that the phratry festival of the Ionians, the Apatouria, was essentially a gathering of kinsmen. That these kinship groupings were also military in character can be shown from a passage in the second book of the Iliad. Here the aged Nestor advises Agamemnon to marshal his troops by phyla and phratries, so that phratry will support phratry and tribe tribe.[134] The advice is ignored, but it could not have been given if Homer did not know of phratries and tribes as military units. From Tyrtaeus we know that the Spartans once marched to war in their three Dorian tribes,[135] and from the words of Nestor we may infer that the Ionians in early times fought in their tribes, each of which was divided into phratries; but when this order of battle was introduced, and how long it lasted, we have no means of knowing. It may well have come into being with the institution of the Apatouria early in the Dark Age, in Submycenaean or Protogeometric times.

The evidence from inscriptions, so far as it goes, suggests that the four Old Ionian tribes together with the Boreis and the Oenopes were most firmly rooted in southern Ionia. North of Teos the tribal arrangements were different, owing to the Aeolian character of the earlier settlers. The existence of tribes is attested in Chios by an inscription of the sixth century, the so-called Constitution of Chios,[136] but their names are unknown. We are not entitled to assume the presence of Oenopes in the island from the name of Oenopion the Cretan founder.[137] At Erythrae there were once three tribes, one of which was called after Chalcis, a part of the Erythraean territory. In Phocaea we can perhaps deduce the existence of three tribes Pericleidae, Teuthadeis, and Abarneis from their presence in the Phocaean colony Lampsacus.[138] Significantly, in none of these northerly cities have any of the Old Ionian tribal names been found; but we have to remember that the evidence is fragmentary.

The contrast between northern and southern Ionia is well illustrated by the speech of the two areas. In the north the dialect is remarkable for the presence of Aeolic forms not found further south. In Chios we find the month name Badromion,[139] an Aeolic form also attested in Lampsacus, a colony of Phocaea.[140] The Aeolic doubling of the nasals is seen in the personal names Dinnys in Chios and Phannothemis in Erythrae; in the name of a mountain in Chios, Pelinnaion; and of a promontory on the mainland opposite, Argennon.[141] In Phocaea the month name Maimakter is also Aeolic[142] (Attic Maimakterion). All these words show that during the Dark Age the line between the Aeolic and Ionic dialects of the coast was further south than in historical times.

Herodotus knew of local differences in the dialects of the Ionians, having perhaps noticed them during his stay in Samos.[143] The system of his classification seems to be geographical. In his first, Carian, group he places Miletus, Priene and Myus. His Lydian group consists of Ephesus, Lebedus, Colophon, Teos, Clazomenae, and Phocaea. Chios and Erythrae, he asserted, had the same dialect, and the Samians one peculiar to themselves. He may mean that Carian words were commonest in the neighbourhood of Miletus, which had the most to do with the Carians of the interior; and similarly that the second group was most affected by Lydian speech: some support for this interpretation of Herodotus can be found in the vernacular of the Ephesian poet Hipponax, which has many Lydian words. Chios and Erythrae have their Aeolisms in common, but these are not enough to distinguish them from Phocaea, as Herodotus does. Perhaps there were no Lydian words in the vernacular of Chios and Erythrae. In their island the Samians came to terms with the Carians very soon after the migration, but what distinguished their speech from that of their Milesian neighbours to the ear of Herodotus we do not know.

Finally it is important when considering the Ionian migration to remark upon the distribution of the dialects of the Attic-Ionic group. If

we had no other evidence for the Ionian migration, the dialects would
show us that it had happened, though they would not indicate whether
the migrants had moved eastwards rather than westwards across the
Aegean through the Cyclades.[144] The existing historical forms of Ionic
show that there was a common Proto-Ionic ancestor in the Mycenaean
age. Fortunately we do not need to discuss whether historical Ionic is a
descendant of the dialect found in the Mycenaean archives.[145] It is
enough to state that historical Ionic had an ancestor spoken in mainland
Greece before the Ionian migration.[146] Attic and Ionic have several
characteristics in common; of which the most obvious are the development of η from $\bar{a}$, which is not found in any other Greek dialect, and the
very early loss of digamma.[147] Central Ionic of the islands is very close
to the Asiatic Ionic, the chief difference being that the rough breathing
is shown in some early inscriptions.[148] The western Ionic of Euboea
shares with Attic the writing of $\tau\tau$, as against the $\sigma\sigma$ of the central and
eastern Ionians, and similarly $\rho\rho$ instead of $\rho\sigma$.[149] In western Ionic
Eretrian is exceptional, in that between vowels σ is not written, but ρ
instead.[150] The close ties between Attic and Ionic seen in the earliest
inscriptions, and their manifest differences from all other Greek dialects,
enable us to postulate a primitive Old Ionic mainland speech spoken
before the Ionian migration; this, it seems, was the tongue of the prehistoric Ionians of Attica, the Argolid, northern Peloponnese, and
Boeotia.[151]

CHAPTER III

Aeolian and Magnesian Settlements

AT THE TIME OF THE IONIAN MIGRATION, COLONISTS FROM BOEOTIA and Thessaly began to move across the northern Aegean to the island of Lesbos and to the Asiatic coastland between the Caicus plain in the north and the gulf of Smyrna in the south. In Lesbos a little Proto-geometric pottery has been found,[1] and the discovery of Protogeometric in Smyrna suggests that Aeolians had arrived there too by about 1000 BC or earlier.[2] We have seen that when Phocaea was founded, Kyme already existed; and since there was Protogeometric at Phocaea,[3] Kyme too must have been in existence by about 1000 BC. The finds of Greek pottery in Dark Age Aeolis are, however, still few, part of the reason for this being that the settlers long continued to use grey monochrome wares like those of their inland neighbours, the Phrygians, and of their Anatolian forerunners of the late Bronze Age. This continuity of Anatolian culture makes the dating of the Aeolian settlements difficult.

Homer implies that there were Greeks in Lesbos during the Trojan war,[4] and the Delian Hymn to Apollo suggests that they may have been Aeolians.[5] So the migrants who, traditionally, came over after the war may not have been the first Aeolians in the island. In their migration Mycenae is given the role taken by Pylos in the Ionic settlements; for the Aeolians are said to have been led by descendants of Agamemnon,[6] and a notable family in Lesbos, the Penthelidae, claimed descent from Pen-thilus, a grandson of the conqueror of Troy. Penthilus,[7] or in another version his grandson[8] Gras, is said to have brought Aeolians to Lesbos. They started from Boeotia;[9] Boeotians were amongst the migrants, and the ties between Aeolis and Boeotia were still strongly remembered in historical times.[10] North of Aulis, from the Locrian shore by Mount Phricium, other colonists sailed for the Asiatic mainland, where in spite of native opposition they founded Kyme,[11] which became the most im-portant of the mainland Aeolian cities. The leaders of this movement, Cleues and Malaos, were also accounted kin of Agamemnon, and one of their descendants may have been another Agamemnon, a king of Kyme.[12] From Kyme some of the colonists moved southwards to Smyrna,[13] which remained an Aeolian city till its capture by Colophonian exiles.

Local antiquarians claimed that Kyme in Asia was founded in 1120 BC, and Smyrna her daughter in 1102,[14] but though these dates may not be far wrong we cannot prove them correct. Nothing is known about the early history of the other Aeolian places on the mainland listed by Herodotus,[15] and some of them have yet to be identified. In time, however, more excavation at Kyme[16] may throw some light on Dark Age Aeolis. It is unlikely that the primary settlements prospered at first, for though the land was good, the natives, especially the wild Mysians dwelling on the coast between the Troad and the Caicus, must have been a constant threat. Herodotus implies that the mainland Aeolians formed themselves into a League of twelve cities, like the Ionians' League to the south;[17] their community of interest is illustrated by the grant of citizenship by all the other eleven mainland cities to the Smyrnaeans, when they were thrown out of their home.[18] The founding of the Aeolian League perhaps dates from before the end of the eighth century BC, but the Aeolian cities of the Troad, the earliest of which were founded about 750 BC, were not members of it. Kyme is likely to have dominated the affairs of this early League. Her interests were at first entirely agricultural. We hear of an early Kymaian king, Telephanes, who encouraged the planting of trees.[19]

In the Dark Age Lesbos was too large to be controlled by any one city. Of the five chief settlements Mytilene, the largest, lay in the southeast of the island, Eresus in the southwest, and Antissa on an island close to the north shore; at Antissa a late Bronze Age settlement was taken over by the Aeolians. Eastwards along the same coast Methymna faced across to Cape Lectum, the southeastern point of the Troad. All these places have names of Anatolian type, a fact suggesting that they had all been occupied before the Greeks arrived. Pyrrha 'the red' however has a Greek name; it was built on a high spur overlooking the northeastern shore of the great gulf of Callone which reaches inland from the south. A sixth city, Arisba, in the fertile plain at the head of the gulf had been destroyed by Methymna before the time of Herodotus.[20] Pliny mentions two cities called Hiera and Agamede, neither of which survived into historical times; the former is perhaps the late Bronze Age settlement at Yera not far from Mytilene.[21] Homer implies that there was also a city called Lesbos, but this has yet to be identified.[22]

North of Lesbos, off the coast of the Troad, lay Tenedos. Legend reported that there had been a king Tenes[23] in the island, and a population of Leleges.[24] At the Aeolian colonisation of Tenedos the settlers were led by Pisander, who was said to have come from Laconia.[25]

Before we leave the migrations, we have to consider one more body of settlers, the Magnesians, who are sometimes called Aeolians.[26] In the view of Hesiod, however, they were not true Aeolians, for he called Magnes a son of Zeus, not of Aeolus, and made him a brother of Macedon, the ancestor of the Macedonians.[27] There were two places called Magnesia in Asia Minor. One lay by Mount Sipylus inland from Smyrna on the way to Sardis. Nothing is known about the early history of this place, but it may have been settled in the Dark Age from Kyme, for there were thought to have been Magnesians from Thessaly in Kyme.[28]

A second Magnesia, beloved by Artemis,[29] lay by the Lethaeus, a tributary of the Maeander, in the hinterland of Ephesus. In Hellenistic times the city claimed that its founders had not come directly from Magnesia but by way of Crete, where, it was said, after the Trojan war some Magnesians settled in the south between Phaestus and Gortyn. This story was known to Plato, who in the *Laws* mentioned that the Cretan Magnesia had been abandoned long before his time.[30]

When the Magnesians arrived in Asia, the story continued, they first settled at a place called Cretinae, which they took from the Carians. Later the colonists made good their hold beside the river Lethaeus, and Cretinae was lost to the Ephesians attacking from the north.[31] The occupation of Magnesia cannot be dated, because the archaic city has not been excavated, but since the place was well inland, the Magnesians followed the Ionians, who took the best sites on the coast. We have to allow for romantic invention in the story of Magnesia's foundation,[32] but the details fit together well, including the sojourn in Crete.

As with Ionic, the distribution of Aeolic dialects supports, or at least does not contradict, the story of the Aeolian migration. The evidence, apart from the poetry of Alcaeus and Sappho, is slight in the archaic period, but inscriptions from the fourth century onwards show clearly that the closest ties of the Lesbian (and Asiatic Aeolic) dialect are with Boeotia and eastern Thessaly.[33] Tradition, as we have seen, told of an emigration from Boeotia and Locris nearby. In Thessaly there was an eastward thrust of Thessalians, who, starting from Thesprotia in northwest Greece, had made their way through the passes of the Pindus range.[34] This thrust drove Aeolians of the great plain of Thessaly into the neighbourhood of Iolcus, whence many of them may well have set out for Lesbos and the Asiatic coast. The abundant Protogeometric remains following the Mycenaean at Iolcus strengthen the hypothesis that eastern Thessaly was a haven for refugees and emigrants in the early Dark Age.[35] The evidence for phratries in Thessaly[36] and for the month Phratrios in the Aeolis[37] shows that the social organisation of the

Aeolians may have been analogous to that of their Ionian neighbours at the time of the migrations.

With the coming of the Magnesians the primary settlement of Ionia and the Aeolis was complete. The Greeks remembered little about the aftermath of the colonisation, perhaps because there was little worth recalling, compared with the stirring events of the Trojan war and the later invasions. Yet the Dark Age fostered the noble art of epic poetry, the origins and growth of which we must next examine; for the creation of the Homeric epic is the greatest achievement of the Asiatic Greeks in the obscure centuries between the fall of Mycenae and the Hellenic awakening of the eighth century BC.

CHAPTER IV

Ionian Epic Poetry

THE GREATEST GIFT OF THE AEGEAN DARK AGE TO THE LATER GREEKS and to ourselves was the oral epic, and the greatest of its epic poets was Homer. There are two questions we may profitably ask about the poet (1) where did he live, and (2) when? There are also two questions which are often asked, but to which no certain answer has yet been given: (3) did he write, or was his poetry written down long after his time and (4) was he the composer of both the Iliad and the Odyssey? The third and the fourth questions are neglected here because they belong to the realm of literary criticism rather than of history; instead, we shall examine the few biographical facts that can be discovered about the poet.

It is obvious that the composer of the Iliad was an Asiatic Greek, who knew much about the Aeolian and Ionian coastlands.[1] He has seen birds flocking beside the river Cayster in the Asian meadow, 'geese or cranes or long-necked swans'.[2] He knows the rock carving of the goddess on Mount Sipylus and calls her Niobe.[3] He has seen the Icarian sea tossed by the blasts of the southeast wind,[4] and his knowledge of the Troad suggests that he had visited Troy[5] and seen the Simois and the Scamander rivers in flood. He knows too that the summit of Samothrace rising behind Imbros can be seen from Troy.[6] The sight of a Maeonian or Carian woman staining ivory blood-red for a horse's cheek-piece was fixed in his memory,[7] and he knew of other Asiatic barbarians, the Leleges and Caucones. Again, he speaks as an Asiatic Greek would of Boreas and Zephyrus blowing from Thrace.[8]

These hints in the poem agree well with ancient tradition about his life. The cities with the best claim to be his birthplace were Smyrna and Chios, with both of which Homer was already linked in the time of Pindar.[9] It was also said that the Chians honoured Homer though he was not a citizen of Chios,[10] a story which suggests that even if Homer had once lived in the island, he was not a native. Good evidence for his connection with Chios is the presence of his descendants, the Homeridae, in the island.[11] Some said that Homer had lived for a time at Bolissus in the north of Chios, where Aeolians had once settled.[12] Possibly he was born in Smyrna and moved later to Bolissus, but it is clear from the Iliad that he travelled far in Asia Minor, and not all of his life can have been spent in Smyrna and Chios. Since Bolissus was Aeolian, Homer may have had Aeolian ties,[13] though the form of his name is Ionic. The language of the Iliad is the formulaic, traditional, speech of the oral bards: it tells us nothing about the dialect used by Homer in his daily life, and since he came from the borderland between Ionia and the Aeolis, it is not certain whether he should be called an Ionian or an Aeolian.

As for his date, it is clear that if he was literate, he did not flourish before about 750 BC, when for the first time the Phoenician script was being adopted by the Greeks for their own language.[14] On the other hand, it is unlikely that he lived after 700 BC, for if he had been a near contemporary of Archilochus more would have been remembered about so great a poet. If he visited Troy, then he is not likely to have gone there before its settlement by Aeolian Greeks about 750 BC.[15] One sign that Homer lived late in the eighth century BC is given by the widespread tradition that Homer was a contemporary of Hesiod. Herodotus thought the two poets coeval (though he dated them about 840 BC),[16] and a fragment of Hesiod, which may even be genuine, asserts that Homer and Hesiod joined in singing hymns to Apollo at Delos.[17] Hesiod's date is reasonably clear: for he mentions Amphidamas, an Euboean noble, at whose wake he sang at Chalcis.[18] Now Amphidamas is almost certainly the warrior of that name who died in the Lelantine war of the second half of the eighth century BC.[19] This was a Panhellenic struggle, in which many states were concerned, but the principal contestants were the Euboean cities of Chalcis and Eretria, who struggled for mastery of the Lelantine plain in the island. Thus if Hesiod lived late in the eighth century BC, and if he competed with Homer, Homer should be dated in the same epoch.

In antiquity other epic poems besides the Iliad and the Odyssey were sometimes ascribed to Homer. Already in the middle of the seventh century BC Callinus of Ephesus attributed to Homer a poem from the Theban cycle, the *Thebais*.[20] Others thought that Homer composed a poem called the *Epigonoi*, on the heroes who sacked Thebes shortly before the Trojan war.[21] Poems on these subjects were popular in Ionia about 700 BC, but we have no proof that Homer composed epics on the Theban wars. Allusions to the Theban stories in the Iliad do show, however, that he was interested in them.

The earliest Ionian epic poet dated by the ancients in the eighth century BC is Antimachus of Teos. He was said to have flourished about 753 BC,[22] and if the date is correct, Antimachus was perhaps older than Hesiod and Homer. He composed a poem on the Epigonoi,[23] and he may

41

also have been the author of a poem on the Nostoi.[24] After him came
Arctinus of Miletus, who was reputed to be a pupil of Homer. He was
born according to Artemon of Clazomenae[25] (whose own date is unknown) in the ninth Olympiad (744/1 BC): Artemon gave the date in his
book on Homer. To Arctinus are ascribed a poem called the *Aethiopis* (a
continuation of the Iliad in which he told how Penthesilea the Amazon
and Memnon came to fight against the Achaeans at Troy) and another
poem on the Sack of Troy.[26] According to the scholar Phanias of Eresus
Arctinus competed with Lesches, an epic poet of Pyrrha in Lesbos, and
was defeated by him.[27]

Lesches himself composed a *Little Iliad*, which to judge from the
summary of it given by Proclus,[28] was packed with detail; for the mad-
ness of Ajax, the return of Philoctetes from Lemnos, the slaying of
Eurypylus by Neoptolemus, and the building of the wooden horse were
all described in the poem. The aim of Lesches, and of Arctinus too, was
to give the order of events as they were found in tradition, not to fix
attention on one episode in the war, as Homer did. The poems of
Arctinus and Lesches may well have been in the mind of the artist who
made the reliefs of scenes from the sack of Troy, including the wooden
horse, on a magnificent pithos dating from about 650 BC, which was
found in Myconos.[29]

Two other Ionian epic poets are no more than names. A certain
Thestorides of Phocaea was said to have composed another *Little Iliad*;
some even said that he stole the poem together with another epic called
the *Phocais* from Homer himself.[30] A third *Little Iliad* was ascribed to
one Diodorus, a poet of Erythrae.[31] Hesiod was said to have been attacked
by a rival called Cercops of Miletus, who reputedly composed a poem on
Aegimius,[32] a hero in whom Hesiod was also interested.[33] The catalogue
of Ionian epic poets is completed by Creophylus of Samos. He was
thought to be a friend and pupil of Homer, and an ancestor of Hermo-
damas, a friend of the great Pythagoras, the Samian sage.[34] Some writers
made Creophylus a son-in-law of Homer, and held that Homer gave him
a poem, the *Sack of Oechalia*.[35] From the family of Creophylus Lycurgus
the Spartan lawgiver was said to have obtained the poetry of Homer,
which he introduced to Sparta.[36]

There is little evidence for the circumstances in which the Asiatic
Greek poets were accustomed to recite their epics. As the Delian Hymn
to Apollo shows, poets performed at the great Panegyris at Delos, where
the Ionians in their long cloaks gathered with their modest wives and
their children to honour the god, while the Delian maidens chanted

hymns and imitated the speech of strangers, choruses performed, and boxers competed.[37] Late in the eighth century BC a chorus came to Delos from Messenia, far away in southwestern Peloponnese.[38]

Hymns and epics may also have been recited at the precinct of Poseidon by Mount Mycale, though the only hint we have of a poet having visited the sanctuary of the Ionians there is a description by Homer of a sacrifice of a bull to Poseidon Heliconius.[39]

It is likely that poets sang in princely houses, as Demodocus and Phemius sing in the Odyssey; for the kings of Ionia and the Aeolis would have been delighted to be reminded of the exploits of their ancestors: Agamemnon of Kyme must have found the story of the Iliad, the great Panachaean expedition to Troy under the leadership of Agamemnon of Mycenae, specially interesting; and the Neleidae in the Ionian cities must have been delighted by the Pylian passages in the Odyssey and the exquisite Pylian epic recounted by the Neleid Nestor in Book XI of the Iliad.[40] Epic poems, or shorter lays, then, were surely recited in the princely houses, as they were in the royal house of Phaeacia and in the Ithaca of Odysseus. But some recitations may have been given in less formal circumstances, amongst the populace, in the private houses of Ionian citizens, and in the clubs of the phratries,[41] to make the longer winter evenings pass pleasantly and to encourage the settlers in their constant struggles against their Anatolian neighbours. Poets strengthened men's wills to fight and survive, they praised gods and famous men, and they entertained. But they were also the first Greek historians. In their minds, and in the minds of their hearers, the *aoidoi* kept alive the traditions of the great Achaean dynasties of the Mycenaean age, of the internecine Theban wars, of the great expedition to Troy, and of the settlement by the Mycenaean remnant in the Aeolis and Ionia. The Greeks never doubted that the events recalled by the poets had occurred, though there was always room for disagreement over details. To the Aeolians and the Ionians of the eighth century BC Homer and his professional associates were the preservers of the historical memory of the Greek people, and in their poems we may observe the beginnings of the first true Greek historical writing.[42] History is the offspring of epic: predictably, therefore, when the first Greek historians began to write in prose at the end of the sixth century BC the pioneers in the accurate study of the historical traditions preserved in the Greek epics were Ionians.

Many of these poets travelled, as Homer did, far beyond their native cities, to festivals outside Ionia, or from city to city like the nameless aged poet, perhaps Homer himself, who in the words of a beautiful fragment 'came to Colophon, a servant of the Muses and of far shooting Apollo, bearing his own well-tuned lyre'.[43] Their poetry is nearly all lost, because much of it was never written down; but we are fortunate to have the Iliad and the Odyssey and the Homeric Hymns, and we may wonder whether any of Homer's fellow Asiatic Greeks were ever his peers in the art of oral poetry.

It is obvious from the complexity of its formulas that the heroic hexameter is very ancient, and originated long before the coming of the Phoenician script to Greece in the eighth century BC. Its complexity shows too that the hexameter cannot have been the primitive and most ancient Greek verse form. That distinction belongs to the *paroemiac* or metre of proverbs. So ancient indeed is the paroemiac that close analogies with it can be found in the early poetry of other Indo-european languages, notably in Irish, Slavic, and Vedic;[44] hence the paroemiac may even have been inherited by the bards from a primitive Indo-european gnomic-epic poetry existing before Greek had become a distinct language.

The Greek hexameter does not have analogies in other Indo-european languages–the Latin hexameter is borrowed from Greek; but we can suggest how in Greece the hexameter grew out of the paroemiac either during the Mycenaean age, or later in the dark centuries before Homer lived.

Many hexameters contain obvious paroemiacs.[45] Hesiod has at the end of a hexameter:

$$\kappa\alpha\iota\rho\grave{o}\varsigma \; \delta'\acute{\epsilon}\pi\grave{\iota} \; \pi\hat{\alpha}\sigma\iota\nu \; \acute{\alpha}\rho\iota\sigma\tau o\varsigma$$

'there is a best time for everything'[46] and many Homeric hexameters can be analysed as two paroemiacs, the distinguishing characteristics of both the paroemiac and the heroic hexameter being the clausula $- \smile \smile \, / - \overline{\smile}$. Thus the proverb:

$$\delta\epsilon\xi\iota\grave{o}\nu \; \epsilon\grave{\iota}\varsigma \; \acute{\upsilon}\pi\acute{o}\delta\eta\mu\alpha, \; | \; '\alpha\rho\iota\sigma\tau\epsilon\rho\grave{o}\nu \; \epsilon\grave{\iota}\varsigma \; \pi o\delta\acute{o}\nu\iota\pi\tau\rho o\nu$$

'put the right foot first into the shoe, the left into the footbath'[47] can be treated as two paroemiacs, or as a hexameter with hiatus at the caesura after the third trochee. Since some hexameters of this last kind rhyme, there may even have been primitive paroemiac rhyming verses; thus we find:

$$'A\rho\gamma\grave{\omega} \; \pi\hat{\alpha}\sigma\iota \; \mu\acute{\epsilon}\lambda o\upsilon\sigma\alpha \; | \; \pi\alpha\rho' \; A\grave{\iota}\acute{\eta}\tau\alpha o \; \pi\lambda\acute{\epsilon}o\upsilon\sigma\alpha.[48]$$

From this analysis it follows that as the hexameter developed out of the paroemiac, so the clausula - ⌣ ⌣ / - ⹀, which was at first obligatory, was modified, and spondaic endings such as - - / - ⹀ were introduced with - - for - ⌣ ⌣ .

There is still no proof that Mycenaean poetry was already hexametric; but an interesting piece of evidence that the Mycenaeans had paroemiacs is provided by the Homeric formula for a silver-studded sword ξίφος ἀργυρόηλον or φάσγανον ἀργυρόηλον, which can hardly have become current much later than the middle Mycenaean period, for after about 1300 BC such swords were rare in Greece, and in the Dark Age they were not used at all.[49] The Homeric formula for a tower-shield σάκος ἠΰτε πύργον belongs to the same category; it is a paroemiac formula of Mycenaean origin, since there were, so far as we know, no tower shields in use later than the thirteenth century BC. Thus Homer and his contemporaries were the inheritors of a gnomic-epic oral tradition of high antiquity,[50] whose origins are lost in the remote past of Indo-european language and metre, and we can be sure that Mycenaean poets used paroemiacs, even if they did not sing in hexameters.

Closely related to the hexameter, and evidently developed from it, is the elegiac couplet of hexameter and pentameter. This was sometimes sung to a flute and was thought by the ancients to have been originally the metre of dirges. Indeed in one of the earliest of Greek elegies Archilochus laments the loss of a ship and its crew at sea.[51] The origin of this verse form is not less obscure, and perhaps almost as ancient, as the hexameter's; amongst the Greeks it is first found in Callinus,[52] and we are told of an ecstatic Ionian poet Theocles of Naxos or of Eretria who is even claimed as the inventor;[53] but Phrygia may well have been a home of elegy. There flute music was much practised, and the reeds for the tongues of flutes that grew by the river Marsyas in Phrygia were famous.[54] Moreover one of the kings called Midas is said to have lamented for his mother in elegy,[55] and the Phrygians who colonised Armenia[56] may well have taken the word ἔλεγος elegy eastwards with them, for there is an Armenian word elēgn meaning 'reed' or 'flute'. But though the *word* elegy may have originated amongst the Phrygians, we do not know that the Phrygians had poems of alternating hexameters and pentameters. The Greeks may have borrowed the name and the music from the Phrygians, but developed the elegiac couplet themselves in the form in which it is found in Callinus and Archilochus. There, for lack of evidence, the matter must rest.

While oral epic poetry flourished in east Greece, epic poets exercised their art on the Greek mainland also. We have no literary evidence for early Athenian epic poets, but in Peloponnese there was a vigorous tradition in the eighth and seventh centuries. Sparta had an epic poet called Cinaethon,[57] and in Troizen a certain Agias composed a poem on the Nostoi;[58] but the greatest of the Peloponnesian bards was Eumelus the Corinthian whose fame reached far beyond his native city. It was he who composed the processional hymn for the Messenians who went to a Delian festival.[59] North of Corinth the Hesiodic school long prospered beneath the Muses' favoured mountain, Helicon. To estimate how much Ionian influence there was upon the mainland poets is hard, for all of them shared, on both sides of the Aegean, in the ancient tradition of oral formulas. One of the most striking features of the early epic fragments, indeed, is their uniformity of language and resistance to local dialects. It is clear that poets travelled far to compete; but how much Ionian poets taught mainlanders or Boeotians taught Peloponnesians is less certain.

This chapter ends, as it began, with Homer himself. The study of his poetry began not later than the end of the sixth century BC with Theagenes of Rhegium,[60] and it has continued ever since. The chief contribution of modern scholarship to Homeric studies is the proof of the oral, traditional, formulaic, character of the poems. To admit Homer's indebtedness to the tradition does not lessen our awareness of his originality, for he transformed the tradition while belonging to it. Homer was an oral poet, but he was also a genius who imposed the stamp of his mind upon the traditional language and stories. Yet so much remains dark: it is sobering, though not disgraceful, to admit that we still do not know how the Iliad and the Odyssey were preserved for posterity. Homer may have written them down, or he may have dictated them; or he may have taught the poems to the Homeridae, who perhaps helped the Athenian tyrant Pisistratus to prepare a text in the sixth century BC.[61] But even if we knew how the Iliad and the Odyssey were saved in writing, our appreciation of them as poetry would not perhaps be any greater. The important fact is that they survived at all.

CHAPTER V

Early Wars and Feuds of the
Asiatic Ionians

WHEN THE ASIATIC IONIANS OF THE DARK AGE WERE NOT FIGHTING
Carians they were fighting each other. Some memories of their petty
disputes survive, and though none of the stories is easily dated, they are
worth mentioning because they help to show how men lived in the
Greek settlements. The finds at Smyrna show that the Aeolians in the
ninth and eighth centuries led austere, but not bleak, lives in their oval,
thatched houses,[1] and their Ionian neighbours cannot have lived very
differently. But there was always the threat of attack; the city might
wake one morning to find the enemy at the gates, his trumpet sounding
to rally the assault.[2] At Smyrna there was a Chian attack on the Aeolians,
who happened to be carrying the holy model ship of Dionysus at a
festival; but the god came to their aid, and the Chians with their fleet
were driven back.[3] Later the Aeolians of Smyrna lost their city. They
admitted some exiles from Colophon inside their walls. The Colophonians then shut the gates on the Smyrnaeans who again were honouring
Dionysus outside the city. Being unable to return, the Aeolians
agreed to leave the place with their gear, and settled in the other cities of
the Aeolian mainland. Smyrna thus became an Ionian city, though she
was not admitted to the League.[4] Amongst those who took Smyrna
were Pylian kinsmen of the poet Mimnermus, who lived in Smyrna
about 600 BC and told of the capture in one of his poems.[5] Smyrna was
already Ionian by 688 BC, but we do not know how much earlier the
Aeolians had abandoned the place.[6] The excavations do not help to date
the change, because there was no destruction when the Colophonians
took over; but the increasing use of Geometric pottery during the ninth
and eighth centuries at Smyrna points to Ionian influence there even
before the seizure.

One Ionian war deserves not to be called petty. This was the war over
Melie near Panionion at the northern foot of Mycale. The Roman
architect Vitruvius remarks briefly that Melie (or Melite as he calls the
place) was removed from the common council of the Ionians at Panionion
after a war against her, which she had brought upon herself by her
arrogance.[7] From the few words of Vitruvius on the war it appears that
Melie lost Panionion because the other Ionians resented her con-

trol of the sanctuary. The architect does not state that Melie was permanently ruined, and in fact remains later than any possible date of the Meliac war have been found there.[8] So the city was removed from the council, but survived the war. When, then, was the Meliac war fought?

A Prienian inscription makes clear that the Cimmerian leader Lygdamis spent some time in the neighbourhood of Mycale during his attacks on Ionia. It is also clear that the attacks were later than the Meliac war. Since Lygdamis was marauding about 650 BC, the Meliac war was earlier than that, but how much earlier is not yet known.

Ancient historians of Ionia were interested in the war and gave differing accounts of it.[9] An inscription of about 200 BC recording Rhodian arbitration in a border dispute between Priene and Samos names eight writers, of whom one, Euagon of Samos, lived at latest in the second half of the fifth century BC.[10] Since the text mentions division of the land of Melie by the victors, it is clear that Melie lost some, perhaps most, of her land, but she could not have survived if she lost it all. The stone also lists exchanges of land, but the details are uncertain. Colophon gave up Anaea–it is surprising to find her holding land south of Ephesus–according to Maeandrius of Miletus; and the same writer asserted that the Milesians gave–to the Samians presumably– a place whose name begins with A, perhaps Akadamis, in exchange for Thebes on Mycale and Marathesium. All but one of the historians cited held that the Samians obtained Pygela, but Maeandrius claimed that Samos was allotted Karion and Dryoussa, places on Mycale.[11] A mention of the Panionian festival suggests that the terms were agreed at the shrine of Poseidon Heliconius, newly wrested from the rule of the arrogant people of Melie. How Priene benefited from the Holy War we do not know; but she was well placed to take over the priestly privileges formerly enjoyed by the Melians.[12]

An Erythraean story about a king of that city called Cnopus comes from the time when monarchs were losing their authority to dissident nobles, and so perhaps from about 700 BC.[13] On the way to the oracle at Delphi Cnopus was trussed up and thrown overboard by three nobles who wanted to set up an oligarchy. The murderers then put in to Chios, and after borrowing a force from the rulers of that island, Amphiclus and Polytecnus,[14] sailed back by night to Erythrae. The city was quickly taken at the sound of a trumpet by Ortyges the chief murderer; and Cleonice, the wife of Cnopus, had to flee to Colophon, many of the king's men having been killed. Ortyges and his friends next overturned the laws, kept the citizens outside the walls, and dispensed summary justice outside the gates. They dressed foppishly in purple cloaks, and even forced the citizens to clean the streets. At last, however, Hippotes, a brother of Cnopus, returned with a force during a festival and overthrew Ortyges and his family. The story comes from the local chronicler Hippias of Erythrae and is genuine, even if allowance has to be made for some exaggeration. Erythrae was also for a time subject to the rule of the Basilidae: Aristotle states that they ruled well, but the people objected to government by an oligarchy and overthrew the family.[15]

Another local squabble between Chios and Erythrae is typical of early Ionian wars. Chian colonists tried to settle at Leukonia in the Erythraea, because the islanders wanted to get rid of some nobles tainted in a blood feud. The trouble had begun when Hippoclus king of Chios had been killed in a drunken riot at a wedding. The Erythraeans however opposed the settlement and tried to force the colonists out by starving them. Encouraged by their womenfolk, however, the Chian settlers held on.[16] In one of their wars against Erythrae the Chians had the help of Miletus, which in turn received Chian aid in her war against Alyattes of Lydia.[17]

In their long struggle to maintain themselves in Carian territory the Prienians looked for help from Samos against the barbarians. This was not granted, however; instead, the Samians derisively sent a Sibyl. She was accepted by Priene as an omen of victory, which duly came.[18]

Feuds marred early Milesian history, as romantic tradition recalled. A Neleid king Phobius kept as a hostage a young man of the royal line of Halicarnassus in Caria, Antheus. Cleoboea, the wife of Phobius, conceived a fruitless passion for the boy, which was not returned. So she killed him and then herself. Phobius then resigned the kingship to Phrygius, thinking himself accursed.[19]

A romantic story was told about Phrygius too. He married a girl called Pieria from Myus, so bringing to an end a long period of mutual avoidance and enmity between Milesians and Myessians, which abated only when festivals of Artemis were held in Miletus and a truce was declared. During one such truce Phrygius had met Pieria.[20] The trouble between Miletus and Myus can perhaps be linked with a story recording the flight of the Neleids' opponents from Miletus to Myus, but we have no means of dating the war exactly.[21]

Iasos which lay on the gulf of Bargylia between Miletus and Myndus was reputed to be a colony of Argos, but it soon fell under Milesian influence. A Neleid from Miletus was brought into Iasos to help the inhabitants in their war against the Carians.[22] Milesian influence may have reached even further along the coast; for the story of Antheus presupposes that the Neleids were strong enough to take a hostage from Halicarnassus, and the city, though a Dorian foundation with a Carian element in its population, was strongly Ionian by the fifth century BC, when its public decrees were all being written in Ionic,[23] and Herodotus the greatest master of Ionic prose was at school there.

Two other early Milesian rulers are recalled in a tale begun by Conon[24] and finished by Nicolas of Damascus.[25] Leodamas and Phitres (or Amphitres), a Neleid, competed for the kingship of Miletus, until the citizens made them agree that the greater benefactor of the city should become king. There were two wars being fought at the time, one against Melos, the other against Carystus in Euboea. Amphitres' campaign against Melos failed, but Leodamas defeated the Carystians. One of the spoils of victory, a woman with child, was dedicated to the Milesian Apollo at Branchidae. Branchus, the eponymous priest in charge of the oracle, adopted the child and appointed him to announce the prophecies, giving him the name Euangelus. The object of the story is to account for the origin of the Milesian priestly family of the Euangelidae; but the competition for the kingship is genuinely historical, and the naval campaigns bear the mark of truth, for they may well have something to do with the fighting in the great Lelantine war, late in the eighth century BC.

The later history of king Leodamas is taken up by Nicolas of Damascus. Leodamas was a most successful king, and was liked by the people, but in the end he was killed by Amphitres on the way to a festival of Apollo. Amphitres and his party thereupon occupied Miletus and held the city by force, but the sons and friends of Leodamas fled by night to Assesus, where they were welcomed by the chief magistrate,[26] who had been appointed by Leodamas. Before long however they were besieged by Amphitres and his army, but they held out, and consulted an oracle, Branchidae presumably, about what to do. The god instructed them to bring helpers from Phrygia, who would avenge Leodamas and rid the Milesians of their troubles; and later in the siege there duly came to Assesus two young men from Phrygia called Tottes and Onnes.[27] They brought the mysteries of the Cabiri hidden in a chest, and when they came to the wall, holding the chest between them, they asked to be admitted to the city, since they were bringing rites from Phrygia for the good of the Milesians and of the Assesians. So the guards recalled the oracle and admitted them, and at dawn the sons of Leodamas and the rest of the citizenry assembled to enquire of the Phrygians who they were and why they had come. When the same reply was given as to the guards at the wall, the people, overjoyed, promised to establish the rites amongst themselves and to honour the Cabiri, if they could get back to Miletus. The ceremonies being completed, the Phrygians ordered them to march out in full force with the priests in the front of the battle line, and when the armies engaged, the troops of Amphitres were put to flight, he himself being killed by the sons of Leodamas. Peace then returned to Miletus, the tyranny being overthrown. This story also fits the end of the eighth century well, when the kingship was being challenged in Ionia, and the influence of Phrygia was felt there strongly for the first time. Another excerpt from Nicolas mentions a Milesian lawgiver called Epimenes.[28] This man was appointed by the *demos* with power to put to death whomsoever he chose, but being unable to kill the children of Amphitres, he seized their property and put a price on their heads. Three men who had taken part in the murder of Leodamas were killed, and the rest were banished by Epimenes; and so the Neleidae were overthrown. Thus it appears that Leodamas was the last Neleid with royal power in Miletus, and Epimenes the first lawgiver (*aisymnetes*) appointed by the citizens. Members of the Neleid family were, however, still powerful at Miletus long afterwards, in the middle of the fifth century BC.[29]

About 700 BC or a little earlier Chalcis and Eretria engaged in their long conflict for the control of the plain between them.[30] This was the Lelantine war, which we have already mentioned. Thucydides says of this war that the rest of Greece took sides.[31] The problem is to find enough allies for each of the protagonists. Asiatic Ionians may well have taken part, for Herodotus remarks that anciently Miletus was the ally of Eretria and Samos of Chalcis.[32] Samos was once an ally of Sparta whom she helped in a war against the Messenians,[33] and the Samians may also have been friends with the Corinthians about the end of the eighth century BC, when Ameinocles of Corinth built ships for Samos.[34] All this evidence is scattered and hard to control, but Samos and Miletus may well have been engaged in the great Euboean struggle, perhaps sending troops to fight in the Lelantine plain. The Milesian help given to Chios in a war against Erythrae could even be an aspect of the same Panhellenic conflict.[35] But our ignorance of these remote events is very deep, and it is hard to tell why the Ionians formed their alliances as they did. The Asiatics' part at least in the Lelantine war cannot be interpreted as a dispute over colonial ventures: in distant trade and colonisation the Asiatic Ionians were late starters. The Euboeans, as we shall see, with their eastern trade at Al Mina already prospering in the first half of the eighth century, were the pioneers. The first Milesian colonies, those in the Propontis, were not planted before about 675 BC.

With their Phrygian neighbours, whose capital at Gordion was flourishing greatly in the second half of the eighth century, the Aeolians were on good terms. Phrygian traders were able to come down to the Aegean at Kyme,[36] whose king Agamemnon married his daughter to one of the Phrygian kings called Midas.[37] Her name was Hermodike, and she is said to have introduced some kind of currency; we have a hint here of Kyme's commercial interests. Phrygia could offer wool, sheep, and slaves, and could export them through Kyme; what she took in return is less clear, but it may have been in Kyme that before 700 BC the Phrygians learnt of and adopted the Greek alphabet. But the reverse may be true; Phrygia may have given the alphabet with vowels to Greece. Ionian smiths in their turn copied or adapted Phrygian metal work–cauldrons, dishes, and bronze belts.[38] The Lydians also traded to the coast through Kyme, as is shown incidentally in a bloody story of court intrigue in Sardis, dated to some time before the fall of the Heraclid dynasty.[39] The story implies that the Lydian kings were levying an impost on traders passing from the interior through Lydia to the mouth of the Hermus near Kyme. Pottery of Protogeometric type found in the excavations at Sardis[40] suggests that some traders were travelling up from the coast of the Aegean even before the eighth century.

Peaceful dealings between the east Greeks and the Lydians did not last. About 685 Gyges a member of the Lydian family of the Mermnadae overthrew the last Heraclid king Candaules and married his wife, Toudo, a Mysian princess.[41] He is said to have had the support of the Delphic oracle[42] and of a Carian force led by a mercenary, Arselis of Mylasa.[43] The Heraclids however were not wiped out: men of the same family claiming descent from a king Ardys were still held in honour at the sanctuary of Apollo at Clarus near Colophon in Roman times.[44] Possibly some of the Heraclids moved to Colophon after Gyges the Mermnad had become king of Lydia.

The new king in Sardis soon tried to dominate his Asiatic Greek neighbours. He attacked Magnesia by Sipylus, using as a pretext the rough handling by the Magnesians of a Smyrnaean poet, Magnes, who was a favourite of his.[45] Magnesia having been subdued, the Lydians were free to turn against Smyrna and Colophon.[46] The prowess of the Smyrnaeans in the war with Gyges was recalled a generation or two later by the Smyrnaean poet Mimnermus, who reminded his fellow citizens of a man who with his ashen spear had checked, in the very front of the battle line, the assault of the Lydian cavalry by the banks of the Hermus.[47]

At Colophon the Lydians carried their arms into the lower city and only the acropolis held out. Theirs was a remarkable feat, for the Colophonian cavalry then had a high repute: it was even said that they determined the issue of every engagement in which they intervened.[48] After Gyges' victory some Colophonians fled to the Siris valley in southern Italy and founded a city called Polieion;[49] and Lydian influence in Colophon itself grew strong, as Xenophanes[50] more than a century later recalled with bitterness: 'They learned useless luxuries from the Lydians, while still they were not subject to hateful tyranny. They would come to their meeting place in purple cloaks—a full thousand of them as a rule, not less—flaunting their comely locks and drenched in scented unguents.' In this age of polished ease the great Colophonian poet Polymnestus introduced to them the mixed Lydian mode of music.[51] Of the poet himself we are told that he visited Sparta, where he composed epic verses during the second phase of musical development there in the seventh century BC,[52] and was praised not long afterwards by Alcman.[53]

Gyges also attacked Miletus, but he is not said to have kept the place:[54] the inhabitants could easily have held out on Kalabak Tepe, even if they had to abandon the harbour town by the temple of Athena.[55] It is odd, since Gyges attacked Miletus, that he allowed Milesians to plant a colony at Abydus in the Troad, over which the Lydians then had suzerainty.[56] Perhaps this was at first not a proper colony, but rather a settlement of Ionian mercenaries[57] placed to watch the Hellespont, across which the Treres, a Thracian people,[58] were shortly to invade Anatolia. The attacks of them and of their allies the Cimmerians we now consider.

Both Cimmerians and Treres were displaced from their homes north and west of the Black Sea by a movement of Scythians.[59] The Treres under their leader Kobos,[60] having crossed from Thrace to Asia Minor, joined forces with the Cimmerian invaders in attacks on Lydia, in which Lycian marauders also took part.[61] The Cimmerians on the other hand had been driven eastwards into the Caucasus and then turned southwestwards into Asia Minor. Meanwhile their Scythian pursuers made their way southeastwards into Media.[62] Assyrian sources report that the people of Urarṭu in Armenia were defeated by the Cimmerians about 714 BC; later the invaders overran central Asia Minor in the time of the

Assyrian king Aššurhaddon, who defeated them on the frontiers of
Urarṭu in 679.[63] They took the Chersonese on which Sinope was founded,
and threw out a small Milesian settlement of people led by Habrondas;[64]
some of the invaders moved on into Bithynia,[65] and also attacked
Gordion in Phrygia, where the power of king Midas, who killed himself
by drinking bull's blood, crumbled.[66] A discovery of silos filled with
grain at Syassos in Phrygia enabled them to feed themselves for a time;[67]
soon they were threatening Gyges in Lydia, in alliance with the Treres.

Gyges looked for help from Aššurbanipal king of Assyria, in vain;
he had been a faithless friend of the Assyrians, and had encouraged
Psammetichus of Egypt to revolt from them, perhaps even sending
mercenaries.[68] In c. 652 Gyges died in battle against the invaders, and
seven years later the Trerians and Lycians sacked the whole of Sardis
except the acropolis.[69] This disaster befel in the reign of Ardys, Gyges'
son.

The Cimmerians under Lygdamis, whom the Assyrians called Dugdamme,[70] also overran Ionia at the time of the fall of Gyges, but
Herodotus[71] states that though the land was plundered the cities were
not wrecked. Lygdamis attacked Ephesus and burned the sanctuary of
Artemis (though some said that the goddess drove him off)[72] and for a
time he settled in the Batenetis land near Priene,[73] whose neighbours,
the Magnesians by the Maeander, were completely ruined. 'I weep for
the woes of the Thasians, not of the Magnesians'[74] said Archilochus at
this time, for distant troubles were less threatening to him; but the utter
destruction of the Magnesians by the Treres became proverbial.[75]
Callinus expressed the terror of the Ephesians when he proclaimed,
'Now there comes upon us the army of the Cimmerians, the dealers in
violence,'[76] and called on Zeus to protect his city in the hour of need.[77]
The call was heeded, and Magnesia, the old enemy of the Ephesians,
was destroyed instead. Her land was then taken by her neighbours,[78]
though the place was later reoccupied. Sometime after the destruction
of Magnesia the barbarians abandoned Ionia and moved eastwards into
Cilicia, where Lygdamis fell ill and was defeated by the Assyrians. His
son Šandakšatra succeeded him and reigned for a while.[79] A few of the
invaders stayed in the west, however, and were able to settle at Antandrus
in the Troad,[80] where they remained for a century till the time of the
Lydian king Alyattes, who finally drove them out.[81] The threat to the
Ionians was past by about 640 BC; but while it lasted, the very survival of
their civilisation was at stake.

CHAPTER VI

The First Ionian Colonies

WE HAVE SEEN HOW THE ASIATIC IONIANS, HAVING STRENGTHENED their hold on the western Anatolian mainland and in Samos and Chios during the Dark Age, fostered a sense of community at Panionion.[1] By the time of the Cimmerian attack their interests were still mostly local and they had not begun to found colonies. The pioneers in trade and colonisation were the Ionians of Euboea and the Cyclades, whose rivalries had by the end of the eighth century plunged them into the great Lelantine war. Before 750, however, Chalcis and Eretria had been working closely together in trade, settlement, and exploration far outside the Aegean, while in the Cyclades Eretria had won for herself a small naval empire including Andros, Tenos, Ceos, and other islands.[2] Both cities were amongst the first to use heavy-armed, hoplite troops towards the end of the eighth century,[3] and the military strength of the Eretrians about that time is recalled by Strabo who mentions a great procession, a record of which was kept in the sanctuary of Artemis at Amarynthus; three thousand hoplites, six hundred knights, and sixty chariots took part.[4]

The earliest Euboean pioneers are not even recorded in the literary sources. They were the men who by about 800 BC had made their way to Al Mina at the mouth of the Orontes in Syria, where they established an emporium.[5] It was perhaps here, about 750 BC, that the Greeks first learnt to adapt the Phoenician script for their own use,[6] but the creator of the Greek alphabet need not have been an Euboean. One of the earliest examples of the Greek alphabet, if not the earliest, is in fact Attic,[7] and some Athenians may have reached the Levant before 700 BC. Naxians from the Cyclades may have come too, but the pioneers were, to judge from the earliest Greek Geometric pottery found there, Euboeans.[8]

The eastern venture was soon followed, not later than 750 BC, by the founding of a colony in the island of Ischia, ancient Pithecusae, where there were gold mines and rich land.[9] Soon afterwards Euboeans crossed to the mainland and founded Cumae, the *oikists* of which were Kratai-menes of Chalcis and Perieres of Asiatic Kyme.[10] Later the inhabitants of Pithecusae quarrelled:[11] their dispute was perhaps part of the bitter troubles of the Lelantine war between Chalcis and Eretria. When Eretrians were forced to leave Corcyra by the Corinthians about 733,[12]

Eretria lost an important staging point on the way to her western settle-ments, and the influence of her Chalcidian rivals in Italy and Sicily must have been greatly strengthened.

At Naxos, on a headland in eastern Sicily, the Chalcidians and other Ionians placed settlers in 734 BC,[13] the year before the Corinthians founded Syracuse. As the name suggests, Naxians also took part in the colony,[14] which replaced a native settlement.[15] In 729 the Chalcidians of Naxos founded Leontini, driving out the natives from the plain of the river Symaethus. About the same time they also founded Catane on the coast nearby.[16] Next the Chalcidian hold on the straits of Messina was secured by the foundation of Zancle on the Sicilian side by tumultu-ary settlers from Cumae, and later from Chalcis.[17] At Rhegium in Calabria Chalcidians from Zancle were joined by Messenians from Peloponnese.[18] The latter were fleeing from the Spartan conquest of Messenia by king Theopompus in the last quarter of the eighth century BC.[19]

Further west the earliest pioneers were Euboeans and Naxians. We hear of Naxian islands[20] off Tunisia, and an Ionian settlement in the neighbourhood of Carthage may also be Naxian.[21] These foundations may well go back to the time of the Naxian and Chalcidian settlements in Sicily before 700 BC, but only excavation will confirm the conjecture. Nearer home we find Naxians planting a colony in Amorgos,[22] and in the seventh century Delos, as the finds of sculpture suggest, was strongly under Naxian influence,[23] and may even have been a Naxian dependency.

It is not easy to determine the motives of these earlier colonial ventures. Lack of land and a growing population at home may have prompted some Euboeans to sail abroad. The need for metals, notably tin (brought from the Cassiterides, Cornwall, to the Rhône mouth and thence to Cumae),[24] may have been great; and we should not forget the fondness of Greeks, in ancient times as well as modern, for travel for its own sake. The hope of profit after hard bargaining in the Levantine emporia must have attracted many ambitious men; while for many a farmer the prospect of rich land to be won from the natives in Sicily and around Cumae must have been very exciting. But no single factor accounts for the pioneering of the Euboeans and their dependents in the Cyclades before the Lelantine war. The significant fact is that they were showing the way already by 750 BC. The leaders of the Greek renascence were the Ionians of Euboea and the Cyclades, who taught the Greeks to look outwards again from the Aegean world after the long introversion of the Dark Age.

In the Aegean too the Chalcidians had been active. Here the dating of the settlements is hampered by lack of excavation; but that the first Euboean colonies had been planted in the northwest Aegean coastlands by the last quarter of the eighth century is shown by the part taken in the Lelantine war by a contingent from that region.[25] In course of time the Euboean colonies in the north were named collectively Chalcidice, for most of them were Chalcidian. The chief of these early settlements were Torone[26] and Amphipolis.[27] Eretria planted settlers at Mende,[28] and the Eretrians whom the Corinthians expelled from Corcyra (*c.* 733 BC) were not allowed to return home; so some of them settled at Methone in the Chalcidice.[29] Since Eretrians from Corcyra were said to have been driven forcibly with slings from Eretria, literally 'slung out', when they tried to return home, it is possible that the mother city was suffering from overpopulation at the time. Excess of numbers then may have been one cause of her intense colonial activity in the eighth century BC.

The active part taken by Delphi in the encouragement and even in the planning of colonial enterprises was not matched by Apollo's shrine in Delos. Even here however interest was not lacking in places beyond the confines of the Greek world as the strange tradition of the Hyperborean maidens shows.

Near the Artemisium in Delos were two tombs of the early or middle Bronze Age.[30] One, the *theke*, behind the Artemisium was thought by the Delians in the time of Herodotus[31] to be the burial place of two Hyperborean maidens, Arge and Opis, who had brought offerings from a remote land in the north long before. On the left side of the entrance to the Artemisium was the *sema*, the tomb of the maidens Hyperoche and Laodice who were said to have reached Delos in the care of five Hyperborean men. Herodotus[32] remarks that when the maidens and their escorts failed to return home, the Hyperboreans sent no more of their own people to Delos but took their offerings in baskets of straw to their own borders—wherever those may have been. Thence the offerings were passed on to the Scythians and from them to Dodona, where they entered Greece. Next they were carried across northern Greece to the Maliac gulf, and then through Euboea as far as Carystus. The Carystians then sent the basket of offerings to Tenos, leaving out Andros, and from Tenos it came to Delos.[33]

Pausanias gives a different route, taking in Attica, but this looks like a less ancient version of the story.[34] Attic embassies to Delos set out from Prasiae and may have begun as early as 600 BC, for there was a law, perhaps the work of Solon the Athenian lawgiver of that time, concerned with the Deliastae or emissaries to the Delian Apollo.[35] The origin of the legend of the Hyperborean maidens remains unexplained, but Herodotus at least makes clear that the offerings came in his time from somewhere in the barbarian world beyond Dodona. The fact that the tombs in Delos associated with the maidens were Bronze Age burials is not evidence however that offerings had already been brought from so far away in Mycenaean times. The five men who accompanied the maidens were called Perpherees and received great honours from the Delians according to Herodotus,[36] whose account of them may mean that there were still officials called Perpherees in Delos in his time.

A hint that the Hyperborean cult in Delos is very ancient is given by its connexion with Olen the Lycian, who according to Pausanias was the author of the oldest Greek hymns.[37] From Herodotus[38] we learn that Olen composed the hymn in honour of the maidens Arge and Opis as well as other hymns sung in Delos, but no reason is given why Olen came to Delos from Lycia. Possibly he was drawn by the Delian cult of Apollo's mother Leto, who was much honoured by the Lycians.[39]

Of all the sacred monuments of Delos one was specially venerated already in Homer's day. This was the palm tree to which Odysseus compared the graceful Nausicaa.[40] Theognis in the sixth century BC mentions that Leto had grasped the tree while she gave birth to Apollo 'beside the wheel-shaped lake',[41] the sacred lake of Apollo upon which his swans floated, not far from the imposing row of nine archaic marble lions.

In Roman Imperial times there was an oracle of Apollo in Delos,[42] but there is no cogent evidence for one having flourished there earlier. It is significant that Delos in the Homeric Hymn to Apollo asks to be granted a fair temple to be an oracle for men, but Leto promises an altar and a temple without a word about an oracle.[43] If there was an oracle of Apollo in Delos in early times it cannot have been very important.

The Ionians of Delos[44] profited so greatly from the visits of pilgrims that they never needed to colonise. Theirs was one of the smallest of the Cyclades, but also the most venerable. Delos in Pindar's words was, 'Daughter of the sea, unmoving marvel of the broad earth, whom mortals call Delos, but the blessed ones in Olympus dark Earth's shining star.'[45] The other islands dancing in a circle about her could not rely on divine bounty: some were forced to colonise.

We have already noticed Naxian colonies. Andros, which before the

Lelantine war had been an Eretrian dependency, had also been forced to send colonists abroad. Andrians and Chalcidians joined in the foundation of Sane on the Athos peninsula. Then they heard that the natives had abandoned Acanthus nearby, but a dispute over who had a prior claim to the empty city arose, and the parties agreed to submit to the arbitration of the Erythraeans, Samians, and Parians.[46] Erythrae and Samos voted for Andros, but Paros for the Chalcidians. So the Andrians were awarded Acanthus, but vowed never to intermarry with the Parians. The date of the settlement is given as 654 BC.[47] The Andrians also settled at Stagira[48] (the birthplace of Aristotle, who can perhaps be claimed as an Ionian) and at Argilus by the Strymon.[49]

About the time of the Acanthus dispute or a little earlier the Parians also established themselves in the northern Aegean, both in the island of Thasos and on the Thracian mainland opposite, the Thasian *peraia*. Some early pottery found in Thasos is East Greek of about 650 BC,[50] but this may be later than the first Parian settlement. The colony was founded at the command of the Delphic oracle by Telesicles, son of Tellis;[51] and the rites of Demeter, who was much worshipped in Paros and had priests called Kabarnoi in the island,[52] were introduced to Thasos by the priestess Cleoboea.[53] Telesicles' chief claim to distinction lies in his being the father of the great lyric poet Archilochus by the slave woman Enipo,[54] but he is likely to have been one of the most notable Parians of his time, since Delphi chose him to lead the new colony. It was Delphi too which predicted to him the fame of the son who was the first to welcome him in Paros on his return from a visit to the oracle.[55] The son was Archilochus.

The vigorous poetry of this astonishing man gives us some precious glimpses of life in Paros and Thasos in the seventh century BC. The poet's date is reasonably clear from his mention of Gyges: he introduces a carpenter, Charon, who says that he is not interested in Gyges and all his gold nor does he long for mighty tyranny.[56] This remark cannot have been written earlier than Gyges' accession to the throne of Lydia about 685 BC. Another pointer to the poet's date is his declaration, 'I weep for the troubles of the Thasians, not those of the Magnesians.'[57] This alludes to the destruction of Magnesia by the Maeander by the Treres, about the time of the death of Gyges c. 652 BC, and shows that the Parians were already fighting for their colony in Thasos by that time. In another fragment Aristotle states that a father is speaking about his daughter to Archilochus.[58] This father need not be Lycambes, whose second daughter, Neuboule, Archilochus loved and hoped to marry. Archilochus makes

59

the father remark that nothing is to be unexpected, now that Zeus has made night in the middle of the day, a reference to a total eclipse of the sun which in the context seems to have been a recent one.[59] There was an eclipse, total at Paros about noon, on 15th April 657 BC[60] and this may well be the one to which Archilochus made the father refer, but the mentions of Gyges and the woes of the Magnesians, not the eclipse, are what enable us to date the poet.

Archilochus became a poet, so it was believed in local tradition inscribed in Hellenistic times in the Archilocheion by the river Elytas in Paros, through the intervention of the Muses.[61] One moonlit night shortly before dawn as the boy was driving a cow from a place called Lissides to Paros town he was met by some women, with whom he conversed laughingly. They offered to give him a just price for the cow, and then disappeared leaving a lyre in payment. A search of the island failed to reveal the cow, and Archilochus understood that the lyre was a gift of the Muses, by whose supernatural agency he was made a poet. Of his early years amongst the 'figs and sailors' life'[62] in Paros little is known: but he lost his brother-in-law at sea,[63] and persuaded the Parians to introduce to the island a cult of Dionysus; the Parians had hesitated at first, but when they were afflicted by a disease of the genitals they consulted Delphi and were ordered to obey Archilochus, the oracle's favourite, and bring in the cult of the wine god.[64]

Another Parian inscription preserves fragments of the poet's verses which had been quoted by the local historian Demeas.[65] Demeas dated events by *Archons* in Paros and Thasos; some of their names he found in Archilochus.[66] Evidently he was able to reconstruct a number of events in seventh century Parian history. The inscription records a wreck of a penteconter in the strait between Naxos and Paros. The ship had been bringing Milesian ambassadors to Paros, and of the party one only, Koiranos, survived.[67] He was said to have been carried to the shore by a dolphin, a story which is not quite absurd in view of the high intelligence of those creatures. A cave where the Milesian landed came to be known as the Koiraneion and was sacred to Poseidon the Horseman.

The details of the Neuboule affair are lost, but the outlines can be recovered. Archilochus loved and wished to marry her. Lycambes however had an elder daughter,[68] and like Laban, father of Leah and Rachel, he may well have insisted on the elder marrying first. Archilochus, who had been admitted to close ties of salt and table with the family of Lycambes,[69] refused to be another Jacob. He wanted the younger daughter and was not allowed her. So he gave vent to his wrath in verses of bitter scorn for Lycambes.[70] Yet there may have been moments of wistful regret too: 'if only I could touch the hand of Neuboule' the poet once declared.[71]

Perhaps after the setback of the Neuboule affair, the poet took the advice of Delphi and joined the Parian colonists in Thasos.[72] He himself tells us how he saved his life but abandoned his shield by a bush during an engagement with the Thracian Saioi.[73] Some fragments of his show that the Naxians also fought under a Neleid leader, in Thasos or on the Thracian mainland, against the Parians. The Thracians had at first welcomed the Naxians, who foolishly turned upon their benefactors and were ruined.[74] The Parians were victorious[75] and no Naxians got a foothold on the northern Aegean coasts, whereas the Parians of Thasos were able to found settlements in their peraia[76] and exploit the local gold mines of the island and the mainland.[77] They had already been fighting against the Chians of Maroneia in Archilochus' time,[78] and were then getting a secure foothold in Thasos itself.

Of his other travels we know nothing certain. He is said to have visited Sparta,[79] he knew of a Milesian whore,[80] and he praised the streams of Siris beside which the Colophonians were settling when the Parians were fighting for Thasos.[81] But we do not know that he lived anywhere except Paros, Thasos, and the Thasian peraia. The oracle given to him suggests that he may have visited Delphi, and his own remark that he would be called a Carian mercenary shows that he may have travelled far as a soldier.[82] We simply do not know. One fragment predicts an outbreak of war in Euboea, but does not prove that the poet took part, or even that there was a war in his time in that island.[83] The little that we do know from his fragments amply confirms his proud claim that he was the servant of the Lord God of War and knew full well the lovely gift of the Muses.[84]

He was killed by a Naxian, Calondas 'the Crow', who incurred the hatred of the Pythia. When Calondas came to the oracle, the priestess declared, 'You have killed the servant of the Muses. Depart from the temple.'[85] The Naxian had to make his way to Taenarus in Laconia before he could be purified from the blood guilt. We do not know on what occasion Calondas killed Archilochus; but in the Pythia's view it was a great sin to kill, even in war,[86] the most gifted poet of the day. If Archilochus died fighting Naxians in Thasos he gave his life for a successful cause. With the secure foundation of the colony in Thasos the first phase of Ionian colonisation may be said to end. Not long after-

wards there was set up in Thasos a monument to the poet's friend
Glaucus who had distinguished himself in the fighting for the island,[87]
and Parian sculptors were at work there.[88] By 625, thanks to the efforts
of Archilochus and his friends, the Parians in Thasos had proved to the
Thracians that they had come to stay, and by 600 they even had a colony
at Neapolis on the mainland.[89]

Further east the Thasians were less successful. A party under Archias
failed to hold on to Archion near Chalcedon on the Bosporus and had to
move to Aenus by the river Hebrus.[90] This settlement too seems to have
been a failure, for Aenus is later found as an Aeolian colony.[91] It had
originally been occupied by Thracians, when its name was Poltymbria,
'Poltys' Town.'[92] East of Aenus Clazomenians under Timesias gained a
foothold, but were driven out by Thracians, according to Eusebius about
654;[93] the Chians at Maroneia however secured their position and built
up a flourishing wine trade such as existed in Chios itself.[94]

While the Parians, Chalcidians, and Chians had been settling in the
northern Aegean lands the Aeolians of Lesbos and the Aeolis had also
been active. Mitylene planted colonists at Sestus[95] and Madytus[96] at the
passage of the Dardanelles opposite Abydus, and farther north was her
colony Alopeconnesus 'Fox Island'.[97] In the Troad the Aeolians of
Tenedos had a peraia of their own, and there were several small
Mytilenian settlements of farmers on either side of the Tenedian
domain in the country inhabited by the barbarian Gergithai, who were
thought to be descendants of the ancient Teucrians.[98] Inland were the
Aeolian cities of Cebren, Scepsis, and Neandria, all of them made
moderately prosperous by their wool trade. Neandria had a fine temple
with Aeolic capitals, Cebren drew profit from an iron mine,[99] and at
Scepsis the ancient dynasty of the Aeneadae continued to rule on the
lower slopes of Ida up the valley of the Scamander.[100] Homer knew of
their renown, for the Iliad prophesies the glory of Aeneas' descendants.[101]
Not only Aeolians but also Milesians settled in the city of this ancient
Trojan dynasty.[102] In Troy itself there had been Aeolians from about
750 BC onwards.[103]

The men of Methymna in Lesbos who looked across to the steep
coast that leads eastwards from Cape Lectum to the gulf of Adramyttium founded along it the cities of Assus, Lamponia, and, from
Assus, Gargara.[104] These places never became great centres of trade,
but their agriculture prospered, and Assus was famous for her lofty
citadel.[105]

The Aeolian moves northward were not followed up. The initiative passed about 675 BC to the Ionians and the Megarians. Amongst the Ionians the Milesians were, after the Cimmerians had passed away, the most energetic traders and colonists, and, partly through their commercial enterprise in the Euxine, their city grew to be the largest and richest of the Greek foundations in Asia Minor.

CHAPTER VII

Colonies of the Eastern Ionians

THROUGHOUT THE DARK AGE MILETUS DEVOTED HERSELF TO SECURING
from the Carians her mainland territory, which consisted, apart from
the city itself, of the *hyperakria*, or limestone plateaux of the peninsula
south of the Maeander mouth, and part of the Maeander plain.[1] We have
seen that she also held land on Mycale at the time of the Meliac war, and
remarked how she put princes of her own into Iasos to rule there. Next
she secured the approaches to the Maeander mouth by placing settlers in
Leros, Lepsia, and Patmos.[2] Icaria west of Samos also became Milesian,
but the Corseae islands were Samian.[3]

One of the first places to be settled from Samos was Minoa in
Amorgos. The colonists were led by the poet Simonides (or Semonides),[4]
who was a contemporary of Archilochus. The poet's stringent criticisms
of women[5] and rather pedestrian notions suggest that the Samian
settlers may not have found his rule enlightened. What his poem on the
Archaeology of the Samians[6] contained we do not know.

The Samian colonies at Nagidus and Celenderis[7] may also be early, as
they lay conveniently on the way to Al Mina, and Levantine bronze
work was reaching Samos by about 700 BC.[8] Only by excavation can the
eastern Samian settlements be dated, but there were already Greeks
along the same coast at Tarsus in Cilicia when the Assyrians crushed a
revolt there in 698 BC.[9] Kymaians too settled on this southern Anatolian
coast, at Side in Pamphylia[10] and Geometric pottery was being imported
to Mersin before 700 BC.[11]

Another early Samian settlement was made in Samothrace. The
excavations in the island show that about 700 BC the Thracians were
joined by Greeks,[12] and Herodotus clearly states that the Greeks of
Samothrace were Ionians.[13] From later writers we learn that they were in
fact Samians, who came at the command of Delphi.[14]

The first Greeks to enter the Black Sea or Euxine were traditionally
the Argonauts. In the eighth century Hesiod already knew of the Phasis
river up which they voyaged to Ocean from the eastern end of the
Euxine,[15] and Arctinus the Milesian poet is said to have mentioned the
White Island off the Danube mouth to which Thetis carried the body of
Achilles.[16] The fragments ascribed to Eumelus, the Corinthian poet of
the late eighth century, mentioning Borysthenes and Sinope[17] are less

cogent evidence for Greek knowledge of those places before 700 BC, but by 650 the Danube (Istros) was known to the Ionians, as the name Istrokles written at that time on a pot from Old Smyrna testifies.[18] Before 700 Hesiod had mentioned the Istros in his *Theogony*.[19]

Though the literary evidence hints at Greek knowledge of the Euxine before 700 BC, there is no Greek material from the Black Sea region so early as that, and we must conclude that any trade there may have been in the eighth century was slight and sporadic. Eusebius dates a foundation at Trapezus on the southeastern shore of the Black Sea in 756 BC. If there was an eighth century settlement here, it may have been made for trade with Urarṭu and is not likely to have survived the Cimmerian invasions. There is however no archaeological support for so early a Greek foundation here.[20]

The Milesians are not likely to have sailed regularly into the Euxine before they were well established in the Propontis, the sea of Marmara. The earliest Milesian settlements here were made in the seventh century, from about 675 onwards. Greek pottery has been found in the Lydian city of Dascylium dating from about 700 BC,[21] but this does not prove that the Milesian colony at Cyzicus nearby was founded so early. There were Milesians in Proconnesus by about 650, for Aristeas the traveller was living there then.[22] This island may have escaped the Trerian incursions, but Milesian colonies in the Thracian Chersonese may all date from late in the seventh century after the Trerian threat had passed; here Miletus founded Limnae,[23] and there were Clazomenians as well as Milesians in Cardia.[24] On the south shore the Erythraeans in Parium[25] and the Milesians in Abydos, Cyzicus and Kios founded a number of secondary settlements, devoted themselves to their fisheries and to farming the hinterland, and with their good havens benefited from the coasting traffic through the Propontis.[26] The Samians, being later, had to take less favourable sites on the north shore at Hera's Wall,[27] Bisanthe[28] and Perinthus[29] west of the Bosporus where Megarians were well established by the middle of the seventh century at Chalcedon and Byzantium.

The only Phocaean colony in the Propontic area was Lampsacus.[30] Here Codrids from Phocaea helped the barbarian king Mandron against his enemies. Later the Greeks, anticipating a plot against them, seized the city while the natives were banqueting outside. The date of the settlement is given as 654 BC by Eusebius. Later still the Lampsacenes won some land from their neighbours in Parium in a boundary dispute. The two cities agreed to settle the matter by sending out at cock-crow two parties, one from each side, and the boundary was to be at the place where they met. The Parians were delayed by some fishermen stationed in their path by the Lampsacenes, and were persuaded to join in a feast and a sacrifice to Poseidon. They dallied so long that the Lampsacenes reached Hermaeum, seventy stades from Parium, before meeting the Parian party.[31]

In the century or so before the Persian conquest of Ionia the Milesians went far towards making the Black Sea a lake of their own. Their only serious competitors were the Megarians who founded Mesambria and Callatis on its western shores and Heraclea Pontica, a convenient haven for mariners making the three hundred mile coasting voyage from the Bosporus to Sinope. But the Megarians were less enterprising than the Milesians, who planted settlements right round the coasts of the Euxine. We now describe the most important of them briefly, travelling eastwards first and starting in the south.

Sinope, whose promontory is the most obvious landmark on the southern shore of the Euxine, was settled by the Milesian exiles Coes and Cretines.[32] It was a fine harbour and was well placed for trade with the interior. A route inland from Sinope leads to Ḫattušaš, the old Hittite capital, which later became an important 'Phrygian'[33] settlement. Since Greek pottery was used at Ḫattušaš from about 600 BC[34] and Phrygian is found at Sinope,[35] regular trade may well have passed to and from the coast by the end of the seventh century. The earliest pottery in Sinope itself, Corinthian and East Greek, comes from a cemetery outside and dates from about 600. A few pieces of about the same date have been recovered from beneath the modern town of Sinop which covers the ancient city. According to tradition the first Milesian settlers under Habrondas[36] were driven out by the Cimmerians who occupied the peninsula; later came Coes, Cretines and their party. But at the moment we have no archaeological proof that Milesians occupied Sinope before the end of the seventh century. Sinope's riches came from the export of timber, a flourishing tunny fishery, and the production of miltos, a red dye.[37]

East of Sinope the Milesians founded Amisus amongst the Cappadocians.[38] The earliest Greek pottery here is a little after 600 BC. Like Sinope, Amisus was well situated for trade, in iron especially, with the hinterland; East Greek pottery has been found with Phrygian about ten miles inland at Ak Alan, and further inland at Pazarlı some clay relief plaques, made to decorate the facades of buildings, reveal East Greek influence of the early sixth century BC.[39] Eastwards from Amisus

Trapezus lies beneath Trebizond and awaits exploration. Colonial life here must have been hard at first, for the local barbarians, Tibarenians and Mosynoeci, were very wild and attacked wayfarers.[40] But the city did profit from the metal trade with the Chalybes and Armenia, and it was able to survive upon its defensible acropolis.

On the eastern coast of the Black Sea in the land of Colchis there were Milesians at Dioscurias[41] and at Phasis,[42] which gets its name from the river at whose mouth it stood. The foundation dates of these colonies are not known, but they enjoyed a flourishing trade with the natives,[43] and the Greeks of Phasis may already have begun to mint silver in the sixth century BC.[44]

Ionian knowledge of inner Asia owed much to the explorations of Aristeas, who composed a poem on his travels, the *Arimaspea*. He disappeared from Proconnesus for over six years, then returned to relate his experiences, and again 'seized by Apollo' went off to the northeast, never to return, though the Metapontines of southern Italy thought that they had seen him some two hundred and forty years later according to Herodotus.[45] Since Herodotus was not writing later than about 430 BC the second disappearance of the poet may not have been later than about 670 BC; Proconnesus would have been founded by that time.[46] Aristeas or his father may have belonged to the first generation of settlers, for the name of his father Caystrobius suggests that he was born or conceived, not in Proconnesus, but by the river Cayster in Ionia.[47] Aristeas, a leading citizen, may well have belonged to one of the founding families of the Milesian colony in the island.

Aristeas heard much about central Asia on his travels, and may even have had word of the Chinese, but he got no further than the Issedonians, and frankly confessed that what he had heard about the regions beyond was hearsay.[48] To have reached the Issedonians, even when driven on by Apollo, was a great achievement, for they lived far from the coasts of the Black Sea on land they had taken from the Scythians, who in turn had dispossessed the Cimmerians.[49] In the time of Aristeas the Issedonians were perhaps living at the head waters of the Ishim, a tributary of the Ob, and there they may well have told him of the central Asiatic mountains and of the peaceful Hyperboreans beyond, who may have been the Chinese.[50] The knowledge brought back by Aristeas spread widely in the Greek world, and Alcman at Sparta some years later spoke of the Issedonians; so perhaps they were well known to his hearers.[51] The best place for Aristeas to begin his journey northeastwards through the steppe was the coast of the sea of Azov, from which he could follow

the river Tanais (Don) inland. In this connexion it is noteworthy that
some of the earliest Greek pottery (c. 625 BC) found in south Russia
comes from Krivoroshie between the Don and Donetz, some 250 miles
from the sea.[52] It may well be that Aristeas pioneered a route later
followed by traders with Greek goods. There was certainly some trade
with south Russia before the Milesians founded colonies there, and it is
significant that some of the earliest Greek finds have been made well
inland, up the Dniepr, Bug, and Don.

From south Russia the Milesians brought grain and dried fish, notably
dried and pickled tunny. Assured of a regular supply of food from the
Euxine settlements, the Milesians had little to fear from the ravaging of
their fields at home by the Lydians, and from 600 onwards the city's
population could increase rapidly. We have no statistics, but at present
the evidence suggests that the growth of Miletus' population was rather
a result, than a cause, of her colonial activity. What the Milesians sent in
return for the food is not clear. Some of the East Greek pottery in the
Pontus may well be Milesian, and wool manufactures for which the city
was famous may have been sent to the Scythians, who would have valued
them in winter. As natives and Greeks intermarried, so there grew up a
market for all the material benefits of Greek civilisation. Amongst the
Graeco-Scythians the Milesians must have found eager customers in the
Callippidae, farmers who lived inland from the colony in Olbia.[53]

Olbia lay on the right bank of the Bug estuary. None of the earliest
Greek pottery dates from before c. 600. Another colony was planted in
Berezan island on the estuaries of the Bug and Dniepr towards the open
sea. This may once have been a peninsula. The earliest pottery, Chian
and Rhodian, may be a little earlier than that in Olbia, and Berezan may
have been the first Greek settlement hereabouts.[54] In the Crimea there
was another group of Milesian settlements clustering about the entrance
to the sea of Azov. The most important of the early ones was perhaps
Panticipaeum,[55] which was settled by the early sixth century; the native
settlement had been already trading with the Greeks at the end of the
seventh.[56] A similar course of events can be seen at Cercinitis 'Crab
City' (Eupatoria) in the western Crimea,[57] where a native settlement
trading with the Greeks was replaced by a Greek colony.

Of the Milesian settlements on the western shore most is known about
Istros,[58] which lay between Tomis, another Milesian foundation,[59] and
the Danube mouth. The coastline here has changed much since antiquity, but it is clear that the first settlement was made on a hill, which
may then have been an island rather than a peninsula. The earliest

pottery is mostly East Greek and Attic, and none of it goes back much before 600 BC.[60] The traditional dating to 657/6 of the foundation may therefore be too high, but more excavation is needed. West of Istros inland the native village at Tariverde had dealings with the Milesian colonists soon after they arrived at Istros.[61] Further north the Istrians founded near Olbia a colony of their own at Istrian Harbour for trade with south Russia,[62] and they were obviously well placed to take part in commerce along the western coast of the Black Sea to the Bosporus. On the south side of the present Istrian lagoon there seems to have been a good haven in antiquity. South of Istros the Milesians at Apollonia Pontica, in what is now Bulgaria, were well established by the early sixth century BC; the epoch of foundation given by Pseudo-Scymnus, c. 610 BC, may even be correct.[63] The earliest Greek finds hereabouts are from Sozopol bay, but the Greek settlement was built on the island of St Kiriak north of Sozopol and on a peninsula by the island. Odessus, at Varna north of Apollonia, was founded about a generation later, the earliest pottery being of the middle of the sixth century.[64] This agrees quite well with the tradition that the place was settled in the time of Astyages the Mede.[65]

In view of Delphi's great encouragement of Greek colonisation it is very remarkable that not a single Pythian oracle survives urging the Milesians to found any one of their many colonies: Apollo of Delphi, it seems, was not concerned in, even if he was not hostile to, the great Pontic colonial enterprise of the Milesians. Apollo of Didyma however did look with favour on their ventures. A Milesian inscription of the second century BC claims that the settlers of Apollonia by the river Rhyndacus and of other places in the Propontis and Hellespont came under the leadership of Apollo himself to those parts, which they won by the spear from the native barbarians.[66] From the inscription it is plain that the men of Apollonia were still proud to recall their Milesian origin about five centuries after Miletus had begun to colonise the Propontis: they had a lively tradition that their city was established by force.

In the west Miletus planted no early colonies of her own. The city did have its agents in southern Italy however, for there were close ties of friendship with the Sybarites, and when Sybaris was destroyed by her neighbour Croton in 510 BC the men of Miletus shaved their heads and went into mourning.[67] It may have been at Sybaris that Milesian wares bound for Etruria were handed over to the Etruscans, who sailed northwards for home after the short journey overland to Laus. When the first Milesians did settle in the west they came not as traders but as privateers, after the Persian sack of their city in 494 BC, and seized Zancle in the company of Samians.[68]

Colophon's colony Siris on the gulf of Tarentum was founded by fugitives from Gyges' attacks.[69] At first it was called Polieion, but the name of the river Siris came to be applied to the city. A loom weight found at Siris was inscribed in the Ionic script in the sixth century and confirms that the place was then Ionian.[70] The Colophonians lasted until the third quarter of the sixth century, when the city was taken by Sybaris, Croton, and Metapontum.

There were thought to have been some Rhodians in Siris before the Ionians,[71] but this tradition cannot be checked. If Rhodians came first, then their settlement may have been very early indeed, for Strabo records that even before the first Olympiad Rhodians were voyaging in the western Mediterranean.[72] The Ionians in Siris dressed quite as luxuriously as the Colophonians themselves, and their girdled tunics became a byword amongst the rustics of the neighbourhood.[73] Endowed with rich lands, Siris obviously prospered during the century or so of Ionian occupation, but her luxury perhaps was her undoing, for she succumbed to her neighbours.

Colophon the mother city was essentially agricultural, in contrast to Miletus, and so it is not surprising that she did not colonise much. Apart from Siris the only oversea settlement of Colophon was at Myrleia on the Propontis.[74]

One of the pioneers in the exploration of the far western Mediterranean was Colaeus the Samian. He was blown off course on a voyage to Egypt about 638 BC and made his way through the straits of Gibraltar, the Pillars of Herakles, to Tartessus. Here he was able to tap an untouched supply of Spanish silver, and on returning home he dedicated a tithe of his enormous profit to Samian Hera.[75] His silver paid for an offering of a huge bronze griffin-head cauldron of Argive type, supported by three kneeling human figures of bronze, each seven cubits tall. In spite of this success, however, Colaeus may not have been the first Greek to reach Tartessus, for offerings of Tartessian bronze are said to have been dedicated at Olympia a little earlier than his voyage.[76]

The Samian initiative was not followed up. In the west the Phocaeans became the most enterprising traders and colonists; before the rise of Etruscan and Carthaginian naval power in the middle of the sixth century they placed a series of settlements on the coasts of what are now southern France and eastern Spain.[77] Here trade definitely preceded colonisation. By about 700 BC Cycladic vases were reaching Marseilles, and by the end of the seventh century the native villages at Saint-Blaise and La Couronne at the mouth of the Rhône were receiving Corinthian and East Greek wares.[78]

Massalia (Marseilles), the most important of the western Phocaean colonies, was founded about 600 or a little earlier on the hill to the north of the Old Harbour. There is a story in the *Constitution of the Massaliots* by Aristotle which purports to show how the city came to be founded. Euxenus of Phocaea was a guest friend of Nanus the king of the district. Petta the king's daughter chose the Phocaean as her husband and changed her name to Aristoxene. Their son was Protis, from whom the Protiadae, a clan in Massalia, took their name.[79] The tale implies that the Greek city was founded with the approval of the native king, but there was also a story that the Phocaeans were ordered to make a settlement at Massalia by an oracle which advised them to take a priestess of Artemis of Ephesus with them. The goddess then appeared to Aristarche, an Ephesian noblewoman, who at her command sailed with the colonists.[80] Artemis of Ephesus was also much honoured in the secondary settlements of the Phocaeans in the west founded from Massalia.

Massalia was a potent force in the civilising of her neighbours. Having fine vineyards of her own, she taught the barbarians the delights of wine drinking, encouraged them to till their fields and to wall their towns,[81] and perhaps had a lively trade in exporting salt to the peoples of the Hallstatt cultures to the north.[82] It was perhaps through Massalia that the spectacular Greek cauldron reached Vix near the navigable limit of the Seine about a hundred miles southeast of Paris.[83] Southwards along the Seine valley and down the Rhône came the Cornish tin needed by bronze workers of the Greek world.[84] Amidst this prosperity the city enjoyed a stable government under a council of six hundred, whose members held office for life.[85]

Massalia founded several cities in southern France, of which Nicaea (Nice) and Antipolis (Antibes) are perhaps the best known today. Westwards along the coast of Spain the settlement at Ampurias (Emporion) has been explored. The earliest settlers took an islet offshore from the native town on the mainland. Later the Greeks moved to the mainland, and later still combined their town with the native settlement.[86] The earliest pottery from Ampurias dates from about 600, and some of it is East Greek. Other Phocaean settlements along the coast of Spain including Hemeroscopium and Mainake formed a chain of outposts conveniently placed on the route through the straits to Tartessus. One of them, Rhode, recalls by its name the earlier presence of

Rhodians.[87] In Spain too trade seems to have preceded colonisation, for
an early Phocaean portulan, parts of which are preserved in the *Ora
Maritima* of the late Roman writer Avienus, fails to mention the
Massaliot colony Emporium, though it knows of trade with Ireland
through the straits.[88] Thus the Phocaean source of Avienus may well
date from the end of the seventh century BC or earlier.

When the Phocaeans reached Tartessus and its 'silver rooted streams',
as Stesichorus called them,[89] in their penteconters, they made friends
with Arganthonius the king, who is said to have lived for one hundred
and twenty years, and to have reigned for eighty. He was so fond of them
that he invited them to settle wherever they liked in his land; after
failing to persuade them he paid instead for the fortification of Phocaea.[90]
The close ties between the Ionians of Phocaea and the Tartessians were
perhaps known to one of the authors of Genesis, who called Tarshish a
son of Javan.[91] Arganthonius was dead when the Persians took Phocaea
about 545 BC.[92] His first dealings with the Phocaeans may have been at
least half a century earlier. Avienus does not prove that the Phocaeans
went beyond Tartessus to the British Isles, but in Tartessus they must
have heard much about the sources of Cornish tin and perhaps of Irish
gold too. Herodotus also tells us that the Phocaeans pioneered in
the exploration of the Adriatic,[93] but this remark has yet to be con-
firmed archaeologically. Another Phocaean, Euthymenes of Massalia,
courageously explored the west coast of Africa beyond the straits.[94]

We turn now to the very different circumstances of Ionian settlement
in Egypt. The first Greeks known to have arrived in Egypt after the
Mycenaean age were mercenary soldiers, Ionian and Carian bronze-clad
warriors who helped Psammetichus I to win back his throne. These men
may have been sent by Psammetichus' friend Gyges of Lydia, who joined
him in opposition to the Assyrians. The mercenaries were rewarded by
the Egyptian king with two strips of land called Stratopeda or 'Camps'
on either side of the Pelusiac branch of the Nile.[95] The position of these
camps has not been fixed.

Also during the reign of the first Psammetichus (664–610) Milesians
built a fort on the Bolbitine mouth of the Nile. Later they sailed up into
the Saite nome and after a battle founded Naucratis ('Naval Victory')
on the east bank of the Canopic branch of the Nile, ten miles from the
capital of Psammetichus I in Sais.[96] In spite of the poor quality of the
excavations here study of the finds has shown something about the time
of the settlement and supports the dating given by Strabo, but the
stratigraphy of the place is past recovery. The earliest datable pottery is

Corinthian of the latter years of the seventh century, with one piece perhaps as early as 630.[97] Since Naucratis was a new foundation, not a native settlement taken over after prior trade with the Greeks, it is reasonable to date the foundation in the last quarter of the seventh century during the last years of Psammetichus' reign. By the end of the seventh century Rhodian and Chian pottery was being used in Naucratis, and Rhodians and Chians may have already settled.

The chief sanctuary at Naucratis was the Hellenium, which, Herodotus[98] reports, was established in common by the following cities; of the Ionians, Chios, Teos, Phocaea, and Clazomenae; of the Dorians, Rhodes, Cnidus, Halicarnassus, and Phaselis; of the Aeolians, Mytilene alone. These places provided *prostatai*, administrators of the emporium. The Aeginetans, Samians and Milesians also had sanctuaries of their own apart from the Hellenium; the first dedicated theirs to Zeus, the second to Hera, and the last to Apollo. All these may have been in existence soon after the city's foundation, though Herodotus,[99] whose words are not clear here, is writing of the time of king Amasis, about half a century afterwards. Amasis made Greeks who arrived to settle in his time dwell in Naucratis; and Herodotus also remarks that 'of old' – in the earliest years of the city presumably – Naucratis was the only emporium in Egypt: any trader who came to any mouth of the Nile other than the Canopic had to swear that he had not gone off course deliberately, and was compelled to make for Naucratis at once.[100]

Naucratis was a genuinely international venture. Many Egyptians were xenophobes, and the Greeks in the city must have looked to each other for mutual support. However, the chance of quick profits compensated for a sense of isolation in a strange country. There was plenty of gain to be had from the export of corn and from the import of wine, olive oil, and silver.

Egyptian interest in the Aegean world was stimulated, however, by the presence of large numbers of Carian and Greek mercenaries in the land. About 608 the pharaoh Neco dedicated his armour to Apollo of Branchidae,[101] and his successor Psammetichus II relied heavily upon Carian and Greek soldiers in his great expedition of 591 BC against the Nubians. Amongst the Greeks who scratched their names on the legs of the colossal rock-cut statues at Abu Simbel were a Teian, a Colophonian and a Dorian from Ialysus in Rhodes. The man who took them upstream as far as they could go was a certain Psammetichus son of Theocles. He seems to have been in charge of the troop ferries and to have been an Egyptianised Greek.[102] Upper Egypt came to be well known to Greeks, for there were Greek mercenaries in the fort at Elephantine north of Abu Simbel, stationed there to guard the approaches to Nubia.[103]

Apries, who reigned from about 589 to 570, is said by Herodotus to have had a mercenary army of thirty thousand Carians and Ionians, who fought bravely against the usurper Amasis but were defeated.[104] Amasis became king, but took no reprisals against the foreigners. Indeed he became friendly with the Greeks, some of whom became his guardsmen at Memphis when the cantonments at Stratopeda were abandoned during his reign.[105]

Amasis gave much proof of his Philhellenism. He took as wife a well-born Cyrenaean, Ladike,[106] and sent an offering to that city.[107] He helped to pay for the rebuilding of Apollo's temple at Delphi with a large gift of alum.[108] He allied himself to Polycrates of Samos, and dedicated to Samian Hera two wooden images of himself.[109] To the Spartans he sent a corselet as a gift.[110] How well he treated the Greeks of Cyprus, which paid tribute to him,[111] we do not know.

One more Ionian settlement in Egypt deserves a mention. Herodotus reports that some Samians of the Aeschrionian tribe, mercenaries perhaps, lived in a town called Oasis, seven days march westwards through the sand from Thebes. To the Greeks the place was known as the Islands of the Blest, a little outpost of Hellenism in the hostile desert. The settlement was there by 525 and still existed in the time of Herodotus,[112] but its time of foundng is not recorded: it may have been the Kargeh Oasis in Libya northwest of Elephantine.

It is obvious that no single explanation accounts for the Ionians' colonising activity. In some colonies the settlers needed land. In others they looked for trade with the natives. Some cities were founded long after trade had begun with the indigenous peoples. Grain from south Russia, Cornish tin from Massalia, iron from Pontus, all found a ready market in the Ionian cities, and distant trade, such as that with Tartessus, was at first indistinguishable from exploration. As the Ionian economy grew, so did the Ionian view of the world, and it is not surprising that the first systematic geographies and the first genuine maps were composed in the most enterprising of the cities, Miletus and Phocaea.

CHAPTER VIII

Ionia in the Time of Alyattes

THE ATTACKS OF GYGES UPON IONIA WERE INTERRUPTED BY THE invasion of the Cimmerians, but Ardys his son was able to continue them when the invaders retreated (*c.* 640 BC). He took Priene and attacked Miletus,[1] and was succeeded by his son Sadyattes after a reign of about thirty-five years.[2]

Sadyattes prosecuted the war against Miletus.[3] His sister, who had been married to a Greek, he forced to live with himself, and when her husband fled to Dascylium, Sadyattes expelled him from there also. Finally the poor man settled in Proconnesus. He was of distinguished lineage, being a descendant of Melas, a connexion by marriage of Gyges. After marrying his own sister, Sadyattes married two other women, who were sisters; by his own sister he had Alyattes, who succeeded him, and by the two other wives Attales and Adramys.[4]

To the reign of Sadyattes or of his successor Alyattes belongs a significant event in economic history, the invention of true gold and silver coinage, which Xenophanes[5] and Herodotus[6] ascribed to the Lydians. That this ascription may well be correct is clear from the fact that the earliest electrum coins are found not only in the Ionian coastlands, but also up country in Lydia and in the Troad, then a Lydian dependency. The earliest coins were pieces of metal sealed with a mark recognisable by the issuer and the receiver, and known to be of sound weight and metal. Occasionally these earliest issues were given little countermarks by money changers to show that they were genuine and acceptable. The earliest Lydian coins have lions' heads upon them. The most ancient datable deposit of coins comes from the Ephesian Artemisium; it lay in the foundation of a building replaced by the temple to which Croesus contributed so generously. Because the other objects found with the coins in the foundation deposit of the pre-Croesan Artemisium suggest a date not before 600 BC, and perhaps a little later, the coins should be ascribed to the beginning of the reign of Alyattes, whose name, in the form *Walwas*, may well be written on one of them.[7] The invention of coinage to facilitate trade and to get rid of the need to test every lump to see that it was genuine, not just lead coated with silver or gold, can hardly be put more than a generation earlier than 600 BC. Sadyattes, then, may well have been the king in whose reign true coinage was invented, somewhere in western Anatolia. Moreover there is no evidence to contradict the statement of Xenophanes that the Lydians were the inventors; rather, the distribution of the earliest lion-issues suggests strongly that they introduced the first coins.

Alyattes inherited the war against Miletus from his father, and regularly invaded the Milesian territory. Whenever the corn was ripe he attacked to the accompaniment of lyres, pipes and flutes, and destroyed the trees and crops, but to the houses in the fields he did no damage.[8] There was no point in camping outside Miletus, because the city could, by relying on its walls and fleet, hold out indefinitely, and he left the houses in the countryside to encourage the Milesians to plough and sow their fields every year, although they had no profit from their labours. This practice continued for eleven years during which the Milesians suffered two great defeats, one at Limeneion and the other in the Maeandrian plain.[9] Six of these annual incursions were made by Sadyattes, five by his son. The Milesians had to oppose them alone, except for the help they received from the Chiots.[10]

In the twelfth campaigning season when the crops were being burned by the Lydian army, the wind carried the fire to the temple of Athena at Assesus and destroyed it. Alyattes returned to Sardis, where he fell ill, and when the disease did not relent, he sent messengers to Delphi to ask about it. The Pythia replied that the sickness would not cease until Alyattes had the temple of Athena at Assesus rebuilt. It was said that Periander tyrant of Corinth heard of this advice of the Pythia and gave his friend Thrasybulus tyrant of Miletus warning of it.

Thrasybulus ordered the people of Miletus to feast and to enjoy themselves, while all the food was gathered in the market place, so that when the herald came from Sardis to ask for a truce he would think that the Milesians were well supplied with food. This duly happened, and when Alyattes heard the report of the herald, he made a treaty with the Milesians, recovered from his disease, and had two temples built to Athena at Assesus to replace the one that had been burned.[11] The warning given by Periander can be explained by a wish for Alyattes and Thrasybulus to be at peace one with the other, for the Corinthian had friendly dealings with both rulers and would not have wished to be drawn into the war between them. On one occasion he had sent a present of three hundred children of the leading Corcyreans to be made eunuchs at Sardis, but the Samians rescued them when the children and their Corinthian captors stopped in the island on the way to Alyattes.[12]

The Lydians under Alyattes also attacked Smyrna, and took the city,[13] an event vividly illustrated by finds made in the excavations there. Many spearheads and bronze arrowheads were found in the level of destruction of the time of Alyattes; a cache of weapons and an iron helmet of oriental type come from the same period. Some of the arrowheads had been shot into the mud bricks from the walls of the houses. But the most impressive reminder of the siege is the great siegemound by the northwestern walls of the city.[14]

The fall of Smyrna to Alyattes cannot be dated exactly, but it most likely happened towards the beginning of his reign, for the pottery found in the great mound of the Tomb of Alyattes[15] himself near Sardis is appreciably later than the latest pottery found in the excavations of the city of Smyrna. By 590 BC Alyattes was engaged in his long war against the Medes, and for the first five years of his reign, during the last decade of the seventh century,[16] the war against Miletus was being fought. The attack on Smyrna, therefore, may be placed between the Milesian and the Median wars about 600 BC or a little later.

We do not know that the poet Mimnermus lived to see the fall of Smyrna, but he had exhorted his fellow citizens to strive against the enemy, and recalled the prowess of their ancestors in their war against Gyges. His poetry, a compound of resigned melancholy tinged with hedonism, suggests that if he saw Smyrna fall he witnessed the destruction with equanimity. Brief is the harvest of the days of our youth, said he, and no man is there to whom Zeus has not given an abundance of evil.[17] When painful old age comes, then it were better to die, for life without the joys Aphrodite brings is not worth living.[18] Zeus made Tithonus immortal, but he also made him eternally old, and that is more horrible than painful death.[19] Yet perhaps he found in the charms of Nanno, the flute girl,[20] some release from the burden of living, for to the ancients the prevailing impression left by his poetry was of sweetness and delicacy.[21]

The victorious Lydians advanced from Smyrna to Clazomenae, but here Alyattes met with a reverse.[22] Herodotus mentions the Lydian defeat in passing without explaining what happened: but evidently the Clazomenian hoplites proved superior to the Lydian horsemen. Such a victory as theirs is perhaps recalled on North Ionic sarcophagi of the late sixth century BC showing battles between footsoldiers and cavalry. Dogs are also shown, but it is not certain that they were used in Ionian battles.[23]

Against Smyrna the army of Alyattes had been successful, against the

Clazomenians it failed: to ensure that Colophon kept quiet, the crafty Lydian employed treachery. He invited the Colophonian knights to a festival at Sardis and had them murdered, thus abusing the principles of guest-friendship and depriving the city of the most powerful cavalry force in Ionia.[24]

Alyattes next turned his army eastwards, where the power of Media presented a growing threat to the eastern Lydian territories. A pretext for war was given by Alyattes' refusal to hand back to Cyaxares, the Median king, some Scythians who had fled from Media and presented themselves as suppliants at Sardis.[25] Fighting continued for five years with both Median and Lydian victories, but in the sixth year there was a total eclipse of the sun during a battle [28th May 585 BC].[26] This unexpected event made both sides more eager for peace, which was achieved by the diplomacy of Syennesis of Cilicia and Nabynetos of Babylon. The treaty was secured by the gift of Alyattes' daughter Aryenis in marriage to Astyages son of Cyaxares, the Median king.[27]

Another marriage tie bound Alyattes to Ephesus in Ionia, where the tyrant Melas was married to one of the Lydian's daughters.[28] Melas was not the first tyrant in the city, for the oligarchy of the Basilidae had been overthrown by a certain Pythagoras, who ruled with great severity while keeping the support of the mass of the populace.[29] Pythagoras killed many of his opponents, even in the temples, and confiscated the property of rich citizens. Some daughters of one of his enemies, however, he dared not kill within a sanctuary to which they had fled; and instead he starved them there, until they hanged themselves to escape their hunger. Thereupon disease and famine afflicted the city, until Pythagoras, having asked Delphi for a remedy, acted on the instructions of the Pythia in burying the dead and building a temple. It is not clear which temple is meant: but if Pythagoras was succeeded by Melas, then the temple may have been begun about 600 BC, and it is worth noting that the foundation deposit of the first great Artemisium at Ephesus dates from this very period.

Like his father Sadyattes, Alyattes took more than one wife, partly because he needed sons to help him to administer his growing empire. By an Ionian woman he had Pantaleon, and by a Carian, Croesus.[30] When Croesus was viceroy in Adramyttium and the plain of Thebe, Alyattes ordered him to parade with his troops at Sardis on an appointed day for a campaign against Priene.[31] Croesus, who had been indulging himself, was not ready, and envious persons were quick to tell his father. The young prince, urgently needing funds to pay his mercenaries,[32]

asked a notable Lydian called Sadyattes to make him a loan, but the
haughty man retorted that if he had to support all the sons of Alyattes
he would have no silver left. Croesus then went to Ephesus, where he
vowed to Artemis that if he became king he would dedicate to the goddess the entire household of the churlish Sadyattes. Now an Ionian
friend of Croesus was Pamphaes of Priene,[33] who, seeing the urgency of
the Lydian prince, persuaded his father Theocharides to give him the
money. The request being granted, the money was given to Croesus,
who, it was said, as king gave his Ionian friend a wagon filled with gold
from the treasuries of Sardis, and dedicated the house of Sadyattes,
foundations and all, to the goddess.[34] With his thousand gold staters
Croesus recruited his army and was the first to parade at Sardis on the
appointed day before the campaign. Priene, however, owing to the able
generalship of her statesman Bias, was able to withstand the formidable
Lydian attack.[35]

The history of Miletus in the time of Alyattes is marred by bloody and
protracted disputes. After the overthrow of the Neleid kings the chief
magistrate in the city was the Prytanis or President. According to
Aristotle tyranny first arose from the great powers possessed by this
official.[36] We do not know the name of the Prytanis who first made
himself tyrant, but by 600 BC Miletus was already being ruled by a
tyrant, the friend of Periander of Corinth, Thrasybulus, whose chief
distinction was the successful defence of the city against Lydian aggres-
sion. At home he was said to have acted ruthlessly against all opposition,[37]
and abroad his navy helped the Corinthians against their neighbours in
Sicyon.[38] Miletus' trade with the west must have benefited from her
friendship with Corinth, as well as from her close ties with Sybaris.

After Thrasybulus came 'tyrants with Thoas and Damasenor', as they
are called by Plutarch.[39] When they were removed, two parties held the
city, the *Ploutis* and the *Cheiromacha*. The men of the Ploutis won. It is
said that when they wished to deliberate on any important matter, they
used to embark in ships and put out from land. After ratifying their
decision they sailed back, for which reason they were called *Aeinautai*
'Perpetual Sailors'.[40] Their behaviour gives point to the cutting remark
of Demodocus[41] the Lerian poet: 'The Milesians are not fools, but they
act as if they were.'

In this sickness of the Milesian city the Ploutis were the party of the
rich and the Cheiromacha the poor artizans. The country landowners, it
seems, wisely remained aloof. Both the new rich and the poor committed
great atrocities; the popular party who were contemptuously called

79

Gergithai by the rich, as though they were no better than barbarians,[42] drove out their enemies, and gathered their children into granaries to be trampled to death by oxen. The rich retaliated by daubing the poor and their children with pitch and setting them alight, whereupon portents appeared in the city and a holy olive tree set itself on fire. The god, whether Apollo of Branchidae or of Delphi is not stated, excluded the rich of Miletus for a long time after this from his oracle, saying that he was 'grieved at the murder of the peaceful Gergithai and at the death of the pitch-daubed men'.[43] The bitter struggle lasted for two generations until the old friends of Miletus, the Parians, came to arbitrate.[44] Reasonably they gave authority to the landowners whose demesnes were best maintained, thinking that they would look after public business as carefully as they had tended their own property. The Parians wisely did not select the new rulers inside the city, where class feeling was bitterest, for that would have perpetuated the dominance of extremists of one party or the other. Their action must have won the approval of the Milesian poet Phocylides, who flourished about this time, in the middle of the sixth century BC. 'If you want to be prosperous' he advised, 'tend rich farmland. For the field, they say, is the horn of Amaltheia.'[45] Evidently civil discord had taught him to avoid political extremes: 'Many things are best for the men in the middle. In the city I want to be a man of the centre.'[46]

In Samos the landowners called Geomoroi took power after the overthrow of a certain Demoteles about 600 BC. During their rule the Megarians sent an expedition against the Samian colony Perinthus, with fetters to bind the prisoners they expected to take; but the Geomoroi dispatched a force of thirty ships under nine generals. Two ships were struck by lightning and destroyed as they sailed out of harbour from Samos. The rest of the force defeated the Megarians, of whom they took six hundred alive.[47]

The victorious Samians now plotted to overthrow the oligarchy of the Geomoroi with the help of the Megarian captives, whom the Geomoroi had ordered to be brought in fetters to Samos. The Megarians were marched into the Council Hall with the fastenings knocked off the fetters, and when the signal was given the supposed captives fell on the Geomoroi and killed them. Those Megarians who wished to become Samian citizens were then allowed to do so; the free Samians constructed a building called the Pedetes in which the fetters were dedicated; and popular government was set up. We do not know how long this lasted, but the tyranny of Polycrates, which began in the middle of the sixth century, marks its end. The Geomoroi however were not entirely destroyed, for they still existed in the island at the end of the fifth century BC.[48]

To the great days of Samian prosperity in the sixth century some verses of the Samian poet Asius son of Amphiptolemus refer: he wrote engagingly of the joyous panache of the Samians as they made their way to the precinct of Hera by the stream of Imbrasus west of Samos city. Their hair was combed, they were closely wrapped in fine clothes, and they covered the floor of the wide earth with their snowy cloaks. On them were golden brooches like cicadas, and their hair in golden bands tossed in the wind, while about their arms were delicately wrought bracelets. Plainly they were quite as elegant as the nobles of Colophon against whose luxury the strict Xenophanes protested. Douris of Samos,[49] not the most sensible of historians, quoted the lines of Asius to illustrate the softness of the ancient Samians, but since we do not know the context of the verses, there is no reason to think that Asius himself called them effeminate.[50] There are hints indeed that they valued their independence and were ready to fight for it, for they overthrew the tyrant Demoteles and continued to resist the family of Polycrates long after his tyranny was firmly rooted.

The refinement of the Ionians was not always held up to reproach, for less doctrinaire men than Xenophanes recognised that valour in war is compatible with elegance in peace. The Cean poet Bacchylides could write of the warrior king of Athens, Theseus, as 'lord of the delicately living Ionians'.[51] The elegant mode of dress of the Old Ionians in Attica lasted until not long before the time of Thucydides,[52] who described their linen tunics and the golden grasshoppers that used to fasten their hair before the Spartans had set a less flamboyant fashion. Thucydides asserts that refinement of dress was copied by the Asiatic Ionians from the Athenians, who were the first to give up the habitual carrying of weapons. How elegant they must have looked, carrying, as Cratinus[53] tells us the early Athenians did, an apple in one hand and wearing a flower at the ear. Moralists of all ages claim that luxury leads to political decline, inferring as usual universal laws from inadequate evidence, but the history of the Ionians does not support their claim: Ionia failed to keep her freedom not through refinement, but from her lack of political unity at the time of the Lydian and Persian threats and from her precarious situation at the edge of a great land mass. As for the early Athenians, Heraclides Ponticus[54] asserted robustly, and with justice, that their city had been greatest and nurtured the most glorious men in her age of luxury, that is to say, before the adoption in the middle of the fifth century of more austere Spartan fashions. The men of Attica who wore golden grasshoppers in their topknots may have been dandies, but they also won the battle of Marathon.

In the sixth century BC the Samians did wear their garments long, as Asius says: this can be seen in a statue of a confident and comfortably fat Samian of about 550 BC whose full cloak is gathered up in his right hand yet still touches the ground behind his heels.[55] The gentleman reminds us of the description in the Homeric Hymn to Apollo of the Ionians dragging their cloaks at the festival at Delos.[56] He wears his hair long, like the young Samian boxer Pythagoras who came in a purple robe to the Olympic games of 588 BC. Being excluded by ridicule from the boy's contest he went at once to the men's and won that.[57]

The women too of Samos were a fine spectacle. The 'Hera' of Cheramyes, is supernaturally tall, with a restrained dignity; her dress clings closely to her back and falls to the ground about her feet, but is drawn back to reveal her toes.[58] When the author of the Hymn to the Delian Apollo said that the Ionians with their women and children would be thought by a stranger to be immortal and unageing, he was not being bombastic: rather was he expressing the truth that the gods and goddesses were made in the image of the Ionian nobility.

Apart from squabbles with Erythrae, little is known about the history of Chios after the decline of the kingship. The earliest Ionian constitutional document does, however, come from Chios, the stele found in 1907 near Tholopotamoi in the southern half of the island.[59] The inscription, which is much damaged, is cut on four sides of a trachyte block, and dates from the middle of the sixth century BC or a little earlier. There are references to decrees of the people, to the office of *demarchos*, to a court of the *demarchos*, and to appeal to a council of the people, which has fifty men from each tribe. It met on the third day after the Hebdomaea (that is, on the ninth of each month) and dealt with verdicts against which there had been appeals during the month. The stone also names 'kings' as well as a person acting as 'king', a fact which shows that there were several *basileis* with a chief *basileus* amongst them. The functions of the *demarchos* remain obscure, but considerable powers were possessed by the *demos*. It could inflict penalties, and in certain cases overrule the decisions of the court of the *demarchos*. The Council is called 'The people's Council', perhaps in order to distinguish it from a Council of the nobility, such as existed in most Greek states in this period. An interesting feature of the code is the assessment of fines or deposits in staters. At this date the sums are less likely to have been paid in coin than in bullion. The goddess Histie is mentioned in the text; perhaps the *demarchoi* are responsible to her for their conduct of the law. Since, despite obscurities, we can see a system of justice at work, designed to ensure the rights of free citizens, this document has a significant place in the study of the origins of democratic institutions.

The Chian historian Theopompus wrote that his countrymen were the first of the Greeks after the Thessalians and Lacedaemonians to employ slaves. 'But they did not acquire them in the same way as the others; for the Lacedaemonians and Thessalians can be seen to have got their slaves from the Greeks who formerly inhabited the lands that they now possess. . . . But the Chians took barbarian slaves for whom they paid a price.'[60] We do not know when the Chians began to acquire barbarian slaves by purchase, but there may be a link between the growth of true slavery in the island and the respect for the legal rights of the men of the *demos* as shown about 550 BC in the inscription from Tholopotamoi.[61] The very possession of slaves may have made the Chians more aware of the rights of free citizens.

In the aftermath of the Trerian sack, Magnesia's territory by the river Lethaeus was taken by her neighbours,[62] but the city recovered, and fighting between Ephesus and Magnesia continued for a long time. The focus of the dispute was the Cretinaeum, which the Ephesians finally won.[63] These local wars are the setting for a remarkable legend about the Ionian sage Pherecydes of Syros.[64] The philosopher was walking near Ephesus when he met an Ephesian. A war was about to break out between Ephesus and Magnesia, and Pherecydes wanted the Ephesians to win. So he ordered the Ephesian to drag him by the legs into Magnesian territory, and to advise the Ephesians to bury him where he lay after their victory. Pherecydes died, and the Ephesians buried him with honours in the place to which he had been dragged: so the Ephesians gained territory by taking the sage's advice. This pretty story is contradicted by another according to which Pherecydes died in Delos;[65] but it does suggest that Ephesus gained land at the expense of Magnesia about the middle of the sixth century BC when Pherecydes flourished.[66]

What little is known about Priene in the sixth century BC concerns one of the seven wise men. Bias son of Teutames – the father's name looks Carian, though the family was of Theban descent[67] – was renowned for his eloquence as a pleader[68] and for his diplomatic powers. He made a treaty of peace with Alyattes after successfully directing the defence of his city,[69] and he also went on an embassy to Samos after a war between

83

the Samians and Prienians on Mycale. Each side had been causing the other moderate damage until in one battle a thousand Samians were killed. Then followed a six-year truce, after which Samos and Miletus in alliance defeated the Prienians at a place called the Oak. After this misfortune, in which the leading Prienian citizens were killed, bereaved women in Priene used to swear by 'the Darkness at the Oak'.[70] On his embassy to Samos, Bias obtained the best terms for the defeated Prienians he could, and fixed a boundary between Samian and Prienian territory at a watershed on Mycale.[71]

Bias is also said to have ransomed some Messenian maidens taken in a war. He brought them up as his daughters, gave them a dowry each, and restored them to their fathers in Messenia.[72] The story suggests that there were still in his time Messenians not subject to the Spartans. A poem of his, said to be two thousand verses long, described Ionia and the manner of rendering it prosperous.[73] He was still active in the reign of Croesus, and when the Persians took Ionia he urged the Ionians to join forces, sail to Sardinia, and found a single city for all of them there. This advice, which Herodotus[74] praises warmly, was not taken, and Bias himself stayed at home. He died peacefully in his grandson's arms at Priene, where the grateful citizens dedicated a precinct to him called the Teutameum.[75] It is a sign of his greatness that even Heraclitus,[76] the most reluctant of men to bestow praise, asserted that Bias was 'a more considerable man than the rest'. We have now gathered the fragmentary evidence for the history of the Ionians in the time of Alyattes and must next discuss their Aeolian contemporaries.

CHAPTER IX

Aeolian Poets and Statesmen

IN THE NOBLE SOCIETY OF LESBOS POETS ENJOYED GREAT PRIVILEGES, for they brought renown to the families who employed them, and many were themselves well born. It follows that the study of their poetry can tell us something about themselves and about the political history of that beautiful and fertile island.

One of the most renowned of the contemporaries of the great Midas amongst the Greeks was the poet Terpander of Antissa, who flourished in the first half of the seventh century BC.[1] He may well have taken over the musical scale of the Phrygian poet Olympus[2] and fitted it to the seven-stringed lyre, which he reintroduced to Greece.[3] A lyre with seven strings such as Terpander's is painted on a late Geometric pot from Old Smyrna of the second quarter of the seventh century BC, the very period in which Terpander flourished.[4] Since Pindar[5] tells us that Terpander invented his lyre, the *barbitos*, after hearing the Lydians' stringed instrument, the *paktis*, at their feasts, the Lesbian poet may have passed through Smyrna on his way back homewards. His knowledge of the Phrygian music of Olympus he may also have got in Lydia, for we are not told that he went to Midas at Gordion. His later travels brought him to Sparta where he was the victor at the first musical contest held at the festival of the Carneia in 676 BC,[6] and before long, as Sappho proudly claimed, Lesbian poets had a reputation unequalled by others: 'pre-eminent as a Lesbian singer over foreigners' was her proud boast.[7] Already in the middle of the seventh century Archilochus calls the Paean Lesbian as though Aeolian poets were known for their songs of triumph.[8] No Paean of Terpander's survives, but we are told that he composed preludes in hexameters,[9] and also, on the good authority of Pindar, that he 'invented' *skolia*,[10] songs to be sung at feasts; but nothing is known of their character. To judge from the fragment of a hymn to Zeus ascribed to him,[11] Terpander was fond of solemn, spondaic, language, but his hexameters show that he also liked swift cadences.

A successor of Terpander was Arion of Methymna, who, according to Herodotus,[12] was a citharode second to none in his time. Not a verse of his poetry survives, and he is famous chiefly for the legend of the saving of his life by a dolphin, which brought him ashore at Taenarus in Laconia, after he had been cast overboard by wicked sailors with whom

85

he was making the voyage from Taras to Corinth.[13] The dolphin had been attracted to the ship when Arion played a last *nome* before being thrown into the waters. It would be pleasant to believe this story, for dolphins are capable of carrying humans on their backs, and are fond of music; and their vocal behaviour reveals a high intelligence.

Arion wrote songs and preludes for epics;[14] and when he was with Periander in Corinth he produced a dithyramb with a chorus.[15] Archilochus already knew of the Dionysiac dithyramb,[16] but Herodotus states that Arion was the first to name it: this may mean only that Arion's dithyrambs had definite themes from which the poems took their names. Since the word *Dithyrambos* is of Anatolian origin,[17] this kind of poetry may have been introduced by Aeolian poets to Greece: Terpander indeed may have been one of them for he told the story of the birth of Dionysus,[18] a dithyrambic theme.

In Mytilene the Penthelidae kept the royal power for themselves, until, not later than the middle of the seventh century BC, their excesses brought about a reaction and they were overthrown; they were not entirely destroyed, however, for we find them still active in Lesbian politics about 600 BC. According to Aristotle the Penthelidae went about striking people with clubs, until Megacles with his friends attacked and overthrew them; and later a certain Penthilus was killed by Smerdes, who had been beaten and dragged away from his wife.[19] From then on the Penthelidae had to share their privileges with the other noble families in the island. The murdered Penthilus may well have been the head of the clan at the time, a direct descendant of Penthilus the founder of the Aeolian settlement in Lesbos; perhaps he was also Penthilus the father of the lady whom the reformer Pittacus married.[20]

The poetry of Alcaeus was used by the ancients, and can be used by us, to reconstruct in outline the disorderly history of Lesbos in the time of the poet. Some dates given by the chronographers may come, through the Lesbian historian Hellanicus, from local tradition, but what is significant is the order of events, which can be recovered. Strabo, who knew the poetry of Alcaeus well, stated that the city suffered from several tyrannies in the poet's time because of factional strife. Amongst the tyrants was Pittacus himself, together with Myrsilus, Melanchrus, the Cleanactidae, and others. 'Alcaeus is not free from suspicion of plotting a revolution. But Pittacus used his personal power to weaken the patrician factions, and when he had done that he gave the city back its own government.'[21]

In Strabo's list of tyrants, or intending tyrants, Melanchrus seems to be the earliest. He was overthrown by Pittacus and his friends with the help of Antimenidas and Cicis, the brothers of Alcaeus, but the poet himself seems to have had no part in the affair, perhaps because he then was still too young for politics.[22] The date is given as the forty-second Olympiad (612/609 BC).[23]

The next ascertainable event in Lesbian history is related by Herodotus,[24] who remarks that the Mytileneans stationed in Achilles' City and the Athenians in Sigeum had fought for a long time, until they were reconciled by Periander son of Cypselus, the Corinthian tyrant, whom they had chosen as arbitrator. He decided that both sides should keep what they had. Hence the Athenians held on to Sigeum, which formerly had been Aeolian.[25] It is plain from Herodotus' narrative that the Athenians later lost Sigeum. The place was recaptured for them by Pisistratus later in the sixth century BC.[26]

In the earlier war Pittacus led the Mytileneans, and Phrynon, an Olympic victor, the Athenian force. Pittacus killed Phrynon in single combat after trapping him in a net he had concealed behind his shield.[27] In one of the incidents in the war Alcaeus, like Archilochus, threw down his arms and fled: 'Alcaeus is safe' wrote the poet to his friend Melanippus in Mytilene; 'but his weapons the men of Attica hung up in the temple of the grey-eyed goddess'–the temple of Athena at Sigeum.[28] The date of Phrynon's death is given as 607/6 BC,[29] which agrees well with the tradition of Periander's arbitration, for the year falls within the period of the Corinthian's tyranny. We do not know what Phrynon and his force were doing at Sigeum. They cannot have easily controlled the Dardanelles from there, and there is no evidence for regular Athenian trade through the Propontis at this time. Phrynon and his men may well have been soldiers of fortune, exiled from Attica in the troubles that followed the Cylonian conspiracy (c. 630 BC). The Athenians in Sigeum formed themselves into a city state with a council chamber of their own, as a Sigean inscription of the first half of the sixth century mentioning their prytaneum shows.[30]

The Sigean war was but an interlude in the struggle for power amongst the patrician factions at home in Lesbos. A new threat was presented by Myrsilus, whose rising power Alcaeus viewed with dread, as though it were a tempest about to ruin the ship of state.[31] We are told that Myrsilus formed a conspiracy against the Mytileneans,[32] and also that on one occasion he returned, presumably from exile, in a boat provided by one Mnamon.[33] This last detail cannot be fitted into the story, but it is clear that Myrsilus became tyrant. Alcaeus and his friends hatched a plot against the tyrant, but it failed and they were forced to flee to Pyrrha.[34] There was an engagement between the party of Alcaeus and the bodyguard of Myrsilus somewhere between Mytilene and Pyrrha.[35] Either at Pyrrha, or during another exile from Mytilene spent somewhere in a remote part of Lesbos, Alcaeus lamented his rustic's life as he 'yearned to hear the assembly summoned . . . and the Council'.[36] Here, perhaps at the sanctuary at Messa at the head of the gulf of Callone not far from Pyrrha,[37] was a precinct of the gods where the Lesbian girls went annually to be judged for their beauty. Evidently exile from Mytilene had its compensations; and even Alcaeus was content to live for a while 'stepping clear of troubles'. Another poem written in exile accuses Pittacus of breaking the holy covenant made with Alcaeus and his friends, that they would either die or kill the tyrants.[38] Myrsilus is named in the fragment, and the covenant seems to have been aimed at him. But when the poem was written Pittacus 'the Potbelly' had forsaken his friends and joined Myrsilus in power.[39] Later, when Myrsilus died or was killed, Alcaeus exclaimed, 'Now must a man get drunk, yea, and drink for all his worth, for Myrsilus is dead.'[40]

The first exile was at Pyrrha, but later Alcaeus went abroad, out of Lesbos altogether. His brother Antimenidas too went oversea, to fight for the Babylonians, amongst whom he distinguished himself by killing a warrior only one palm's breadth short of five royal cubits.[41] Alcaeus himself went to Egypt,[42] and Sappho also was forced into exile after 605/4 BC but before 591/0 BC–the exact date is missing on the Parian Marble where the flight to Sicily is recorded.[43]

Alcaeus and his friends were at one time given some support by the Lydians, who supplied two thousand staters, a very large sum, in the hope that they would enter 'the holy city'. The identity of this city is uncertain, and equally obscure is the 'crafty fox' who predicted easy success and thought that he would not be marked.[44] Here it is worth recalling that Croesus may already have been crown prince in Adramyttium at the time of Alcaeus' exile from Lesbos offshore.[45]

Pittacus was called a Thracian by the Hellenistic historian Douris of Samos,[46] with the implication that he was also a plebeian. It is true that the name Pittacus is found in Thrace,[47] but the Lesbian leader came from a noble family. Alcaeus, who was fastidious in such matters, would not readily have taken as a comrade a man of base birth, nor is it likely that Pittacus would have been able to marry a daughter of the ancient house of Atreus if he had been a commoner. His father Hyrras, moreover, is called a 'king' of the Mytileneans;[48] hence it is likely that the reformer was a noble son of a noble father. The charge of base birth originates in the abuse of Alcaeus, which is not to be taken as objective evidence.

The threat posed by the exiles was so serious that the people of Mytilene entrusted Pittacus with unlimited powers to protect them. 'The low born Pittacus', complained Alcaeus, 'they have set up as tyrant of the spiritless and doom-laden city, as all together they proclaim his praises.'[49] Aristotle calls Pittacus both tyrant and *aisymnetes*,[50] a title the philosopher defines as 'elective tyrant'. Pittacus was now a monarch, as Strabo calls him,[51] but he was a legitimate ruler holding power with the consent of the *damos*. He ruled soberly, and even, it was said, when Alcaeus came into his power, set him free with the words, 'Mercy is stronger then Vengeance.'[52] It is said that he imposed double fines for offences committed when drunk.[53] The laws he changed in detail, not the entire constitution,[54] and he may well have left the assembly and the aristocratic council, in which the father and the grandfather of Alcaeus had sat,[55] unaltered. He was said to have governed for ten years and to have lived for another ten in retirement.[56] It was also said that he declined a subsidy from Croesus.[57] To illustrate his clemency the following tale was related: his son was sitting in a barber's shop in Kyme when a smith came in and struck him dead with an axe. The Kymaians sent the murderer to Pittacus, who set him free with the words, 'Mercy now is better then repentance later.'[58]

Pittacus like Alcaeus was a nobleman. But his greater awareness of the obligations of nobility led the people to trust him with power. We may praise the force and spirit of Alcaeus' poetry, but should recognise that in the political contest the better man won. It is pleasing to think of the aged statesman Pittacus passing his declining years in the estate given him by his fellow citizens. Most of it he dedicated as sacred domain.[59]

The luxuriantly passionate poetry of Sappho of Eresus is not the first source to turn to in the quest for details of political history. Yet Sappho was forced into exile, her poems do hint at the disorder of the times, and an examination of them reveals a little about life in Lesbos about 600 BC. In one fragment she complains, as though she was in exile, that she has no gay headband for her daughter Cleis, and knows not whence one shall come; and then she goes on to speak of the exile of the Cleanactidae,[60] who were enemies of Alcaeus.[61] Another fragment suggests that Sappho was hostile to the Penthelidae.[62] Perhaps her sympathies were with the friends of Alcaeus, who himself wrote about her with respect and admiration.[63]

About her family a little more is known. She was the daughter of

Scamandronymus,[64] whose name suggests that his parents had interests in the Troad. She had three brothers, one of whom, Larichus, she often praised for pouring wine for the Mytileneans in the *prytaneion* or City Hall, a privilege reserved for young men of the nobility.[65]

Charaxus, another brother, was engaged in the trade to Naucratis in Egypt, where he formed a liaison with an expensive courtesan, Rhodopis; she became celebrated for her charms amongst all the Greeks and flourished in the reign of Amasis of Egypt,[66] that is after 570 BC. This remarkable lady was reputed to be the fellow slave of Aesop the writer of fables;[67] she was brought to Egypt by Xanthus the Samian; and there she made a great fortune as a courtesan. Overwhelmed by her charms Charaxus bought her freedom at a high price, but Rhodopis, with a fine business sense, stayed in Egypt, and sent a tenth of her wealth to Delphi as a dedication in the form of iron spits. Some Greeks were so taken with her that they called the Pyramid of Mycerinus the work of Rhodopis, an absurd notion which Herodotus[68] was at pains to correct.

Sappho may have had a monetary rather than a moral objection to her brother's wasteful affair with this lady, whom she calls Doricha: she prays that Doricha may not be proud to tell how Charaxus came a second time to her longed-for love, and that the Cyprian goddess will release him from his sufferings.[69] Finally on his return home she tried to bring him to his senses by mockery, with what success we do not know.[70]

Sappho's deep love for her daughter Cleis is revealed by her own words: 'A beautiful daughter is mine, who looks like the golden flowers, Cleis my beloved, whom I would not exchange for all Lydia or lovely ...' and there the fragment ceases.[71] The riches and power of Lydia had impressed her deeply. She mentions Lydian chariotry[72] and the mitra, a headdress in fashion amongst the ladies of Sardis.[73] Her interests are patrician and womanly – in the well-being and reputation of her family, in high fashion, and in the rest of the Lesbian nobility.

She was also capable of feeling, and of expressing gracefully in verse, deep passions towards persons of her own sex. It would be absurdly impertinent to censure her for this. She had favourites, and she had rivals in the love of young girls, many of whom had come to Lesbos from abroad. Anactoria came from Miletus, and then, to Sappho's sorrow, departed.[74] Gongyla came from Colophon.[75] Another girl, a friend of Atthis, went away to Lydia where, Sappho claimed, she surpassed the women in her beauty as the moon the stars.[76] The poetess had to comfort gentle Atthis for the absence of her friend. Later Atthis came to hate the thought of Sappho, and flew off to Andromeda, who was perhaps, like Gorgo, the leader of a rival group of women.[77] In the leisured and emotionally charged society of Lesbos such shifts of affection must have been frequent: we need not take them too solemnly. The significant point is, as Strabo insisted, that as a woman and as a poetess there was none to match her.[78] She recognised the primacy of the passions, and would have been genuinely puzzled at any suggestion that she should disguise them. 'You came . . . , and I was pursuing you: you cooled my heart that burned with yearning.'[79] 'Once did I love you Atthis, long ago.'[80] 'Again love loosens my limbs and makes me giddy, the bitter-sweet, irresistible creature.'[81] Her poetry reminds us that true history is not only political history.

Testimony to the riches that supported the elegant society of Sappho and her contemporaries is given by the remains at Klopedi, where a sanctuary lies on rising ground north of the great plain at the head of the gulf of Callone. Here were two temples, the larger of which, though it was unfinished, must have been a magnificent spectacle, for it was thirty-seven and a half metres long and its peristyle had forty-six columns adorned with fine Aeolic capitals.[82] Here perhaps was the sanctuary and oracle of Apollo Napaios, who takes his name from Nape, a place in the territory of the Methymnaeans.[83]

The history of the mainland Aeolians in Sappho's time barely exists. Some time after the reign of Agamemnon the kingship in Kyme was replaced by an aristocratic council, but magistrates called 'kings' still exercised authority after the overthrow of the monarchy, and were accountable to the council for their actions. The chief magistrate was the *aisymnetes*.[84] When the council met at night to consider the kings' actions, a magistrate led the kings out by the hand and guarded them until the council, casting their votes in secret, had decided whether they were guilty of wrongdoing or not. Another magistrate, called a Guardian (*phylaktes*), was normally in charge of the prison.[85]

The laws and customs of the Kymaians were archaic. In one of their rituals a woman taken in adultery was set up on a stone in the market place in public view and then mounted upon a donkey to be led around the city, before being set on the stone again. The stone was later cere-monially purified, and the woman became known as the 'rider upon the donkey'.[86] Another quaint law enacted that if in a case of murder the accuser produced in support of his charge a certain number of his own kinsmen as witnesses, the accused was guilty.[87]

The Kymaian oligarchy was increased in numbers, or the franchise was made less exclusive, when a certain Pheidon gave political rights to all who possessed a horse;[88] his arrangements may be compared with the oligarchy of knights at Eretria.[89] Pheidon's census of horsemen was changed when a certain Prometheus, 'an energetic man with a ready tongue',[90] introduced an oligarchy of one thousand. These details are all that is known of the mainland Aeolians in the early sixth century BC. If the Kymaians had done more, it would have been worth recording; the lack of evidence suggests, though, that they neither emulated the elegance of the Lesbians nor aspired to the intellectual distinction of the Milesians. They were content to enjoy the fruits of their fields and the taxes levied upon the trade with Phrygia and Lydia passing through their harbour.[91] But of originality or brilliance they give no sign.

CHAPTER X

The Birth of Natural Philosophy

THE GREATEST GIFT OF IONIA TO THE INTELLECTUAL TRADITION OF mankind was the creation of a rational view of the world. The Ionian thinkers drew on Hesiodic and near eastern cosmogonies and stripped them of much of their crudity and anthropomorphism; then, inspired by the belief that Nature is intelligible to the mind of man, they attempted to explain the origins and the present structure of the world about them. When in the sixth century the Ionians had leisure to think deeply about the world, they were not afraid to do so. The ferment of Ionian society provided the right climate for free ratiocination, a climate which did not last. The Athenians' persecution of the philosopher Anaxagoras would have been inconceivable in the Miletus of Thales and Anaximander.

(A) PHERECYDES

There are signs that Mimnermus was interested in cosmogony,[1] but the earliest Ionian thinker deserving to be called a natural philosopher was Pherecydes, whose alleged help to the Ephesians in their war against Magnesia we have already noted. Pherecydes, son of Babys, from Syros in the Cyclades flourished in the time of Alyattes and was said to have been born about 600 BC.[2] He wrote a book on the reigns or births of the gods,[3] which was said to have been written in prose. The story of his life is surrounded by fanciful legend, and there were tales connecting him with Pythagoras, whose master Pherecydes was thought to have been.[4] One story states that Pythagoras attended Pherecydes in Delos during his tutor's last illness. Ion of Chios in the fifth century BC named Pherecydes and Pythagoras together in the same sentence of a poem,[5] but this does not prove that the two sages had anything in fact to do with each other.

The work of Pherecydes is characterised by bold cosmogonical speculation and is still in the tradition of Hesiod's *Theogony*. In his scheme of things there was no primal creation, for Zas, Chthonie, and Chronos (Time) had always existed.[6] Chronos, who seems to be quite distinct from Kronos the father of Zeus, created numerous offspring of gods from his own seed, which he had placed in five recesses.[7] It was perhaps from this seed that there was born a snake-like creature Ophioneus, who, with his own offspring the Ophionidae, attempted to

93

defeat Chronos. The usurper was vanquished, however, and Chronos forced Ophioneus into a region called Ogenos;[8] it may well be that Ogenos was the primeval Ocean in Pherecydes' view. The story of a fight between a chief god and a monstrous snake is found in Hurrian and Hittite mythology,[9] and Pherecydes may have borrowed his version of the battles from a near eastern source, perhaps indirectly through a Greek cosmogonical forerunner. In antiquity it was even believed that Pherecydes had read certain Phoenician secret books.[10]

Zas, the philosopher said, made a cloth upon which were pictured Earth and Ogenos; and this he presented to his bride at the time of their marriage,[11] an act perhaps intended to symbolise the creation of the world. Pherecydes also described a winged oak, and it is possible that this was intended to represent the created world floating through boundless Chaos;[12] but the precise significance of the oak remains obscure.[13]

The introduction of Time as an uncreated primal element is distinctly sophisticated, but the creative act of Chronos is as anthropomorphic as anything in Hesiod. The few surviving fragments of his work bear out Aristotle's estimate that he was a 'mixed' theologian,[14] one who did not say everything in mythical form. Pherecydes' book may well have been written later than the physical researches of Thales, but his work stands at a much earlier stage of thought than the thinking of the great Milesian. There was supposed to have been a rivalry between Pherecydes and Thales,[15] but the evidence for this is doubtful: the methods of the two sages were however very different, and each may have felt little sympathy with the other.

(B) THALES

The great reputation of Thales as a statesman and thinker, and the exaggerated claims that have sometimes been made on his behalf, do not hide the fact that very little was known about him, even by the industrious Hellenistic scholars who put together all the traditions they could find. He was thought to have been equally at home in practical matters and in the realms of cosmogonical speculation, as a story in Aristotle makes plain (though Aristotle thought it had no basis in truth): 'When he was reproached for his poverty, as though philosophy were useless, they say that after observing from the study of the heavens that there would be a large olive crop, he borrowed a little money when it was still winter, and paid deposits on all the olive presses in Miletus and Chios, hiring them cheaply since no-one bid against him. But when the harvest time came, many people had a sudden need for the presses, and so he hired them out on his own terms, thereby proving that it is easy for philosophers to be rich if they wish, but that it is not money-making which interests them.'[16] This, if not true, is certainly well invented, and much more in character than the amusing story in Plato's *Theaetetus* of the Thracian serving girl who teased him for having fallen into a well while gazing up at the stars, saying that he was keen to know the things in the sky but failed to see what was at his feet.[17]

Herodotus remarks that Thales was by descent a Phoenician,[18] a tradition which may only mean that his ancestors came from Thebes, the seat in the late Bronze Age of the dynasty of Cadmus the Phoenician. Cadmeans, we recall, were amongst the early settlers in Ionia.[19] The name of Thales' father Examyes, however, is not Phoenician but Carian, and may be compared with Cheramyes, the dedicator of the veiled 'Hera' in the Samian Heraeum. Evidently Thales' ancestry was mixed, but he was of noble descent and a member of the family called Thelidae.[20]

In his wisdom Thales recognised that the political weakness of Ionia was due to the lack of a unified foreign policy and of a central government. He therefore advised the Ionians to create a single council, to place it at Teos in the middle of Ionia, and to regard the other cities of Ionia as though they were *demes*, local settlements subordinate to the central government.[21] This was a counsel of perfection, rather like asking the colleges of Oxford to give up their autonomy and to transfer all their assets to the University; but the advice was sound, for if taken it would have led to the political union of Ionia into a state not so large as to cramp the enterprise of individuals, yet large enough to offer powerful resistance to Lydia and to vie with Sparta for the leadership of Hellas. But Ionia did not unite, and the opportunity was lost for ever in the great revolt from Persia in 499 BC.

The tradition of a visit to Egypt by Thales is at least plausible, for he may have had occasion to join the Milesians in Naucratis.[22] Several stories purport to illustrate his interest in Egypt. Thus he was thought to have explained the Nile flood by the action of the Etesian winds in raising up the river's water through the pressure of the sea coming against it,[23] a view scornfully rejected by Herodotus, who however does not link Thales with it.[24] The assertion that Thales was the first to bring the study of geometry from Egypt to Greece is simply an inference from his having been the earliest known Greek geometer:[25] it is doubtful that Thales ever brought back any geometrical theorems from Egypt, since Egyptian mathematics never had the axiomatic character of the

Greeks', and Herodotus'[26] suggestion that the art of land-measurement came to Greece from Egypt was cautiously expressed. A visit to Egypt is implied by the story that Thales measured the heights of the pyramids by their shadow, having observed the time when the shadow of an object is equal to its height.[27] Plutarch improves on this by making Thales use the principle that as the height of the pyramid is to its shadow so the height of *any* object at the same time of day is to its shadow.[28] Use of triangles is also made in the construction ascribed to Thales for finding the distance of a ship at sea, but it is doubtful that he ever stated the underlying theorem.[29] Thales was chiefly interested in elementary mensuration, not in axiomatic geometry, which did not become a coherently organised body of knowledge before the fourth century BC.

Thales' practical knowledge of astronomy won the admiration of Xenophanes, his younger contemporary,[30] and Herodotus even remarks that Thales predicted the total eclipse of the sun that happened during the war between the Lydians and the Medes, 'setting as its limit the year in which the change from day to night actually took place.'[31] Now it may well be that Thales had some knowledge of cycles of *lunar* eclipses, for these were already known to the Babylonians of his time, from whom indirectly he may have obtained some astronomical knowledge. But his prediction, if he made it, of the year of a solar eclipse was only a fortunate guess: for there is no cycle of solar eclipses visible at any one point on the earth's surface, successive eclipses of the sun in a cycle being total at different latitudes.[32] The eclipse foretold by Thales is that of 28th May 585 BC,[33] which happened in the course of Alyattes' Median war, as we have seen. But it would be wildly extravagant to claim that Thales had predicted the eclipse to the nearest day.

His interest in astronomy was, like his geometry, motivated by practical needs; that he studied astronomy as an aid to navigation is shown by the tradition that he marked out 'the little stars of the Wain by which the Phoenicians sail'.[34] Possibly the Milesians had earlier, like Odysseus,[35] relied on the Great Bear.

Thales is also said to have discovered the variable lengths of the seasons;[36] he may well have tried to determine the exact time of the solstices, a problem which also interested Anaximander and Cleostratus of Tenedos his younger contemporaries, but we have no evidence that he proved the apparent motion of the sun between the solstices and equinoxes to be unequal. A connexion between Thales' work on solstices and that of Cleostratus may lie behind the statement that Thales died in Tenedos,[37] and Cleostratus may have been thought to be Thales' pupil. Some claimed that Thales wrote two works *On the Solstice* and *On the Equinox*,[38] but if these works ever existed, they may not have been genuine, and even the *Nautical Star Guide* which some thought to be the only genuine work of Thales was by others ascribed to an otherwise unknown Phocus of Samos.[39]

For knowledge of Thales' cosmogony we are almost entirely dependent on Aristotle. Thales taught according to Aristotle that the earth stays in place by floating on water like a log or some other such thing.[40] Secondly, Thales taught that water was in some sense the 'principle' or 'beginning' (*arche*) of all things. Aristotle clearly did not know what relation this principle had to the physical world in Thales' cosmogony, for he is forced to guess why Thales held water to be the principle– 'perhaps taking this notion from the nurture of all things being moist'.[41] His allusions to Thales' teaching are so vague that we cannot determine whether Thales meant that all things *were* water or that all things *originated* in water. Either alternative suggests that Thales had abandoned anthropomorphic cosmology, an innovation which entitles him to be called the father of philosophy. Nor is it a slight achievement to have looked for an unifying principle within the structure of the physical world.

It is possible that his doctrine of the earth floating on water comes from Mesopotamian, Egyptian or Palestinian cosmology, in each of which the notion of water lying around and under the earth is prominent. In the Akkadian story of the creation Apsu and Tiamat are the male and female principles of the primeval water. Marduk splits the body of Tiamat to create the sky and the earth, and Apsu becomes the waters under the earth.[42] In Egyptian cosmogony Nun is the primordial, boundless, original expanse of waters, out of which a hillock arose, like the muddy land after the Nile flood, and upon the hillock sat Atum the creator.[43] If Thales heard this story in Egypt, he would have been reminded of the land appearing from the sea at the silt-filled mouth of the Maeander near Miletus. Again, in Hebrew cosmogony Tehom is the deep water lying beneath the earth,[44] and God creates the earth upon the waters.[45] Thus it appears that Thales follows these near eastern cosmogonies, not the early Greek cosmogony in which Ocean surrounds the earth,[46] whose roots extend indefinitely downwards towards or into Tartarus.[47] Earthquakes he explained as the rocking of the earth as it rode like a ship in the moving waters.[48]

Aristotle cautiously ascribes to Thales the view that all things are full of gods.[49] It is also said that Thales gave a share of soul to inanimate things, offering as evidence the magnetic stone and amber.[50] This, as Aristotle[51] saw, suggests that Thales thought of souls as the source of motion. It is not clear, however, that Thales thought of everything that can move or cause movement as possessing soul; he may have considered that some things, for instance amber, had a greater share of soul in them than others, or that some objects had no soul in them at all.[52] Again, when he said that all things are full of gods he may not have meant that there is a god in every single thing. We do not have enough evidence to form a coherent view of his animism, but what there is suggests that soul had an important part in his doctrine of movement and change. Here too, as in all his thinking, observation and theory are closely linked.

(C) ANAXIMANDER

The pioneering work of interpreting rationally the physical world was carried on by Thales' successor Anaximander, whose intellect is pre-eminent in the history of Milesian philosophy. From the few surviving accounts the range and penetration of his thought are still obvious.

Much of the evidence about his doctrines comes to us from the work of Theophrastus on the history of philosophy. From summaries of Theophrastus' account we learn that the Unlimited (*Apeiron*) according to Anaximander had no beginning, for it is – in what may have been Anaximander's own phrase – 'eternal and unaging'.[53] He thought of the *Apeiron* as divine,[54] and held it to be in motion and the cause of motion in the heavens.[55] The value of the concept of the Unlimited lay in its generality.

From the *Apeiron* there was in some way drawn off or separated out an entity productive of hot and cold; from this entity arose a spherical shell of flame round the vapour enclosing the earth, 'like a bark round a tree' – the simile may be Anaximander's own.[56] When the sphere of flame disintegrates, it breaks up into circles concentric to the earth. We would see the fires in the heavens as bands or rings, but for the interposition of the mist surrounding the earth. The heavenly bodies show themselves because there are breathing holes, like pipes, in the mist through which the fires shine. When the holes are blocked there are eclipses, and similarly the phases of the moon are due to the closing and opening of a hole. The circle of the sun is furthest from us, and it is twenty-seven or twenty-eight times the size of the earth in diameter.[57] The aperture of the sun is the same size as the earth, however:[58] it is 'like a chariot wheel with its felloe full of fire, and showing the fire through an opening as though the nozzle of a bellows'–the simile from the workshop may well be Anaximander's.[59] Nearer to the earth are the moon and planets on their circles of fire; nearest of all are the circles of the fixed stars.[60]

He conceived the earth to be like the drum of a column, cylindrical in shape, with its depth one third of its width.[61] On one of its plane surfaces we walk. The earth stays where it is because it is established at the centre, fixed by necessity, equally far from all extremities.[62] Nothing at all displaces it. The remarkably sophisticated idea of a body in equilibrium staying motionless because all forces were acting on it equally, or because no force acts on it at all, was a wonderfully original advance upon Thales' doctrine of earth supported by water. Since it was reached by the exercise of the intellect, not by the aid of empirical observation, Anaximander may perhaps be claimed as the first theoretical physicist, and in this astonishing abstraction we may discern the birth of physics on the shores of Asia Minor.

Simplicius takes from Theophrastus a quotation from Anaximander.[63] Since this is not in Ionic and cannot therefore be verbatim, Theophrastus may have taken it from a commonplace book of physical opinions, not from any work purporting to be by Anaximander; indeed we do not know that Anaximander's writings survived the sack of Miletus by the Persians, or that any of them circulated outside Miletus before the destruction of the city. The Suda[64] assert that he wrote books *On Nature*, the *Circuit of the Earth*, *On the fixed stars*, a *Celestial Globe* and other works, but even if any of these titles are genuine there is no proof that the books themselves were read by Theophrastus or the scholars of Alexandria.

The fragment in Simplicius[65] runs as follows: 'And the source of coming-to-be for things that are is that into which decay also happens *according to necessity; for they pay penalty and retribution to each other for their injustice according to the assessment of Time*, as he puts it in rather poetical language.' The words in italics may well represent the phrasing of Anaximander. Here the reference seems to be to opposites–notably to heat and cold, dry and moist–created, either directly or through an intermediary, by the *Apeiron*. Each opposite encroaches upon the other, and each pays its penalty in the trial conducted by Time. Anaximander regards Time's verdict as inevitable, for it ensures that in the perpetual strife of opposites no one element will permanently prevail. Thus while he thought that the earth as we see it now is drying up,[66] there would inevitably follow a new deluge to restore the rights of the moist element in things.

The persistent strife in nature is obvious in the realms of the air immediately above the earth. Thunder, lighting, thunderbolts and violent winds he traced to the action of wind which, owing to its lightness and fineness, forces its way out of thick cloud with a noise; at the same time a flash comes through the rift in the cloud,[67] presumably from the rings of fire beyond. Rain he thought to be due to the exhalation of moist vapours upwards, which are then condensed by the sun.[68] But the condensation was not equal to the exhalation for Anaximander believed the earth to be drying up in his time.

From moisture the first living things were generated. They lived in thorny barks, and as they grew older came forth into the drier places; then the bark broke off and they lived a different kind of life.[69] Man alone amongst creatures, he observed, needs a long period of nursing. Therefore he would not have survived if he had originally been so weak; he must then, reasoned Anaximander, have been born in the beginning from a different kind of creature. These beings were fish or very like fish, in which men and women grew like embryos until they were able to support themselves.[70] The whole theory is a brilliant attempt at a theoretical biology. It may not be true science, but in such disciplined imaginings the natural sciences had their origins. There is no need to labour the significance of Anaximander in the history of thought: his speculations and his observations show that he had the imagination to wonder at Nature and to ask questions of her. He believed the world to be intelligible; the same belief, taken over from the Greeks, lies at the root of all true scientific endeavour today.

Apollodorus,[71] using evidence now lost, maintained that Anaximander was sixty-four years old in 547/6 BC, and that he died shortly afterwards. If that is right, then Anaximander was a little younger than Thales, but died about the same time. Apollodorus also stated that the *floruit* of Anaximander was in the time of 'Polycrates tyrant of Samos',[72] by which he may mean an elder Polycrates, father of the Polycrates who was crucified by the Persians about 522 BC. The mention of Samos in this context by the chronographer suggests that Apollodorus may have connected Pythagoras with Anaximander in some way.

His astronomical work, like that of Thales, was concerned with the solstices and equinoxes; to study them he employed a gnomon,[73] a device for showing the angle and direction of the sun, examples of which had long been in use in Egypt and in Babylonia. Herodotus remarks that the Greeks learned from the Babylonians of sundials and their pointers and the twelve parts of the day,[74] but though Anaximander is even credited with the invention of the gnomon[75] it is not clear that he introduced it to the Greeks. When Thales studied the solstices, then he too may have used a gnomon; but he could equally well have studied them by observing the successive positions from day to day of the rising sun near midwinter and midsummer against a clearly defined horizon, such as a mountain ridge. This method was used by Cleostratus of Tenedos, who late in the sixth century BC watched the sun rise over Mount Ida, and by Matricetas of Methymna in Lesbos who observed the rising of the sun from behind Mount Lepetymnus in that island.[76]

Anaximander is also remarkable for having been the first Greek map maker, as a fragment of Eratosthenes informs us:[77] the idea of making a map of the world was later taken up by Hecataeus of Miletus at the end of the sixth century. If Herodotus' criticism of these early maps is fair,[78] they were all schematic and rudimentary, rather like the Babylonian maps of the time. Whereas Hecataeus is said to have given a drawing with the rest of his writings,[79] Anaximander used a tablet;[80] the character of his map is unknown, but bronze maps were employed by Milesians a generation or so later.[81]

Like Thales, who is said to have been a kinsman of his,[82] Anaximander may have exercised authority in Miletus. He is even said to have conducted colonists to the Pontic Apollonia,[83] but the story is most implausible as Apollonia was founded about 610 BC and Anaximander would not then have been old enough to lead the first settlers; possibly he led out a later body of colonists, but another Anaximander may have been responsible: the name is found in archaic Milesian inscriptions,[84] none of which needs refer to the philosopher.

There is a tradition that he visited Sparta, where he was said to have predicted an earthquake[85] and to have set up a gnomon at a place called 'Sundials'.[86] This was perhaps used by him to determine the solstices, for he studied the course of the sun in the ecliptic, and is even said to have discovered its obliquity.[87] He is also said to have estimated the interval between the autumnal equinox and the morning setting of the Pleiades:[88] the study of the rising times of stars had a long tradition in Greece going back to Hesiod, and the Babylonians of Anaximander's time and earlier were also very interested in the subject. But it cannot be proved that Anaximander had any knowledge of Babylonian astronomy. He is said to have written on the Sphere;[89] perhaps he used an astronomical globe to distinguish true from apparent rising times of stars. Such patient observations as his of the heavens led in time to the creation of the exact sciences. He seems to have been an amiable man, with the modesty that goes with true intellectual distinction, if we may believe an anecdote about him. When some boys laughed at his singing, he replied: 'Then to please the boys, I must improve my singing.'[90]

(D) ANAXIMENES

Anaximenes son of Eurystratus of Miletus was reputed to have been a friend, pupil, and successor of Anaximander.[91] He hit upon the idea of explaining the differing densities of things by rarefaction and condensation of a single primordial entity, which he took to be 'air' (i.e. Homeric $ἀήρ$, vapour or mist). At its finest air becomes fire, and then, in increasing degrees of density, wind, then cloud, then water, then earth, then stones. From these constituents all other things come into being (if Theophrastus' account is to be relied upon here). In general Anaximenes held that that which is condensed is cold, and that which is 'relaxed' ($χαλαρόν$) is hot, thus invoking condensation and rarefaction to explain changes in temperature.[92] The primordial entity is divine, and the gods arise from it;[93] but they seem to have had no part to play in his cosmogony. Motion there had been for ever in the air,[94] and this motion, he perhaps maintained, caused the original condensation, from which there came into being the earth. The earth is flat or table-like and rides on air which extends infinitely all around it.[95] Exhalations from the earth generated the heavenly bodies. They are flat like leaves and can thus float upon air.[96] They do not pass under the earth but revolve around it 'like a cap revolving around our head' as Anaximenes put it.[97] The sun is hidden at night by the higher parts of the earth, which, it appears, form great mountain ranges to the north blocking the sun's light on his journey between sunset and dawn from west to east.[98]

He explained thunder and lightning by the action of wind, in this following Anaximander. Other meteorological events were held by him to be due to varying densities of air. Clouds are caused by the thickening of the air. Further compression squeezes out rain. When the falling water freezes, there is hail, but when wind is added, snow.[99] Earthquakes are not due to air, but to excessive droughts or deluges which cause the earth's surface to disintegrate.[100]

In living things the soul is of air also, but the paraphrase of Anaximenes' words on this subject does not show clearly how air holds bodies together.[101] He seems to have drawn an analogy between air enclosing the whole world and air, as breath, controlling us, permeating us through and through until we die.

Anaximenes was the last of the great Milesian philosophers of the sixth century BC; of his life nothing is known, but since he is said to have used a simple and unaffected Ionic speech,[102] his work may have been read by later scholars, having survived the sack of Miletus. It is noteworthy that Theophrastus wrote a special work on Anaximenes,[103] but not on Anaximander, presumably because he had more evidence about the former from Anaximenes' own Ionic writings. Later a paraphrase of them may have been made: Aetius claims to quote Anaximenes, but the quotation is not in Ionic.[104]

The cosmology of Anaximenes is less significant than his theory of variable densities, which reveals some physical insight. The account he gives of rain and hail is reasonable, and his search for a single primordial substance was, like Thales', a prelude to the same enquiry in modern physics; but we must not make the historical mistake of awarding high or low marks to the Milesians according to the likeness of their ideas with those of contemporary physicists. Milesian thought has to be studied for its own sake. That some of their ideas correspond with modern physical notions is interesting and perhaps significant: but Milesian philosophy would be just as worth studying if there were no similarities at all. The merit of the Milesian intellectual aristocracy lies less in the details of the theories they advanced than in their shared belief that Nature is intelligible; for this belief is at the root of all rational and exact enquiry to this day. Miletus was indeed fortunate that for much of the sixth century BC she was governed by some of the best minds in Ionia,[105] men who, like Thales, turned easily from responsible government to bold ratiocination, and made their city an adornment to Greece.

(E) PYTHAGORAS

The doctrines of Pythagoras of Samos, whom Herodotus called 'by no means the weakest sage amongst the Hellenes',[106] are not easily recovered, even in their barest outlines, for notions which may have been introduced by his followers in southern Italy were often said to come from the master himself. The earliest evidence, however, is found in Xenophanes and Heraclitus, neither of whom was far removed from him in time; each of them was critical of his claims. That Pythagoras believed in the transmigration of souls is clear from a satirical fragment of Xenophanes, in which the Samian sage claims to hear the soul of a friend giving tongue in a puppy as it was being whipped.[107] Heraclitus thoroughly disapproved of Pythagoras and his claims: 'the learning of many things,' he maintained, 'does not teach good sense; for if it did, it would have taught Hesiod and Pythagoras, and Xenophanes too, and Hecataeus.'[108] 'Pythagoras made scientific enquiries more than all other men,' said the Ephesian sage, 'and making a selection of those writings he claimed as his own a wisdom which was really dabbling in many subjects and sharp practice.'[109]

The facts about his life are few and obscure. According to Apollodorus Pythagoras flourished in the time of Polycrates about 547 BC.[110] It is said that when he saw the Samian tyranny coming into being, he left Samos and travelled to Egypt and Babylon for the sake of study. When he returned home, he saw that the tyranny of Polycrates was more firmly established. He therefore departed to Italy at the age of forty, as Aristoxenus, a historian of Pythagoreanism, remarks.[111] He settled at Croton, where he became a legislator and a person of importance. He and his three hundred followers became in effect an oligarchy,[112] but when later the men of Croton revolted against him, he retired to Metapontum where he died.[113] Supposed similarities between the teachings of the Pythagoreans and those of the Egyptians, Phoenicians and Chaldaeans were taken by ancient scholars as proof that Pythagoras travelled widely in the near east, but there is no proof that he did so.[114] Whatever he may have owed to the Orient he may have learnt in Samos. Yet the story of his having been taken captive to Babylon from Egypt by Cambyses was persistent.[115]

His most likely debt to the Orient was in mathematics. The so-called Pythagorean theorem is certainly not the discovery of Pythagoras. For the 'Pythagorean' property of square numbers was well known in Mesopotamia in the Old Babylonian period.[116] It is moreover possible that Pythagoras formulated the theorem arithmetically, as the Babylonians did, not geometrically as it appears in textbooks from Euclid onwards.[117] The interest of the early Pythagoreans in supposed mystical properties of numbers seems to go back to the master himself, whose arithmetical studies were thought to have led him to venerate ten above all numbers: ten, the sum of the first four integers, is a triangular

number, for the integers can be arranged thus: .: : The Pythagoreans

venerated ten as the Tetractys of the Decad and took their most solemn oaths by it, considering it to be the fount of nature.[118] Thus they had a closely coherent view of the world, in which number and nature were linked. Such a unitary conception of the scheme of things points to the workings of a single mind: and we may perhaps trace the origin of Pythagorean arithmetical doctrines to the master himself. It is different, however, with the rules of abstinence and the primitive taboos, which may have been adopted over a long period and piecemeal by his followers.[119] Pythagoreanism persisted for long in antiquity because it appealed strongly to a deep need for a unitary view of the world. Nor in spite of much obscurantism can the teachings of the Pythagoreans be regarded as wholly deleterious. We must refrain, however, from claiming for Pythagoras a prominent place in the history of science, partly because so little is known about his teachings, partly because he cannot be proved to have been the mathematical originator he is often claimed to be. Greek mathematics in the sixth century BC, before and after Pythagoras, was not more advanced than the mathematics of the Babylonians more than a millennium earlier. But Pythagoras was a true philosopher, a word he is said to have invented.[120]

(F) XENOPHANES

The first problem in the life of Xenophanes is to date it. Of himself the philosopher asserts, 'Already there are seven and sixty years tossing my thought about in the land of Greece; and from my birth there were twenty-five to add to them, if I know how to speak truly about these things.'[121] Thus he reached the age of ninety-two at least. A fragment of his elegies mentions a conversation by the fire in winter when somebody lies on a couch, drinks his wine, and nibbles chickpeas: 'From what land do you come?' he asks, 'What is the number of your years, good sir? How old were you when the Mede arrived?'[122] Here the poet mentions the Persian conquest of Ionia. He was expelled from his native Colophon, but whether that happened before, at the time of, or after the coming of the Mede we do not know. Timaeus[123] the Sicilian historian claimed that Xenophanes lived in the time of Hieron, who reigned in Syracuse from 478 to 467 BC: his assertion may be true, since we have the poet's own word that he lived to a great age. Xenophanes is said to have lived in Zancle and Catane after his exile,[124] and to have had connexions with Elea, the Phocaean colony founded about 540 BC in southern Italy–he said that if Leucothea was a goddess, then the men of Elea ought not to lament for her; if a human being, then they ought not to sacrifice to her.[125] He is also credited with a poem on the colonisation of Elea, and a historical poem on the founding of Colophon.[126] Since he mentioned Pythagoras[127] and was mentioned by Heraclitus,[128] he was active in the second half of the sixth century, and the whole span of his ninety or more years may have extended over a century from about 560 BC onwards. He is an acute, observant and profound student of men and of the world of nature.

Some of his most striking work was geological. He thought that the earth was being mixed with the sea, and that in time the earth is dissolved by the moist. He had observed shells inland and in the mountains; and at Syracuse in the quarries he claimed that he had seen the impression of a fish and of seaweed. In Paros there was an impression of a bay leaf in the depth of the rock, and in Melite flat shapes of all things that are in the sea. These, he said, came about when everything long ago was covered with mud, and the impression was dried in the mud. All men are destroyed when the earth is carried down to the sea and becomes mud; then there is another beginning of coming-to-be, and this forms a foundation for all the worlds.[129] Thus he has a cyclical theory of the history of the earth, and sees flooding as the cause of the destruction of living things. Another geological fragment refers to water dripping down in caves: the context is obscure, but the reference may be to stalactites.[130] Volcanoes also interested him: he thought that Stromboli erupted every seventeenth year.[131]

All things have their being from earth and water, and we all originate in those two elements.[132] Clouds, winds and rivers are all begotten by the great ocean.[133] The parts below the earth at our feet extend indefinitely downwards.[134] These details are reasonably clear, but his opinions about the heavenly bodies are less coherent. The sun is said to come into being daily from little pieces of fire gathered together,[135] but another tradition attributes to Xenophanes the view that the sun and the stars arise from ignited clouds.[136] The rainbow too is a cloud, 'what they call Iris . . . purple and red and yellow to behold.'[137] A confused passage in Aetius mentions Xenophanes' puzzling doctrine of eclipses, according to which the sun's disc is said to be banished to some part of the earth not inhabited by us and as it were 'treads on nothing when producing the eclipse',[138] perhaps by stepping into a hole. What Xenophanes may have meant by the statement that the sun goes forward indefinitely, but seems to move in a circle because of the distance, is not clear. He did not mean that the sun went on *ad infinitum*, because he has just said that it is renewed every day.[139]

To his study of the physical world he linked the study of the gods, the conventional view of whom he attacked vigorously. 'Homer and Hesiod' he complains, 'have attributed to the gods everything that is a shame and

a reproach amongst men, thieving and committing adultery and de-
ceiving each other.'[140] Mankind's mistake is to create gods in their own
image, considering, 'that they are born and have clothes, speech and
bodies like their own,'[141] so that, as he remarks, 'the Æthiopians say that
their gods are snub-nosed and black, and the Thracians that theirs have
light-blue eyes and red hair.'[142] Why, he continued to press the argument, 'if cattle and horses and lions had hands and could paint with their
hands as men do, horses would paint the forms of the gods like horses,
and cattle like cattle, and they would make their bodies like their own
bodies.'[143]

If then the gods are not like men, what are they like? There is, he
says, 'one god, greatest amongst gods and men, in no way like mortals
either in body or in thought.'[144] The one true god is an unmoving per-
cipient being. 'All of him sees, all thinks, and all hears.'[145] 'Ever does he
he remain in the same place, without any movement. Nor is it fitting for
him to change his position at one time and another, but without effort he
shakes all things by the thought of his mind.'[146] Aristotle unfairly calls
this conception 'somewhat uncouth';[147] it was, on the contrary, a great
feat of abstract reasoning to strip true divinity of all attributes except
cognition. Since the mind of the one god reaches everywhere, he does
not even need to move. It is an austere, yet awesome, conception,
compelling in its simplicity.

The one god is beyond the comprehension of mortals. Even if a man
chanced to say the complete truth about the gods and all that Xenophanes spoke of, he would not know that he had done so. 'Appearance is
wrought over all things,'[148] yet we must not give up the quest for truth.
'The gods have not revealed all things to mortals from the beginning,
but by searching men find out better in time.'[149] Our defect lies in the
fallibility of the senses: 'if god had not made yellow honey, men would
claim that figs were far sweeter.'[150] Not even Xenophanes after his deep
thought and patient observations could knowingly propound the truth,
but (he thought) mortals can at least try to recognise error, and show
what is not true. Only God knows; man opines.[151]

Man, for all his weakness, may enjoy himself, and has a right to do so.
One of the longest elegiac fragments describes a pleasant feast with
garlands, the mixing bowl is ready, and there is a bouquet to the wine.
The table is piled with cheese and honey, the altar decked with flowers,
and people are dancing in the house. Then will men first sing hymns to
the gods and make their prayers. There is no harm in a man drinking if
he can get home afterwards without an attendant, and is not so old that

he needs one anyway. He will not, if he is wise, tell the ancient myths about the battles of Titans, Giants and Centaurs or speak of disputes and factions.[152]

For the cult of sport he has nothing but scorn. It is useless to the city and utterly without profit, unlike his wisdom which is better than the strength of men and horses.[153] To prefer strength to sound intelligence is, he claims, not just. With what distaste would he look upon that outstanding characteristic of our civilisation, the fanatical and nationalistic cult of competitive games.

CHAPTER XI

Croesus and the Ionians

WHEN ALYATTES DIED, THERE WAS A BITTER STRUGGLE FOR THE kingship of Lydia amongst his sons Pantaleon and Croesus. Croesus, the son of a Carian mother, had been appointed successor by Alyattes, but Pantaleon, the son of Alyattes by an Ionian woman, still hoped to rule, and he was supported in his ambition by a rich Lydian;[1] this man was perhaps Sadyattes, who earlier had refused to lend Croesus staters to raise troops for an expedition of Alyattes.[2] In spite of an attempt by a stepmother to poison Croesus,[3] however, Pantaleon's cause failed, and Croesus became king. The date of his accession is close to 560 BC: Croesus was then thirty-five years old.[4] His first action was to murder the insolent partisan of Pantaleon by having him drawn over a spiked carding machine;[5] then his riches were dedicated in fulfilment of Croesus' vow to Artemis of Ephesus, where golden bulls and drums of columns with inscriptions recorded that he set them up.[6] He was lavish also in his dedications at other Greek shrines: a great golden shield dedicated to Apollo Pythius bore witness to the continuing friendship of the Mermnads towards Delphi; a golden tripod was sent to Ismenian Apollo at Thebes in Boeotia and gifts were made to Apollo's oracle at Branchidae near Miletus.[7] Yet another gift was made to the Spartans; he gave them gold for the statue of Apollo at Thornax in Laconia, though they had offered to pay for it.[8]

The Lydian's friendship towards Artemis of Ephesus did not carry with it immunity for the city, however. Croesus determined to bring Ephesus within his empire by overthrowing the tyrant Pindarus, a grandson of Alyattes. When the Lydian army attacked the walls of Ephesus, and caused one of the towers to collapse, the defenders dedicated the city to Artemis by tying a rope from the columns of her temple to the wall of the old city, a distance of seven stades. Croesus, amused at the stratagem, agreed to grant immunity to the Ephesians, but insisted upon the exile of Pindarus.[9] The tyrant thereupon departed to Peloponnese with some of his friends, but left his son and most of his assets in the care of a certain Pasicles. This man became chief magistrate (*archon* or *aisymnetes*) of Ephesus; but he was killed at the Ephesian Heraeum, where his mother was priestess, by a certain Melas and his friends.[10] Melas may well have been a son of Pindarus and a grandson of the tyrant Melas to whom Alyattes had married one of his daughters.[11]

Shortly after this, about 550 BC when Cyrus the Persian and Harpagus overthrew Astyages the Mede, a certain Aristarchus was invited to Ephesus from Athens as monarch by some kinsmen of his.[12] He is said to have ruled well for five years; his reign must have ended about the time of the Persian conquest of Ionia.

The cities of mainland Aeolis and Ionia now for the first time paid tribute to Lydia, but Croesus did not build ships to subject the islanders, on the advice, it was said, of Pittacus or Bias, who pointed out that the Lydians would be as ineffective at sea against an Ionian navy, as the Ionians were on land against the horsemen of the Lydians. Instead of attacking therefore Croesus made a treaty of friendship with them, and campaigned in Asia Minor instead.[13] A memory of one of his campaigns on the mainland is found in Strabo, who recalls an attack by Croesus on the little town of Sidene in the Troad.[14] Miletus on the mainland was thought to have refused on the advice of Thales an alliance with Croesus,[15] a decision which was to her advantage when Cyrus overthrew the Lydian empire.

That empire in the time of Croesus was one of the most powerful states in the near east. Apart from the Cilicians[16] and the hardy Lycians, Lydia had subjected all the other peoples of Asia Minor 'within the Halys river'. Herodotus[17] lists them to prove his point: Lydians, Phrygians, Mysians, Mariandynians, Chalybes, Paphlagonians, Thynian and Bithynian Thracians, Carians, Ionians, Dorians, Aeolians, and Pamphylians. Moreover, Croesus formed alliances with several great powers, so as to confront the rising might of Persia. One of his sisters was married to Astyages the Mede;[18] he made pacts with Amasis of Egypt and Nabun'aid of Babylonia, and he allied himself to the most powerful Greek city, Sparta.[19] None of these alliances in fact brought Croesus security, but about 550 BC his military position seemed to himself and to his neighbours very strong indeed. The Mermnad succession, however, was not secured.

Croesus had two sons, one of whom was dumb and unfit to rule; the other was a boy of great ability called Atys, whose tutor was a Phrygian of the royal line, Adrastus a son of Midas son of Gordius, living at Sardis in exile because he had killed his own brother. When Adrastus killed Atys by mistake during a boar hunt on Mount Olympus in Mysia, Croesus lost a fit successor to the throne. The king did not punish Adrastus, but the miserable Phrygian was driven by despair to kill

himself upon the young prince's tomb.[20] Croesus is said to have mourned
for his son for two years, until the news that Astyages had been overthrown by Cyrus prompted him to check the growing power of Persia
before it was too late.[21]

It is clear that the Mermnadae were friendly with some Athenians
as well as with Sparta, though we hear of no Lydian treaty with Athens.
The Athenian nobleman Alcmeon, who had helped Lydian emissaries at
Delphi, had visited Sardis and taken his fill of gold from the treasuries;[22]
and there was also an Athenian Croesus, who may have been an
Alcmeonid named in honour of the Lydian king.[23]

Miltiades the Athenian founder of a colony in the Thracian Chersonese, who built a wall across the Isthmus from Cardia to Pactye to
defend it from the Apsinthians, was also a friend of Croesus. When the
Lampsacenes captured Miltiades, Croesus ordered them to let him go,
threatening that if they did not obey, he would destroy them like a pine,
which alone of trees does not send forth shoots when it is cut down, as
Herodotus explains.[24] The threat was apt, for a poetical name of
Lampsacus was Pityoessa, the city of pines,[25] and Croesus was heeded.[26]
Evidently Miltiades too, like the Alcmeonidae, had close ties with
Croesus. Miltiades had a dislike of the tyranny of Pisistratus in Athens,[27]
but we do not know that Croesus shared it.

Some evidence for life in Ionia in the time of Croesus is found in the
poetry of the Ephesian Hipponax, son of Pytheas and Protis. He
flourished about the time of the fall of Sardis to Cyrus according to the
Parian Marble,[28] a dating which may be too low, as there is no mention
of Medes or Persians in any of the fragments. Croesus himself however
is named, in connexion with Dascylium.[29]

The poet was banished to Clazomenae by the tyrants Comas and
Athenagoras,[30] for what cause we do not know. He was chiefly remembered for his bitter dispute with the Chiot sculptors Bupalus and Athenis,
who had made caricatures of him. He lampooned them mercilessly, and
even, fertile imaginations asserted, drove them to suicide.[31] The details
of the 'Bupalean battle', as Callimachus called it,[32] are lost, but competition for the favours of the fair Arete may have been the cause.[33] The
lady, it seems, had abandoned Hipponax for Bupalus. The sculptor's
father Archermos had also been distinguished in the same art and his
name has been found on dedications in Athens and Delos.[34]

Fragments of the verse of Hipponax hint that Lydian influence was
strong in Ephesus. The Lydian god Candaules he identifies with the
Greek Hermes: the name, he said, meant 'dog-throttler'.[35] He knows

another Lydian god Malis,[36] and introduces a woman speaking to a man in Lydian.[37] The poet describes in detail, as though he knew the country well, the road overland from the neighbourhood of Sardis to the coast.[38] He bids someone to pass by various monuments of the Lydians including the mound of Gyges, and what, in a corrupt line, seem to be the great late Bronze Age rock monuments at Karabel, along the road to 'Smyrna . . . turning your belly to the setting sun'. Smyrna here means a part of Ephesus, as another fragment of Hipponax shows, in which he states that somebody 'lived behind the city in Smyrna between Rough Hill and Scabby headland'.[39]

Phrygians and Thracians too are well known to him. He mentions the Phrygian goddess Cybebe,[40] uses a Phrygian word for bread,[41] and describes Phrygian slaves sold to grind barley in the mills at Miletus.[42] He knows the Thracian goddess Bendis and the Thracian king Rhesus.[43]

Ionian allusions abound. He mentions an eunuch in Lampsacus[44] and Bupalus and Arete in Erythrae;[45] Bias is well known to Hipponax for his advocate's powers;[46] there is a mention of Branchus or Baranchus, the founder of the Milesian sanctuary of Apollo at Didyma;[47] and of a painter Mimnes and a sculptor Bion.[48] At all times the poet kept his eyes open to life about him, and all manner of things were fit subjects for his keen observation and wry comment.

Hipponax is the earliest author to mention the ritual of the *pharmakos*,[49] which is found in parts of Ionia and in Athens. The pharmakos was an expiatory victim, led out of the city in the month Thargelion at the festival of the Thargelia.[50] At Athens two men were led out to be purifications for the city, one for the men, the other for the women. Sometimes the victims were beaten to death.[51] This horrid and barbarous ritual warns us not to regard the age of Ionian enlightenment as all reason and clarity. Milesian rationalism flourished in the midst of a society still deeply imbued with cults that were ancient, elemental and bloody.

The limping iambics of Hipponax with their spondaic endings were also used by another Ionian poet, whose city is unknown. Ananius the Ionian lived not later than the middle of the fifth century, for the Sicilian poet Epicharmus who lived then quotes his opinion that in springtime the fish called *chromis* was the best of all.[52] Ananius recommends the fish *anthias* in winter; the tunny 'makes a good dish'; and goat's meat is pleasant to eat in the autumn. Full grown pigs, hares, foxes and dogs can be eaten then too. He even swears by food: 'by the cabbage' he exclaims to a friend, 'I like you by far the best of all men.'[53] Some of the poetry ascribed to him is claimed for Hipponax also: one of them calls upon Apollo, whether he be in Delos, or at Delphi, or Naxos, or Miletus, or holy Clarus, or on a visit to the Scythians, making sure that the god will hear, wherever he may be.[54]

Ananius could afford to despise money, saying 'if anyone keeps a lot of gold at home, and a few figs and two or three men, he will know how much better figs are than gold'.[55] Hipponax, who once asked Hermes to give him sixty staters of gold[56] would not have agreed. Nor would another Ionian, Pythermus of Teos, who asserted that 'nothing but gold is of account'.[57]

When Astyages son of Cyaxares the Mede was defeated at Pasargadae and overthrown by Cyrus the Achaemenid Persian in 550 BC,[58] the eastern parts of the Lydian empire were endangered by the growing power of the Persians. Croesus may have already determined to destroy, or at least to check, Cyrus before it was too late; but he wished to be sure that Apollo expected his campaign to go well, and to know whether he should have the support of an allied army. The oracles at Delphi and at Thebes declared that if he marched against the Persians he would destroy a great empire; and also that he should make the most powerful of the Greeks his friends.[59] Croesus then made his alliance with Sparta, and was confident that he would defeat Cyrus. The Spartans meanwhile were delighted by the alliance, and sent a great krater of bronze as a gift to the Lydian king; but unfortunately the bowl was captured by the Samians at sea or, as the Samians claimed, was sold in Samos by the Spartan emissaries when they heard that Sardis had fallen and Croesus was captured.[60]

Croesus, his military preparations completed, marched against the Cappadocians, whose boundary with the Lydian territories was the Halys river. Expecting to add Cappadocia to his empire, the king crossed the Halys. It was said that part of the river was diverted so as to make the rest fordable, half the water flowing in the old bed and half in the new. Some held that this was the work of Thales but Herodotus believed that the army crossed by bridges which were already there. After entering Cappadocia the Lydian army ravaged the land and expelled the inhabitants, though, as Herodotus says, they had done Croesus no harm. The Cappadocians who lived inland from Sinope were by the Greeks called Leucosyri or White Syrians. Their capital, the city of Pteria, Croesus captured, and made its people slaves.[61]

Cyrus had marched quickly through Assyria westwards to intercept the Lydians. Ahead he had sent messengers urging the Ionians to revolt, but they heeded him not. Battle was joined finally near Pteria; the armies fought till nightfall, bloodily but indecisively; and then according to the Lydian version Croesus decided to withdraw his forces westwards, and to call on his allies Amasis of Egypt, Nabun'aid of Babylon, and the Spartans to appear in Lydia with their armies 'in the fifth month', after the winter, which was near at hand.[62] It was said that an Ephesian, Eurybatus, was sent to hire mercenaries in Peloponnese, but instead deserted with the pay to Cyrus.[63] Cyrus with his tough soldiery would not wait out the winter. When Croesus had dismissed his mercenaries, thinking that there would be no need for them until spring, the Persians made straight for Sardis before the troops could regroup, and to the Lydians' astonishment appeared before the city.[64]

Croesus led his Lydians out to the fight in the Hermus plain, relying chiefly upon his cavalry, but against them, at the suggestion of Harpagus the Mede, Cyrus used a clever stratagem. The Persian infantry were placed behind the camels, but in front of the cavalry. When the Lydian cavalry charged, the smell of the camels, which was highly offensive to the horses, caused them to retreat, and they were quite useless to Croesus. The horsemen leapt off their mounts, however, and fought valiantly on foot, but in the end the Lydians had to give ground. Croesus and his troops were then forced to take refuge in the acropolis of Sardis.[65]

When the Lydian envoys reached Sparta, they found the Lacedaemonians engaged with the Argives in a war for the Thyrea, a territory between them. Sparta promised to send help as soon as possible. Soon news came that Sardis was besieged, and ships were ready to sail with a relief force when it was learnt that the citadel was taken and Croesus a captive. With good sense the Spartans thereupon abandoned the expedition, though greatly distressed at the fall of Lydia.[66]

Cyrus had promised a reward to the first man to get over the wall, but the days passed without success. On the fourteenth day of the siege however a Lydian soldier was seen by Hyroeades a Mardian to drop his helmet over the edge of the acropolis on the south side facing mount Tmolus. When the Lydian climbed down and recovered his helmet, Hyroeades at once saw that the citadel could be entered at that point. So he took a party in with him and many others followed. Sardis was taken, and as the Pythia foretold a great empire was overthrown.[67] The Sibyl of Ephesus too proved friendly to Cyrus.[68]

It was said that to make the city impregnable the Heraclid king Meles[69] at the suggestion of the oracle at Telmessus[70] had carried a lion, born from a concubine of his, around the walls of the citadel to make them proof against any enemy. But at the part of the wall where Hyroeades entered, Meles had failed to carry the lion and Croesus had not placed a strong guard, thinking one needless.

Croesus was brought alive to Cyrus, as the Persian had ordered. In Herodotus' narrative the captive king is placed on a pyre, but is reprieved by Cyrus at the last minute, becomes an adviser of the great king, and accompanies him on later campaigns. We have no proof that Cyrus burned him to death; and it is perhaps unlikely that the Persian king would have defiled the sacred fire by burning a living man upon it.[71] Yet somehow the story of the pyre arose: it appears in Attic vase painting early in the fifth century BC,[72] and a little later in the poetry of Bacchylides whose version told how Apollo rescued his favourite from the flames in which the king had tried to immolate himself.[73] Perhaps Croesus had wanted to destroy himself by fire in his citadel, and failed.

The date of the fall of Sardis to Cyrus is still disputed. Herodotus implies that it happened in the autumn, but of which year? The Nabun'aid-Cyrus Chronicle reports that Cyrus in 547 BC, the ninth year of Nabun'aid, marched against the land of *Lu-* (the text is damaged at this point) and killed its king.[74] If *Lu-* is Lydia, then the date of the defeat of Croesus is fixed to the year 547 BC, which agrees well with the Apollodorean date for the fall of Sardis, 547/6 BC.[75] However Herodotus clearly believed that Croesus survived the fall of Sardis and accompanied Cyrus as his adviser. Either Herodotus was wrong in supposing that Croesus survived the fall of Sardis: or the Chronicle is incorrect in stating that the king of *Lu-* was killed, if *Lu-* is Lydia: or the Chronicle does not refer to the fall of Sardis in the passage describing the ninth year of Nabun'aid. The Chronicle may be wrong in stating that the king of *Lu-* was killed; and even if we neglect the evidence of the Chronicle altogether and deny that *Lu-* is Lydia, 547/6 may still have been the year of the fall of Sardis, since that date comes from the fine scholarship of Apollodorus.

According to Ctesias,[76] whom scholars trust at their peril, Cyrus saved Croesus and gave him a city called Barene, said to be near Ecbatana, to live in. There may be truth in this, but the story is found in Ctesias only and we have no means of checking it. Besides, the fact, if fact it is, of Croesus' survival has little historical significance. He was no longer king, his dominions were taken from him, and the riches of

Lydia and her dependent territories now helped to fill the treasuries of the Great King of the Medes and Persians. The power of Cyrus now reached nine hundred miles westwards from Media almost to the shores of the Aegean and the Great King of Babylon, Nabonidus, heard with dread that his Lydian ally was overthrown.

CHAPTER XII

The Persian Conquest of Ionia

WHEN THE LAST OF THE MERMNAD KINGS WAS OVERTHROWN, THE
Ionians and the Aeolians sent messengers to Sardis, asking Cyrus to have
them as his subjects under the same terms as Croesus'. But Cyrus,
angry because they had rejected his request to revolt from Lydia,
pointed out that they were like fish caught by a flute player, who danced
for him only when he had brought them ashore in his net. So the Great
King refused the pleas of all of them except the Milesians, with whom
he made a treaty. The other Ionians returned to their cities to fortify
them, and an assembly at Panionion decided to send ambassadors to
Sparta to beg for help.[1]

Pythermus of Phocaea, the leader of the Ionian delegation, in which
there were also Aeolians, urged the Spartans to come to the help of the
Asiatic Greeks; but they were neither convinced by his arguments nor
impressed by the purple cloak which he hoped would draw many
citizens to hear his histrionic appeal. However, the Spartans did send
a party in a penteconter to Phocaea under Lacrines, who went up to
Sardis to warn Cyrus to leave the Greek cities alone. Cyrus was genuinely
puzzled by this gesture: 'Who are the Lacedaemonians?' he is said to
have asked.[2]

Croesus' Egyptian mercenaries were treated leniently by Cyrus, who
settled them in the Aeolis.[3] Then after entrusting Sardis to a Persian,
Tabalus, and appointing Pactyes a Lydian to gather the gold of Croesus
and the other Lydians, the Great King departed for Ecbatana, taking
Croesus with him according to Herodotus. He ignored the Ionians
because Babylon, Bactria, the Sacae, and the Egyptians offered more
pressing threats.[4] But when Cyrus was safely away from Sardis, Pactyes
made the Lydians revolt from Tabalus, and going down to the Aegean
hired mercenaries with the gold in his care. He also brought men of the
coast inland with him to besiege Tabalus in the citadel of Sardis.[5]

As soon as Cyrus heard of the revolt he sent Mazares a Mede to put it
down, with orders to disarm the Lydians and to enslave the force hired
by Pactyes, who was to be brought alive to the Great King.[6] When
Mazares reached Sardis with part of Cyrus' army, Pactyes made off to
Kyme as a suppliant. Mazares ordered the Kymaians to hand Pactyes
over, but they hesitated to break the law of suppliants, and first asked

Apollo of Branchidae, whose oracle was regularly consulted by Aeolians as well as Ionians, what to do.[7] The Kymaians could easily have consulted Apollo at his oracle of Gryneium nearby,[8] but preferred the more famous to the closer shrine. The god ordered them to give back Pactyes to the Mede, but when the Kymaians were about to do this, Aristodicus son of Heraclides, a notable citizen, told them to desist, because he disbelieved the oracle and thought that those who had consulted it were not speaking the truth. Aristodicus then went with a second deputation to Branchidae, but the oracle again commanded them to hand over the suppliant Pactyes. Aristodicus then deliberately went round the temple pulling down the sparrows' nests and the young birds that lodged there, until a voice from the shrine cried, 'Most profane of men! How dare you plunder my suppliants from the temple?' To which Aristodicus promptly replied, 'Lord, do you help your own suppliants but order the Kymaians to betray theirs?' To which the god, determined to have the last word, answered, 'Yes, I do order you, so as the quicker to ruin you, and stop you pestering my oracle in future with enquiries about suppliants.'[9] Perhaps Aristodicus considered that Apollo, the favourite god of Croesus, had been too eager to go over to the cause of Lydia's enemies. The Persians indeed were well aware of the favours shown to them by Apollo. In a copy of a letter, recorded in an inscription found near Magnesia by the Maeander, from Darius to his 'slave' Gadates, who seems to have been satrap of the Ionian province, the Great King threatens to punish him for taxing the sacred gardeners of Apollo and forcing them to cultivate profane land. 'You are unaware' the king adds, 'of the goodwill of my ancestors towards the god, who spoke unerring truth to the Persians . . .', and there unfortunately the damaged text ends.[10]

In their distress the Kymaians, not wishing to face a siege, sent Pactyes to Mytilene, where the people were ready to hand him over to Mazares for a price; but when the Kymaians got word of this, they sent a ship to take Pactyes to Chios. There the miserable Lydian was dragged from the sanctuary of Athena Poliuchus and sold, the price of his return being the cession to Chios of the land of Atarneus in Mysia opposite to Lesbos.[11] Mazares then attacked the army besieging Tabalus at Sardis, enslaved Priene, plundered the whole plain of the Maeander, and Magnesia too. He was then taken off by a disease.[12]

Harpagus, his successor, was also a Mede, having formerly been a high officer of Astyages. He attacked each of the Ionian cities in turn with siege mounds, assaulting Phocaea first, where the long circuit wall had been built with generous grants from old king Arganthonius of Tartessus.[13] Harpagus' terms of surrender were moderate: the removal of one bastion and the dedication of one house. To consider them the Phocaeans obtained a truce of one day during which Harpagus agreed to take his army away from the walls. Then, as the Mede had foreseen, they drew their penteconters down the slipways, put their children, women and gear aboard, and took the statues and other offerings from the shrines, leaving only works in bronze or stone and paintings; then they embarked and sailed for Chios.[14] The Persians thereupon occupied the abandoned city.[15]

The Chiots did not grant the Phocaeans' request to sell them the Oenussae islands nearby, for they feared competition from a trading post at the approaches to Chios:[16] so the emigrants, led by Creontiades,[17] sailed to Corsica, where twenty years earlier they had, in obedience to an oracle, founded the city of Alalia. They did not go to Tartessus because Arganthonius was now dead.[18] Before leaving the Aegean, however, they descended upon Phocaea and murdered the Persian garrison. They also sank in the sea a lump of iron, swearing solemnly that they would not return to Phocaea before the iron floated. The break with the Ionian past was to be complete. The oaths were soon neglected, however, when over half the citizens, overcome by a longing for home, decided to sail back.[19] Those who left Ionia for good joined the earlier settlers at Alalia, where they stayed five years, founded sanctuaries, and plundered their neighbours.[20] Some of the emigrants from Phocaea may also have joined their kinsmen in Massalia.[21] The Carthaginians and the Etruscans, however, determined to ruin the intrusive colony at Alalia, and sailed against it with sixty ships each. The Phocaeans sailed out to meet them with sixty of their own and barely won a victory off Sardinia in which they lost forty ships. The remainder were made useless when their rams were bent back. Crippled by this battle, the Phocaeans decided to abandon Alalia; they again put all their people and their belongings aboard and went to Rhegium; from there they sailed to Hyele or Velia in southern Italy where they founded a city at the suggestion of a man of Poseidonia.[22] There is an unfortunate gap in the text of Herodotus just after his account of the abandoning of Alalia, but the sense is that the Etruscans of Caere (Agylla) stoned to death some Phocaean prisoners; the land where this outrage had been committed thereafter produced men, cattle, and sheep which had twisted limbs or were lame or threw fits, until the Pythia being consulted ordered the men of Caere to offer sacrifice to the dead and to hold games for athletes and horsemen.[23]

When Harpagus raised a siege mound against the wall across the promontory on which Teos stood, the citizens abandoned their homes and sailed to Thrace, where they established the city of Abdera. Here more than a century earlier Timesias of Clazomenae had founded a settlement but had soon been driven out by the Thracians. His memory was preserved by the Teians in Abdera who worshipped him as a hero.[24]

The life of the Teian nobility in their estates did not leave them much time to be pioneers in the intellectual and mercantile advances of Ionia in the sixth century. Yet the city had a share in Naucratis. One Teian who forsook, long before the Mede came, the cakes and fish for which his city was famous to become a mercenary was Elesibius, one of the Greeks who scratched their names on the left leg of the colossal statue of Rameses II at Abu Simbel in the time of Psammetichus II.[25] But the most famous Teian was Anacreon, son of Scythines, who had grown to manhood before Harpagus took the city. The poet's words 'but now the crown from the city is destroyed'[26] may even refer to the taking of the walls by the Mede. When the Teians fled to Abdera, Anacreon went with them,[27] before going on to Samos to enjoy the patronage of the tyrant Polycrates; but some of the Teians were homesick and returned to their old city, subject to Persia though it now was.[28] Not even the rich ploughland and fine vineyards of Abdera could keep them in Thrace.[29] Others went from Teos to found Phanagoreia on the Cimmerian Bosporus.[30]

The remaining Ionians withstood Harpagus, but all were defeated in a series of battles which may have continued for a number of years. The defenders were brave and fought well; yet most chose subjection to Persia, not emigration. Meanwhile the Milesians, protected by their treaty, kept quiet and bided their time, and the islanders put themselves in the power of Cyrus.[31] What this nominal capitulation entailed is not clear: Samos with her strong navy hardly needed to sacrifice her freedom. But the Chiots may well have thought, once Harpagus had put down the Ionians of the mainland, that their turn would soon come, and so they gave back Pactyes. It was during Harpagus' campaigns that Bias urged the Ionians assembled at Panionion to abandon their lands and found in freedom a new city in Sardinia; but no-one heeded him.[32] Some Aeolians and Ionians were now conscripted into the army of Harpagus for his expedition against the Carians, Caunians, and Lycians of southwestern Asia Minor.[33] During this campaign the Dorians of Cnidus gave themselves over to Harpagus without a fight: they had tried, while Ionia was being conquered, to make their isthmus an island by digging a canal, but the rock splintered and hurt the eyes of the excavators. Delphi when consulted advised them to submit: 'Defend not the Isthmus by wall or channel, for Zeus would have made an island had he wanted.' So the Cnidians ceased to dig.[34] The Halicarnassians must have given themselves up about this time, though Herodotus does not say so. Harpagus had now subdued all the Greeks of the Asiatic mainland and had received the submission of some of the islanders also. Most of the Carians were swiftly subdued, though those of Pedasa near Halicarnassus put up a stout fight in their fortress on mount Lide. The Lycians too were defeated; amongst them the Xanthians fought desperately, and after having burned their own families in their acropolis, died in battle, every man of them, except for a few families who happened to be out in the countryside. Caunus too fell to the triumphant army of Harpagus.[35]

The Asiatic Greeks were now gradually brought within the Satrapy system, which Cyrus may well have inherited from the Medes, for the form of the title *khshathrapan–, from which Greek satrapes comes, is Median.[36] Already under Cyrus the Persian policy of supporting tyrants in the subject Greek cities had begun. We hear for instance of a Cyzicene, Pytharchus, a friend of Cyrus who gave him seven cities to rule as his own. Pytharchus attempted to capture Cyzicus also and rule there, but seems to have failed in the enterprise.[37] The satrapies, together with the taxation districts of the empire, were reorganised by Darius in whose time the Ionians were assessed for payment with the Magnesians of Asia, the Aeolians, Lycians, Milyans, and Pamphylians. Whether the same arrangement had already existed under Cyrus is not quite clear. Darius assessed 'those by the sea', the Hellespontine Greeks and their neighbours in Asia Minor, separately from the Ionians; and Lydia with Mysia and other inland areas formed a third taxation district.[38] There was a satrap in Dascylium, and another in Sardis,[39] who also had a residence at Magnesia by the Maeander.[40] The Ionians and Aeolians were now part of an empire many times greater than the Lydian; but at first life may not have seemed very different from the old times when the Mermnadae attempted to dominate the Asiatic Greek cities. For some Ionians the coming of the Mede meant an enlargement of opportunity. Ionian craftsmen were valued for their skills by the Persians, and Cyrus summoned Greeks, most probably Ionians, to carve the sculptures in the building of the new royal residence at his ancestral home, Pasargadae, in Persis, over twelve hundred miles from Ionia.[41] Later Darius brought Ionian masons and sculptors, and perhaps architects too, to work in the magnificent new palace at Persepolis, and there must have been already in the time of Cyrus many opportunities for enterprising Greeks to travel about the Persian dominions between the Aegean and the confines of India and from the Caspian to the Persian Gulf. We shall see the effect of the growing knowledge of Asia amongst the Ionians when we come to the work of Hecataeus of Miletus.

Thucydides in an obscure passage mentions naval successes of the Ionians in a war against Cyrus.[42] He cannot have the mainland Ionians in mind here, for Harpagus had little difficulty in defeating them. The islanders too, according to Herodotus,[43] acknowledged the supremacy of Cyrus, being fearful of him; but elsewhere Herodotus states that neither they nor the Lesbians nor the Tenedians had anything to fear.[44] Their submission then can only have been nominal, if it was offered at all. As for the naval successes against Cyrus, Thucydides may have Samian piracy in mind or even the Phocaean assault on the Persian garrison in Phocaea. But there is not enough evidence to explain his remark. The island Ionians, it is true, were flourishing mightily in the time of Cyrus and Cambyses, and the achievements of their tyrants must next be described. From the reign of Cyrus onwards the history of Asiatic Greece is a part of the history of the Persian empire. Our concern is with local, not imperial, history, however; and we shall consider only those actions of the imperial government or of its agents in the west which immediately concerned the eastern Greeks in the first half century of their subjection.

CHAPTER XIII

The Islanders in the Age of Polycrates

FROM THE TIME OF THE IONIAN MIGRATION NAXOS HELD A DOMINANT
position in the Cyclades. We have seen that she was an early contender
for colonial sites in the West, and suggested that Naxians pioneered with
Euboeans the route to Al Mina in Syria. The fighting with Paros in the
time of Archilochus brought reverses to the Naxians, but does not seem
to have weakened the economy of the island. Naxos prospered exceed-
ingly in the century from *c.* 640 BC to *c.* 540 BC, during which costly
offerings were made at Delos by the Naxian nobility,[1] and their sphinx
was, about 560, set on its column at Delphi.[2] Delos indeed may well for
a time have been ruled by her larger neighbour.

There is evidence that Miletus, the old friend of Paros, fought a war
against Naxos. The Milesian force was helped by men from Erythrae led
by a certain Diognetus, who lost his heart to a Naxian lady Polycrite. It
was said that she agreed to give herself to Diognetus on condition that
she was granted a place called the Delion, which the Erythraean force
had occupied. On oath Diognetus consented, and Polycrite at once gave
the Delion to the Naxians. After that the Milesian position became
untenable, and both sides came to terms.[3]

Some of the Naxian notables lived in the city, others in the countryside; amongst the countrymen was Telestagoras of the village Lestadae,
a man highly regarded by the populace. When he and his daughters
were roughly treated by some young bloods he had entertained, the
Naxians angrily took up their arms and attacked the youths. When the
fighting became widespread, Lygdamis, a nobleman, put himself at the
head of the people, seized power, and became tyrant. Aristotle mentions
this action of Lygdamis to illustrate the overthrow of an oligarchy by one
of its members; it is plain therefore that Lygdamis belonged to the
ruling class in the island.[4] These oligarchs were called *pacheis*, 'the fat
ones', so rich were they.[5]

Amongst the Naxian nobility were the family of the Promethii; they
took their name from the Neleid Promethus of Colophon who had spent
an exile in Naxos not long after the Ionian migration.[6] Of this family was
Cydippe, whom Acontius of Ceos saw and loved at a festival at Delos.
Determined to marry her he put in her way an apple on which was
inscribed the oath 'By Artemis, I shall wed Acontius', and when Cydippe

read this aloud, she was bound by oath to marry him. Fortunately, as Callimachus who tells this pretty story shows, the two were happily matched, and Cydippe was pleased to marry into the noble Ceian family of the Euxantidae.[7]

The riches of the Naxians are well illustrated by their buildings and dedications at Delos. One Naxian dedicator to the Delian Apollo was the the lady Nicandre, who in the middle of the seventh century had a Daedalic female statue set up and inscribed 'as the ox ploughs' (*boustrophedon*). She states proudly that she is the daughter of Deinodicus of Naxos, the sister of Deinomenes, and now the wife of Phraxus.[8]

In the marble quarries of Naxos great statues of young men (*kouroi*), sometimes called Apollos, were cut, and then moved to be set up elsewhere. One such statue, bearded and so perhaps of Dionysus, proved too difficult to move and was left unfinished in the quarry. The most famous of the *kouroi* however was the colossal Naxian Apollo set up in Delos early in the sixth century BC. As the inscription says, the base and the statue were of the same stone, which presumably was cut apart in the quarry and then brought across from Naxos in two pieces.[9] It is obvious from their *kouroi* and from their buildings at Delos that the Naxians commanded a large force of labour and prized their architects and sculptors highly. One of their architects, Byzes,[10] was said to have invented marble roof tiles. Once dedications were used by Lygdamis as a means of raising capital: he drove some of the Naxians into exile while their offerings were lying half-finished in the workshops, and then sold them back to the exiles or to anyone else who wanted to have his name inscribed on them.[11]

After Lygdamis became tyrant, he helped his friend the Neleid Pisistratus with troops and money to return finally as tyrant of Athens, and took part in the decisive battle of Pallene in Attica.[12] Lygdamis was well repaid by Pisistratus, for later the Naxian lost his place as tyrant in Naxos; Pisistratus conquered the island, set up Lygdamis as tyrant there once more, and placed in his charge children of the Athenian nobility to ensure the good conduct of their parents in Athens.[13] Pisistratus also took over Delos, which, prompted by some oracles, he purified by digging up the skeletons from all the tombs that could be seen from the altar of Apollo and moving them to another part of the island.[14] The motives for the Athenian tyrant's interest in Delos are unclear, but it may well be that he hoped to dominate both the religious and the political life of the islanders through control of Delian cult. While Athenian influence in Delos grew, the Asiatic Ionians, now subject to Persia, began to lose interest in the festival of Apollo and by Thucydides' time they no longer gathered at Delos, but met instead at the Ephesian panegyris.[15] When Thucydides states that 'of old' there was a great gathering in Delos of 'the Ionians and the neighbouring islanders', he may mean that Dorians from Melos and Thera besides the Ionians of the islands and of the Asiatic mainland came to Delos in the sixth century and earlier. Pisistratus must have been quick to see the great political opportunity given to him by control of the cults in Delos. But Athenian power did not last there: Delos soon was ruled by the Samian Polycrates, a friend of Pisistratus' ally Lygdamis the Naxian.

We hear of Lygdamis helping Polycrates to seize power in the city of Samos and become tyrant.[16] Later, sometime after Polycrates was firmly established in authority, Lygdamis was overthrown by a Spartan expedition.[17] This may have happened when the Spartans failed to expel Polycrates from Samos (about 525 BC) or when they are said briefly to have dominated the Aegean with their navy (from 517 to 514 BC according to Eusebius).[18] When Lygdamis was overthrown the island was again ruled by the local nobility and continued to prosper. The remains of the great temple, which was being built in the time of Lygdamis, still testify to the riches and industry of the Naxians under the rule of their tyrant.

When Eusebius gives to the Naxians a thalassocracy of ten years immediately after the Spartans', he may be recalling a genuine tradition of Naxian naval power after the fall of Lygdamis, for Herodotus suggests that about 500 BC Paros, Andros, and the other Cyclades were dependent on Naxos.[19] At this time the oligarchy of the nobles was being opposed, and was finally expelled, by a populist party.[20]

About the middle of the sixth century BC the Samians began to dominate with their navy their neighbours in the islands and on the mainland of Asia Minor. Some Greeks thought of the Samians as little better than pirates, but the Samians themselves, especially during the tyranny of Polycrates, aimed at the creation of a naval empire in the Aegean with a capital worthy of it in Samos; a force of one hundred penteconters and a thousand archers enabled the tyrant to impose his will.[21]

Polycrates himself became tyrant during the thirties of the century, and his father (or grandfather) Aeaces may well have been powerful before him.[22] Polycrates himself did not, however, inherit the tyranny: he had to win it by arms. It is said that with fifteen hoplites, and in another story with the help of Lygdamis of Naxos, he seized power in

Samos;[23] then he ruled in the island jointly with his brothers Pantagnotus and Syloson. Before long Polycrates made himself monarch by killing Pantagnotus and by driving Syloson, the youngest brother, into exile.[24]

We hear of two other early rulers of Samos. One of them, Phoebias, is called an *aisymnetes*, and so may have been elected to power.[25] The other seized it. He was another Syloson, son of Calliteles, who seized the tyranny with the help of sailors from the Samian triremes during a war with the Aeolians, on the occasion of a festival of Samian Hera.[26] The date of this Syloson, and his relationship to Syloson, brother of Polycrates, is unclear, but the mention of triremes, if genuine, suggests that his coup should not be dated earlier than about 530 BC, when the first triremes began to be used. The triremes in the story may, however, be anachronistic.

Amongst the islands dominated by the Samians may well have been Rhodes: for the orator Himerius mentions a Polycrates 'of Rhodes' who loved music and song and begged his father to let him indulge his love of them. His father therefore sent for the poet Anacreon to be his son's tutor.[27] It is possible, then, the Anacreon spent some time with the young Polycrates in Rhodes, where the Samian was perhaps viceroy. A hint that Anacreon was interested in Rhodes is given by his mention of the blue shielded men of Ialysus,[28] but the context is unknown. Anacreon was still with Polycrates in Samos shortly before the tyrant was killed by by the satrap Oroetes in Magnesia about 522 BC.[29] Another poet who came to the Samian court was Ibycus of Rhegium who on arriving there claimed that his poetry would bring Polycrates undying glory.[30]

Amongst the islands taken by Polycrates with his fleet was Delos, which he won sometime after its purification by Pisistratus. He also seized Rheneia nearby and dedicated it to Apollo by tying it to Delos with a chain.[31] Then he instituted a festival on Delos, and wondering whether to call it Pythia or Delia consulted Delphi. The priestess, who evidently did not think highly of Polycrates and his naval imperialism, said 'Pythia and Delia are all the same to you', meaning perhaps that the tyrant counted for nothing for his days were numbered.[32] She may also have disliked the setting up of a rival festival to the Pythian games of Delphi by the most powerful monarch in the Greek world, as Polycrates had become.

Many of his naval successes may have been due to the introduction of the trireme, his reign being the most reasonable period in which to date the first construction of these vessels.[33] He may not have had many of them, however, for Thucydides states that the Corcyreans and the Sicilian tyrants, shortly before the Persian wars, were the first to have numbers of triremes,[34] and Polycrates' navy may well have consisted for the most part of penteconters. His crews proved their worth in a war against the Milesians, who were soundly defeated together with the navy of Lesbos which had come to help them. Many prisoners were taken, and Polycrates put them to work in fetters to dig a great trench around the wall of Samos city.[35] On the west side, where the city wall was most vulnerable, the trench was dug eighteen feet wide into the rock.

To protect his fleet a mole was built out into deep water for a quarter of a mile, and to ensure that there would still be a supply of water during a siege a great tunnel was dug through the hill on which part of the city was built.[36] The water came from a spring outside the wall, in pipes hidden, underground, to the hill; then it flowed in a channel set in the floor of the tunnel to within the circuit of the city.[37] The tunnel is three thousand four hundred feet long and for much of its length six feet high and six feet wide. The excavators worked simultaneously at both ends and met in the middle with only a few feet of error. Thus the builders under their architect, Eupalinus son of Naustrophus of Megara, had a considerable knowledge of surveying. It has been estimated that the tunnel took at least ten years to construct;[38] the work was probably finished by the time of the Spartan attack about 525 BC when the Samians withstood a siege lasting forty days.

The third of the great public works in Samos mentioned by Herodotus was the new temple of Hera, begun under the direction of the Samian architect Rhoecus.[39] The first dipteron was started not later than the middle of the sixth century, but was destroyed by fire soon after completion, perhaps in a Persian attack.[40] A new temple was then begun in which drums from the first dipteron were used, but it was not completed. It was the largest temple known to Herodotus. Rhoecus was perhaps the architect of both the earlier and the later temples. With him worked Theodorus, who is reputed to have invented the surveyor's level,[41] to have made a great silver krater given by Croesus to Delphi,[42] and to have engraved the famous emerald ring of Polycrates.[43] Together Theodorus and Rhoecus invented the hollow casting of bronze statues.[44] Both men travelled widely: Theodorus built an assembly hall at Sparta, the Skias,[45] and Rhoecus worked on the new Artemisium at Ephesus, where he cast a bronze image of a woman called Night by the Ephesians.[46] Both men may have had a part in the introduction of Ionian architecture and sculpture to Sardis.[47] A dedication at Naucratis by a Rhoecus may even have been made by the architect.[48]

Polycrates and the Samians aimed to make their city impregnable, and their precinct of Hera the noblest sanctuary in Ionia. Ibycus and Anacreon sang the praises of the tyrant, his ships dominated the Aegean, he had ambitions to conquer mainland Ionia, and his Milesian and Lesbian enemies were defeated. Yet there were critics at home, and the policy of keeping his subjects quiet by busying them with public works[49] was not a complete success. Of some critics Anacreon said to a friend: 'In the island, Megistes, the Chatterers hold sway over the sacred town.'[50] The island is Samos, and the Chatterers (Mythietai) were a faction led by a certain Herostratus, whose followers were called Halieis (fishermen). Of their fortunes we are told nothing.

In the time of Croesus Samian pirates had seized the krater which the Spartans were sending to the Lydian king, and in the previous year they captured the linen corselet which Amasis of Egypt sent to Sparta.[51] Amasis in his desire to create a front against Persia chose to overlook the insult, and made an alliance with Polycrates.[52] This lasted only so long as Polycrates found it convenient; for when he saw that the ageing Egyptian king would not be able to throw back a Persian invasion, he secretly opened negotiations with Cambyses, who was preparing his attack.[53] When about 525 BC Cambyses urged Polycrates to send ships to help in the Egyptian campaign, the tyrant manned forty triremes with persons whom he suspected of plotting a revolution against himself, and secretly sent word to Cambyses not to return them home. Some said that the Samians reached Egypt and escaped, but others held that they sailed as far as Carpathus where they decided to go no further.[54] They returned to Samos, defeated Polycrates at sea, and landed; but once ashore they were defeated, because, as Herodotus points out, they had no chance of success against the mercenaries and archers of the tyrant. Moreover Polycrates had put women and children of the Samians in the shipsheds, threatening to set fire to them if any of his subjects betrayed him to the attackers.[55]

When the Samian exiles reached Sparta, they begged for help, presenting their case at inordinate length. The magistrates replied, 'We have forgotten the first part of your speech, and do not understand the last.' The next day the Samians appeared simply with an empty bag saying, 'Our bag has no meal in it.' 'Your bag is not necessary' the Spartans replied, and their request was at once granted.[56]

Until c. 550 BC Samos had been importing more Laconian pottery than any other Greek state and the ties between Samos and Sparta were close.[57] Polycrates who was at odds with the Samian nobility and with their Spartan friends cannot have favoured close commercial links between Samos and Sparta: it was perhaps a desire to restore those ties, not less than a sense of obligation to the old regime in Samos for its support of Sparta against the Messenians,[58] which prompted the Spartan government to send a force to attack Polycrates at his enemies' request. Moreover, the naval power of Polycrates posed a real threat to Spartan ambitions to control Peloponnese and be the principal state of Hellas.

The Spartans with Corinthian help[59] soon gathered a large expedition and attacked Samos on the seaward side. Here they were repulsed, Polycrates himself leading the defence;[60] but up on the hill at the other side of the city they had more success, since they drove back a sally of Samians and mercenaries, and killed them as they withdrew. Two Spartans, Archias and Lycopes, followed the fleeing defenders so closely that their own retreat was cut off, and they were killed inside the city. Herodotus had heard about their bravery at Pitana in Sparta from the grandson of Archias, a second Archias. The grandfather had been buried at public expense by the Samians – by the pro-Laconian party in the state perhaps; and his son, the father of Herodotus' informant, was called Samius in his honour.[61] When, after a siege of forty days, the Spartans had made no progress, they returned to Peloponnese.[62] The Samian exiles, too, abandoned the siege, and sailed to Siphnos, being greatly in need of money.[63]

The Siphnians had become very prosperous owing to their rich silver and gold mines; they had a splendid council chamber and meeting place built of Parian marble, and from the tithes of their mines they had built a fine treasury in Delphi. The Samians sent a single ship to the city to demand ten talents, which were refused, for the Siphnians did not know how great was the enemy fleet. The Samians then ravaged the island, defeated the Siphnians, captured some of them, and extorted one hundred talents ransom for the captives.[64] Next they sailed to the Argolid, where they were sold the island of Hydrea by the men of Hermione; having placed this in trust with the Troizenians, they sailed for Crete and took Cydonia. There they remained, building sanctuaries and the temple of Dictyna, until in the sixth year the Aeginetan navy defeated the Samians at sea and sold them into slavery. So the opponents of Polycrates met a bad end after all, and the Samians' attack on Aegina made in the time of their king Amphicrates was at last avenged.[65]

The undoing of Polycrates was swift, and due entirely to his own cupidity. Oroetes the satrap in Sardis fostered the military ambitions of the tyrant by offering him money with which to make possible more conquests.[66] The wily Persian had come down to Magnesia by the Maeander, whence he sent a Lydian, Myrsus son of Gyges, to Samos with his proposals, while in Magnesia he himself waited to see if Polycrates would take the bait.[67] Polycrates was hooked: he first sent his secretary Maeandrius to inspect the money being offered. On his return Maeandrius reported that there was plenty of gold. Then, against the advice of his priests, his friends, and his daughter, Polycrates went up to Magnesia with his private physician Democedes of Croton, and there the tyrant was crucified by Oroetes, in a manner quite unworthy of himself and of his ambitions, as Herodotus says;[68] for apart from the Sicilians there was no Greek tyrant to compare with him in magnificence. He died shortly before the end of the reign of Cambyses, son of Cyrus, that is not later than the summer of 522 BC.[69] The satrap let the Samians in Polycrates' retinue go, but enslaved their foreign attendants.[70]

Oroetes had been prompted to get rid of Polycrates by the taunts of Mitrobates, satrap of Dascylium.[71] Having done so, he killed Mitrobates and his son Cranaspes;[72] then, taking advantage of the disorder that intervened in Persia between the death of Cambyses and the accession of Darius, he made himself an independent ruler of Phrygia, Lydia, and the Ionic district.[73] He had a mounted courier of Darius ambushed and killed, but retribution soon followed, when Bagaeus an agent of Darius came to Sardis and, with the help of letters under the seal of the Great King, persuaded Oroetes' bodyguard to kill him.[74]

Meanwhile Syloson, the younger brother of Polycrates, was still alive. He had, according to a tale in Herodotus, given a red cloak to Darius at Memphis in Egypt when the future king was a member of the bodyguard of Cambyses; the gift was not forgotten by Darius when Syloson asked to be restored as ruler of Samos. Whatever the true reason for Darius' favourable view of Syloson may have been, his request was granted, and Otanes was sent down to the Ionian coast with a force to attack Samos.[75] The island was then being ruled by the agent of Polycrates, Maeandrius, who with the best of intentions wished to restore freedom in the city, and had set up outside an altar of Zeus the Liberator. He next addressed the citizens, promising them equality before the laws, but demanding six talents of Polycrates' money for himself and the priesthood of Zeus the Liberator, which, he claimed, should be hereditary; but his claims were rejected by a noble called

Telesarchus. When Maeandrius saw that if he laid down his authority another would rule as tyrant in his stead, he retired to the acropolis of Samos, to which he invited his opponents one by one with the promise of a share in Polycrates' money. Once within his power they were seized and put in bonds. A disease then overcame Maeandrius who was thought by his brother Lycaretus to be about to die, and Lycaretus therefore killed the prisoners in order to make the government of the island easier for himself. At this point in the turbulent affairs of Samos the Persians with Syloson arrived.[76]

Maeandrius and his party agreed to leave the island without a fight, but there happened to be another brother of Maeandrius, Charilaus, a man of violent disposition, who was then being kept in a dungeon. Furious that no-one had fought the Persians, he demanded to be brought before Maeandrius, who was persuaded to permit an attack by Samian mercenaries on the unsuspecting Otanes and his party. Many Persians were killed, and Otanes, forgetting the order of Darius that Samos was to be handed back unharmed to Syloson, commanded his troops to kill everyone they captured, even the children. This they did, even in the sanctuaries. Maeandrius meanwhile escaped by a secret tunnel from the acropolis to the sea.[77] When the Persians had finished their bloody work, they handed over Samos empty of people to Syloson: hence the saying, 'There's plenty of space now thanks to Syloson.'[78]

Maeandrius sailed straight for Laconia, where he tried to win king Cleomenes' support by bribing him with gold and silver cups. But Cleomenes resisted the temptation and told the Ephors that the Samian ought to leave Peloponnese before he or any other Spartiate was corrupted. So they drove Maeandrius out.[79] Of him we hear no more from Herodotus, but later (c. 513) his brother Lycaretus was made ruler of Lemnos by the Persians.[80] As for Syloson, he, and later his son Aeaces, ruled in Samos as Persian nominees, and Otanes helped them to repopulate the island.[81]

In the western Aegean the affairs of the Euboeans were not less disturbed than the Milesians' under the *Ploutis*. Once a man called Tynnondas made himself tyrant in the island. The name with its ending in *-ondas* looks Boeotian.[82] We hear of another, Chalcidian, tyrant, Antileon; when he was overthrown, an oligarchy was set up in his place.[83] On yet another occasion the notables in the city joined the populace in overthrowing a tyrant called Phoxus.[84] The Eretrians too were not free from tyranny in the sixth century, for the oligarchy of the knights was overthrown when a certain Diagoras, who had been injured in a dispute over a marriage, rose up against them.[85] This man was greatly respected by the Eretrians, who set up a statue in his honour when he had died at Corinth after a visit to Sparta.[86]

At Cerinthus on the east coast of Euboea there had also been civil troubles, as we learn from Theognis: 'Cerinthus is ruined,' the poet complains, 'the fair plain of Lelantum with its vines is wasted. The nobles flee, and rogues govern the city. May Zeus wreck the family of the Cypselidae.'[87] The lines suggest that a branch of the Cypselid family, who once had been tyrants of Corinth, were ruling at Cerinthus, having seized power there. The allusion to fighting on the Lelantine plain is obscure, but may mean that Chalcis and Eretria were again in the sixth century BC quarrelling over the rich land lying between them, just as they had in the eighth.

In 506 BC the Hippobotae of Chalcis suffered a great setback when the Athenians, having first overcome a Boeotian army on the mainland, crossed the Euripus and on the same day soundly beat them. After this victory four thousand plotholders were settled by the Athenians in the land of the Hippobotae.[88] Eretria's friendship for Athens, which had been strong in the time of Pisistratus, must now have been very close indeed. Proof of it was given a few years later when the Eretrians joined Athens and the other Ionians in the attack on Sardis; and not later than 475 BC Eretria had a democratic constitution,[89] which may well have been copied from the new Athenian democracy.

'I am well known' Pindar makes the island of Ceos say, 'for I offer the Muse abundantly; and if my land bears something of Dionysus' life-giving cure for trouble, I have no horses and know naught of the herding of oxen.'[90] Here the people of the four cities–Iulis where the poet Simonides was born in 557/6 BC,[91] Carthaea, Coresia with its sanctuary of Apollo Sminthaeus, and Poeessa, near which was the shrine of Athena Nedusia, said to have been founded by Nestor on his way home from Troy[92]–cultivated their vines, exported their red dye,[93] and trained the choirs that were sent to sing hymns to Apollo in competitions in Delos, where they kept a banqueting house near the Artemisium.[94]

Apollo was the chief god of Ceos, but Zeus was worshipped too in the guise of Zeus Aristaeus, so named because he was identified with a local demigod Aristaeus, who saved the island by causing the Etesian winds to blow for forty days when the Dog Star was parching it. The Euxantiadae, Callimachus suggests,[95] were the priests of this beneficent local divinity. Dionysus too received due worship from the islanders, devoted as they were to the tending of his vines: aptly grapes and amphoras are found in the sixth century on the island's earliest coins.[96]

Though Ceos had once formed part of the Eretrian naval dominion,[97] in the sixth century the islanders may well have ruled themselves, each city independently of the others. Life was simple, and the laws severe, in this rocky land poorly endowed by nature. Expensive funerals were penalised,[98] and men of sixty are said to have been required to commit suicide.[99] It is not surprising perhaps that Simonides of Iulis spent his old age abroad. Yet the Ceans could, for all their severity, afford to adorn their island. An inscription cut when Simonides was in middle age, before 500 BC, records a dedication to Athena, the work of a Siphnian Alcidamas;[100] a fine lion was carved early in the sixth century in a rock not far from Iulis;[101] and Athena's temple at Carthaea had a store of treasures including a golden crown dedicated by the leader of a choir.[102] Bacchylides had such a prize in mind when he wrote in an epigram to Lady Victory, 'may you ever watch with favour over the lovely choir of the Carthaeans and place about the head of Bacchylides the Cean, in the midst of the Muses' delights, many a crown.'[103]

Bacchylides had the name of his grandfather, an athlete. His father Meidylus or Meidon had married the sister of Simonides.[104] Both poets, uncle and nephew, came from Iulis, where Simonides belonged to the clan Hylichidae.[105] Leoprepres, Simonides' father, a notable in the island, had a name found at the head of a list of the Hylichidae much later than his time;[106] it may have been common in that clan. Other clans at Iulis were the Thyssidae, the Leoidae, and, surprisingly, the Coresii; these last were perhaps men of Coresian origin resident at Iulis.[107]

One of the earlier poems of Simonides, composed perhaps when he was still in Ceos before he joined the tyrant Hipparchus in Athens, was the epinikion for Glaucus of Carystus who won the boys wrestling match at Olympia in 520 BC.[108] As a grown man Glaucus could punch a coulter into a plough, and even as a boy his strength was more than heroic, for Simonides said of him with genuine admiration that 'neither mighty Polydeuces, nor the iron offspring of Alcmena (Herakles) would raise their hands against him'.[109] Another Euboean known to the poet was Lysimachus of Eretria for whom he composed a dirge.[110] Eretria, indeed, seems to have interested him greatly. He mentioned Tamynae, a place in the Eretrian territory in a poem,[111] and Eualcidas, an Eretrian athlete and general, who died in the Ionian attack on Sardis in 498 BC, was said to have been praised many times by Simonides.[112] One of his epigrams was written for men killed beneath Dirphys, a mountain overlooking the Euripus, which flows between Euboea and the Boeotian mainland.[113] They had perhaps fallen in the battles between Athens and the Chalcidians in 506 BC. Ties between southern Euboea and Ceos have always been close: it is fitting therefore that some of the earliest poems of Simonides were composed for men of Eretria and Carystus.

Of the remaining Cyclades Paros alone can be said to have any history at all in the sixth century BC. She never rivalled Naxos in prosperity, but her trade was continuous and far-ranging. Egyptian scarabs and faience reached the Delion in Paros, and Parian coins made their way to Egypt.[114] Trading ties with the Thasian colonists in the northern Aegean continued to be close, but there is no evidence of a political union between Paros and Thasos. A certain Akeratos, it is true, had been archon in both places about 520, but this is not evidence of sympolity between them at that time.[115] There are hints that a body of Pythagoreans was early established in Paros:[116] one of them, Thymaridas, who perhaps lived in the fifth century BC, was a considerable algebraist,[117] but there is no sign that the Parian Pythagoreans shared the political ambitions of their colleagues in southern Italy. The suggestion that the Parians who arbitrated in the Milesian civil strife were Pythagoreans is nothing more than an unsupported conjecture.[118] The strong Ionian consciousness of the Parians is well illustrated by a sacral law of the island, dating from the second quarter of the fifth century, in which slaves and Dorians are forbidden to take part in the rites of Persephone;[119] this was presumably an ordinance of the Kabarnoi, a caste of priests of Demeter in Paros.[120] Seriphos is quite without history. There are deposits of iron in the island[121] but it has yet to be proved that they were being worked before 500 BC. Siphnos nearby, however, as we have seen, enjoyed the rewards of a flourishing industry in metals. From the Dryopians of Kythnos, the Andrians, and the Samians and Naxians in Amorgos we have no evidence in the age of Polycrates. In Tenos, unusually amongst Ionians, there was a Heraclid tribe;[122] Icaria was famous for its Pramnian wine:[123] and it is possible that Syros was betrayed to the navy of the Samians.[124] But such details are not matter for narrative history; without more ado we leave the Cycladic Ionians and turn again to their Asiatic kinsmen.

CHAPTER XIV

The First Ionian Historians

IN THE SIXTH CENTURY BC IONIANS TRAVELLED INTO PERSIA FAR TO
the east, southwards to Nubia, and westwards beyond the pillars of
Herakles to the kingdom of Tartessus; they not only speculated about
the origins and structure of the earth, but sought also to describe its
extent. And so they created together with the natural philosophy of
Thales and his followers the first systematic geography, which when
combined with their own traditions gave rise to the first critical, secular
history men had ever written.

The origins of Ionian historical writing lie far back in the epics.
Homer and his contemporaries never doubted that there had been
Theban and Trojan wars; Simonides of Amorgos and Asius wrote on
Samian Archaeology;[1] and other Ionian poets recalled to their hearers
the achievements of the founding fathers, Neleus, Androclus, and their
followers. Xenophanes continued the traditional approach to history
with his poem on the founding of Colophon,[2] and innovated when he
composed a poem on the settlement of the Ionians in Velia in Italy,[3] for
this was contemporary history. But critical history, like critical philosophy, begins with the writing of prose by the Milesian thinkers, men
possessing wondrously acute and observant minds. What Anaximander
did for the origins of natural science, Hecataeus, another Milesian
nobleman, did for the writing of history.

Hecataeus is reputed to have had a predecessor in the writing of
historical prose – Cadmus of Miletus,[4] who is vaguely dated to the time of
Pherecydes of Syros, himself a prose writer.[5] To Cadmus is ascribed a
work on the founding of Miletus and of all Ionia. He existed, we need not
doubt; that he wrote prose is likely; that he wrote on his native city and Ionia,
possible; and that nothing more can usefully be said about him, certain[6].

The language of the earliest Ionian historians was according to
Dionysius of Halicarnassus in his essay on Thucydides, 'clear, simple,
unpretentious and concise, appropriate to the matter, but not showing
any elaborate art in composition.'[7] He adds however that their writings
had grace and charm. The little that we have of Hecataeus' own words
bears out the critic's judgement. He used the Ionic dialect as an elegant
but powerful instrument for stating facts clearly and for the critical
treatment of Greek traditions.

Some traditions he accepts, others he rationalises, others again he rejects with scorn. A book of his opened with the words: 'Thus proclaims Hecataeus of Miletus: I write these things as they seem to me to be true; for many and ridiculous, so they seem to me, are the tales of the Greeks.'[8] This confident, not to say arrogant, opening does not mean that he rejected all tradition. In his *Genealogies* he examined the stories on their merits in the light of his own judgement and set them down because they were worth recording. He conducted a *historie*, an enquiry into the evidence for past events, and submitted it to critical examination, as no epic poet had ever done. His critical spirit made him a genuine historian.

An instance of his rationalising method in the *Genealogies*, which sometimes are called simply *Histories*, is his treatment of Cerberus, the dog of Hades at Taenarus. This was, he said, not really a dog, but a snake called Hades' dog, because a person bitten by it died from the poison at once. This snake was brought by Herakles to Eurystheus.[9] Hecataeus considered that the oxen of Geryon which Herakles drove to Mycenae could not possibly have come all the way from Spain, as some claimed: so he transferred Geryon and his cattle to the mainland of northwestern Greece, maintaining that even to have brought the cattle from there was no mean feat.[10] His account of the Herakles legend he continued into the next generation, for there is a fragment in which Ceyx refuses help to the hero's sons: 'Ceyx being distressed at once ordered the Heraclidae to leave: "I cannot defend you. Therefore that you may not be ruined nor harm me, depart to some other place." '[11] The Greek is tragic in its simplicity. Ceyx knows that he is morally bound to help the sons of Herakles against Eurystheus, but he is afraid to do so.

Other books of the *Genealogies* dealt with the descendants of Deucalion; with the Argonauts, whose travels interested him as a geographer; with the royal line of Danaus at Mycenae, and the Argive wars against Thebes. He had the Argonauts sail from the Euxine up the Phasis river to the Ocean, whence they came at length to the Nile and so to the Aegean.[12] Thus both rivers in his view extended to the circumambient Ocean, and the Nile flowed from somewhere on the coast of the Atlantic south of the Pillars of Herakles to Egypt. He must have learnt about the Nile flood when he was in Egypt, but his explanation of it does not survive. Euthymenes of Massalia explained that the flood was due to the tides of Ocean,[13] and Hecataeus may have accepted this theory, since he believed the river to extend to Ocean. He would then have had to meet the objection that the Phasis does not flood like the Nile.[14]

We come now to his *Periegesis*, 'The Tour of the Earth' a work in two books, 'Europe' and 'Asia'. When Hecataeus was writing this comprehensive work the Carthaginians were attempting to close the western Mediterranean to the Greeks, at the time of the first Carthaginian treaty with Rome of 508 BC.[15] His information about the far west may come from earlier, Phocaean navigators, for there is no evidence that he went there himself. He knows of a city Eliburge in the kingdom of Tartessus,[16] and accurately describes Massalia as a Phocaean colony in the Ligurian land towards the territory of the Celts.[17] His method was to name places in geographical order along the coasts of the Mediterranean and the Euxine, listing settlements inland together with their neighbours on the coast. The same system is found in Herodotus' account of Libya, which may come without much change from Hecataeus.[18]

In the *Periegesis* the Aegean limit between Europe and Asia was drawn close to the coast of Ionia, so that Chios and Lesbos were placed in Europe.[19] For the lands northeast of the Euxine he may have relied on the poem of Aristeas, and eastwards from Greece his horizon extends to Parthia, Chorasmia, and India,[20] for his knowledge of which he must have been indebted to Scylax of Caryanda who helped to survey the river Indus for Darius.[21] To the south, Egypt, Ethiopia, and Libya (which in his view included all of Africa west of Egypt) were described after Asia in the second book. Thus the *Periegesis* began in the land of Tartessus or beyond it to the north, and ended in Libya beyond the straits to the south, on the west African coast.

The *Periegesis* contained far more than the bare names of peoples and places. In his account of the eastern Persian dominions he described the dress of the Cissians; this was the Persian *kypassis*, a kind of cloak.[22] The people of Hyope, a city of the Matieni, 'wore the same costume as the Paphlagonians' he reported.[23] Vegetation also interested him: 'To the east of the Parthians,' he wrote, 'dwell the Chorasmians, who have plains and mountains in their country; and on the mountains are trees growing wild, "prickly artichokes", poplar, and tamarisk.'[24] The artichokes are mentioned again in his description of the forest-covered mountains around the Hyrcanian sea in central Asia.[25] One fragment comes from the narrative of Scylax: 'amongst them dwell by the river Indus the Opiae, who have a royal fort. The Opiae reach thus far, but from that point on there is a desert as far as the Indians.'[26] Some of

Hecataeus' knowledge of the East may have been brought back by Ionian and Lydian architects and masons who went to work at Susa for Darius;[27] the name of one of them is known from Pliny–Telephanes of Phocaea.[28]

Though Hecataeus was called a much-travelled man by the ancients, the only country he is known to have visited outside his native Ionia is Egypt, which he vividly described as 'the gift of the river'.[29] Herodotus, whose rather scornful attitude to Hecataeus did not prevent him from making use of his work, states: 'When Hecataeus the writer was in Egyptian Thebes he expounded his ancestry tracing it back to a god in the sixteenth generation, and the priests did for him what they also did for me, though *I* did not expound *my* ancestry.'[30] They pointed out to him the colossal wooden statues of the high priests. Each statue was set up by the high priest in his own lifetime, and the priesthood came down from father to son. There were, Herodotus claimed, three hundred and forty-five statues, but still the priests did not believe that the earliest was the son of a god or a hero. It is unlikely that the Egyptians convinced the proud Milesian nobleman that he was not of divine descent, but the evidence that Egyptian history began long before the Greeks' was not lost upon him. A span of sixteen generations at three generations in each century amounts to about five hundred years: thus the first remembered mortal member of Hecataeus' family may be dated about 1000 BC, soon after the Ionian settlement of Miletus. We are not told which god was his ancestor; Apollo is likely since *Hekatos* was an epithet of him; but Hecataeus' name could be taken from the Carian goddess Hecate.

The treatment of his native Ionia in the *Periegesis* was, as we would expect, very detailed, several places unknown to history being mentioned in the fragments. Thus we find, 'Coloura, where the Prienians settled,' Sidele, Sidussa, Cybeleia, 'cities of Ionia'.[31] Mount Latmus inland from Miletus he proposed to identify with Homer's Mount Phtheires,[32] and Miletus is carefully described as 'a renowned city of the Ionians in Caria',[33] not without a touch of patriotic pride.

Hecataeus never wished to rid himself of the influence of the Homeric epics. He treated them as evidence for early history to be examined in the light of common sense; and his instinctive wisdom in so doing has been shown by modern archaeology, which has demonstrated that the great epics recall historical events, and that the heroes lived in cities proved by excavation to have been powerful in the age to which the Greeks dated the Theban and Trojan wars. The critical study of Greek legend inaugurated by Hecataeus continues to this day; for him, and for

us, it is a legitimate branch of historical enquiry, but we have archaeological evidence for Mycenaean Greece in an abundance of which
Hecataeus never dreamed. He was a genealogist who criticised tradition,
and a geographer who was also a historian. To those subjects he applied
the sound intelligence that also characterised his statesmanship during
the Ionian revolt.

CHAPTER XV

Heraclitus

IN EPHESUS, WHICH HAD NO FLEET AND FOUNDED NO COLONIES, MEN looked more constantly to the great powers of the East than to the open world of the Aegean, and Hellenism rarely prevailed over the rooted traditions of Anatolia. Here in the time of the Mermnadae, Artemis dominated the spiritual life, and Lydian gold the material concerns, of the citizenry. Trade and religion fostered each other and brought security. Few Ephesians can have been zealous for revolt against Darius, the successor of Lydia, for of what value was a freedom that threatened ruin, and what sense was there in stopping the monies of the goddess by breaking ties with the East? To them the call to freedom must have seemed an illusion, for under the satraps of Darius they enjoyed some independence in the government of their own city.

The cunning or prudence of the Ephesians was held by a distinguished citizen to be smugness and complacency. Heraclitus the philosopher came of the royal line of Androclus,[1] but held political power in low regard. He persuaded a certain Melancomas to give up his tyranny,[2] resigned his own hereditary rights as *basileus* to his brother,[3] and, it was said, left the city for the countryside, so little did he care for the Ephesians' company.[4] Some claimed that he also rejected an invitation to the court of Darius.[5] When his friend the lawgiver Hermodorus was exiled, Heraclitus bitterly attacked the Ephesians who, 'ought to be hanged, every man of them, and the city be given over to the government of children, for they have expelled the best man amongst them with the words, "Let no one be best amongst us; or if one must be best, let him be elsewhere and with other men." '[6] These words do not prove that the Ephesians had established a democracy: they show only that they disliked persons of exceptional ability; by them conformity was counted the greatest virtue, and criticism of established ways, such as Heraclitus persistently gave, seemed a sin.

Heraclitus kept up his attacks, writing his gnomic utterances in a book which he deposited in the temple of Artemis.[7] The work may not have survived the great fire that destroyed the temple in the fourth century BC, and so the Alexandrian scholars may have had little of his work to study. The few fragments that survive cannot easily be arranged into a coherent system; but they fully confirm his reputation for darkness.[8]

His style was fashioned after Apollo's: 'The Lord whose oracle is at Delphi neither speaks nor conceals, but gives a sign.'[9] Heraclitus too did not wish the deep meaning of all his utterances to be immediately obvious. The words of the Sibyl, whose terse, unadorned speech he imitated, could tell more than an explicit statement about the inner truth in things.[10]

The world is a combination of opposites, which compose its underlying unity. It is an unity formed by Logos,[11] the ordering of things that holds them together. Heraclitus believed that he had a true understanding of the Logos, of which most men are uncomprehending; for if they understood it they would agree that all things are one.[12] Men who have 'barbarian souls' are misled by their senses of sight and hearing,[13] but, said Heraclitus, 'the things of which there is seeing and hearing and understanding, them do I prefer':[14] for his own soul was capable of critical interpretation of the senses.

The unity of the world is illustrated by the oppositions within it. 'The path up and down is one and the same.'[15] 'Sea is the most pure and the most defiled water; for fishes drink it and are preserved by it; but to men it is undrinkable and ruinous.'[16] The unity of opposites is divine. 'God is day night, winter summer, war peace, satiety hunger. . . .'[17] To understand this unity men must be patient: 'he who does not expect the unexpected will not discover it, for it is not to be sought out and is hard to comprehend' and, 'the nature of things tends to hide itself.'[18] As in a bow and a lyre, the tensions of opposition create stability, so that what is in conflict yet agrees with itself. Thus, since strife and change lie at the heart of things, war is not unnatural. It is part of the essential order of the world: 'you must know that war is common to all, and right is strife, and all things happen by conflict and necessity.'[19] This is true also of the world of men, for 'war is the father of all and king of all, and some he shows as gods, others as men; some he makes slaves, others free'.[20] The doctrine of opposites is forced onwards to this brutal, bitter, conclusion, because Heraclitus believed that opposites are necessarily in conflict with each other; but it is hard to see why this should always be so. According to Aristotle[21] Heraclitus rejected the Homeric sentiment, 'Would that strife were destroyed from gods and men,' claiming that there would be no musical scale unless high and low existed, nor living creatures without female and male which are opposites.[22]

According to Plato Heraclitus illustrated his doctrine of perpetual change by saying that you could not step into the same river twice, but it has been doubted whether he ever in fact made this celebrated remark.[23] The quotations show only that he wished to explain how a river which is in constant flux maintains its identity: 'upon those who step into the same rivers different and different waters flow. . . . It scatters and . . . gathers . . . it comes together and flows away . . . approaches and departs.'[24] Thus the image of the stream illustrated the doctrine of unity depending upon change through the action of Logos. However, when Cratylus said that you cannot step into the same river even *once*,[25] he may have had his predecessor Heraclitus in mind; Plato then may be right in attributing to Heraclitus the words, 'You cannot step into the same river twice.' A rather different approach to the problem of change is seen in his assertion that the sun is new every day and in the remark that the stars cease to exist when they set.[26]

The world is composed of an everlasting fire, now kindling, now going out, from which sea and earth are formed.[27] The three elements, fire, sea, and earth, are not created by any god: they perpetually maintain a balance with each other by exchange, but to fire primacy is assigned: 'thunderbolt' he says, 'steers all things.'[28] Not only does fire compose the soul of the world, but men's souls are fiery too. Water is death to the human soul,[29] but nobler, drier souls gain better portions after death. Such souls are those slain in war, which are purer than the souls of men who die from disease:[30] it seems that he held the souls of warriors to retain some of their fire, and so to be reunited with the soul of the world, whereas diseased souls cease to exist, for they become watery at death. When a man is drunk, his soul is made watery,[31] and this is an earnest of death, for the fire is dimmed within him.

Where the bright gaseous matter of the world is gathered together, heavenly bodies are formed, of which the brightest and hottest is the flame of the sun.[32] As in Stesichorus,[33] the sun travels in a bowl, and it is, in some way not clearly explained, eclipsed when the bowl turns sideways to us. The same primitive hypothesis was made to account for lunar eclipses and phases.[34] The movements of the heavenly bodies well illustrate the rule of Logos; 'The Sun will not transgress the measures; otherwise the Furies, who are the servants of Justice, will find him out.'[35] Justice, as in Anaximander, is personified.[36] Her servants will not allow the sun to scorch the earth or to upset the seasons of the year.

The regularity of the seasons and the intervals of human generations were combined into a great year, by which Heraclitus illustrated the harmony of human and cosmic soul-fires. Taking the year's length as 360 days, and a generation of men as 30 years, Heraclitus held the product in years of the two numbers, $360 \times 30 = 10,800$, to be the length of the cosmic year.[37] Within this period the cyclical regularity of the fire's action would in theory be observable: but never would the fire overstep its bounds. There is no evidence in Heraclitus for a periodical conflagration of the entire world, such as the Stoics, who shared some of his doctrines, later postulated.[38]

He seems to have been less interested in the systematic observation of the heavens than his Milesian forerunners. The one genuinely astronomical fragment mentions the Bear to the north and 'the bounds of Zeus in the sky'.[39] The latter expression may mean 'the south' but it is not clear what the 'bounds' are, nor that the Sun is to be identified with Zeus. The name Zeus was, it seems, reserved for something of greater cosmic significance than the Sun, because, as Heraclitus paradoxically claims, 'one thing, the only true wise thing, does not and does consent to be called by the name of Zeus.'[40] This one thing may be the Logos, which is somehow to be identified with the archetypal fire, since fire steers or governs all things.

Heraclitus savagely attacked the Magi and other purveyors of mystery religions.[41] Yet he admitted that cult, for all its absurdity and illogicality, sometimes conveys truth. Delphi is mentioned with approval,[42] and the Sibyl is said to be a genuine instrument of the god;[43] but, he claimed, the secret rites customarily practised among men are performed in unholy ways,[44] and to pray to a statue is as foolish as to converse with a house;[45] a man who does that fails to see the true character of gods and heroes.

Political life must be informed by the order that constitutes the power of the Logos. Above all, men must obey the laws of their city, for these are fostered by the divine law: 'the people must fight for the law as though for the city wall.'[46] But, he must have added, the law they are to obey is the law prescribed by noble souls, who choose one thing above all else, 'eternal glory amongst mortals'; the masses, he declared with scorn, are 'sated like cattle'.[47]

To many the political outlook of Heraclitus must seem inhumane, distasteful, and dangerous, or at best irritatingly aloof. Yet there is a certain dignity in the oracular confidence of his philosophical utterances which is far from arrogance. His endeavour to see order in the midst of the tensions of the observable world was a genuinely rational undertaking, and his insistence upon the careful interpretation of the evidence of the senses marks him out as an opponent of mere intuition. Obscure but not an obscurantist, he is wronged if we dismiss him as an enemy of reason; but he cannot be placed with the great Milesians in the van of the Ionian enlightenment.

CHAPTER XVI

Ionian Tyrants and the Ionian Revolt

WE HAVE SEEN THAT AFTER THE CONQUESTS OF HARPAGUS THE
Persians imposed tyrants on the Greek cities of Asia and ruled through
them. How thorough was this policy is shown by Herodotus' account of
the Scythian expedition of Darius,[1] in which he names the tyrants left to
guard the bridge over the Ister.[2] Miltiades the Athenian, tyrant of the
Chersonesus on the Hellespont, was by this time, c. 513 BC,[3] a subject of
the Persians, Darius having invaded Europe. He favoured a proposal of
the Scythians to destroy the bridge, thus cutting off the Persians and
liberating Ionia; but Histiaeus tyrant of Miletus opposed him, pointing
out that each one of them ruled in his city by courtesy of Darius, and if
the Great King were killed, none of the Greek tyrants would have any
authority left. For each city preferred popular government to tyranny.
Histiaeus' argument prevailed, and the others voted with him. They
were Daphnis of Abydus, Hippoclus of Lampsacus,[4] Herophantus of
Parium, Metrodorus of Proconnesus, Aristagoras of Cyzicus, and Aris-
ton of Byzantium, all from the Hellespontine region. From the Aeolians
there was Aristagoras of Kyme, and from Ionia Histiaeus himself,
Strattis of Chios, Aeaces of Samos (the son of Syloson), and Laodamas
of Phocaea. Thus by c. 513 BC there were tyrants owing their positions to
the Persians in all the principal areas of Greek settlement in western Asia
Minor and on the north shore of the Hellespont. Later Darius made
Coes, son of Erxander, tyrant of Mytilene, rewarding him for helpful
advice given at the bridge over the Ister; for he had suggested leaving a
guard there.[5] Histiaeus too was rewarded for his loyalty, being allowed
to build a city near the mouth of the Strymon, amongst the Edonians;[6]
here he began to build fortifications in the expectation of drawing an
income from the Thracian mines and forests, while Darius' general
Megabazus was campaigning from Perinthus to the borders of Mace-
donia.

Soon however it became obvious to Megabazus, who may have
envied the Ionian's privileges, that Histiaeus was becoming too powerful
in Thrace.[7] Histiaeus was therefore summoned to Sardis by Darius, and
taken with him to Susa, where a friendly watch could be kept upon him
and use made of his political experience. Artaphrenes the brother of
Darius was left behind to be satrap at Sardis, while Otanes took over the

mopping-up of Greek resistance in Asia Minor and the Hellespont. In his campaigns he took Byzantium and Chalcedon, and in the Troad Antandrus and Lamponium.[8] Later with the help of the Lesbian navy he captured Lemnos and Imbros, both of which were occupied by barbarians. In Lemnos the natives (Pelasgians or Tyrsenians) put up a stiff fight, but they were subdued, and Lycaretus the Samian was made their ruler. He governed severely and was soon murdered, his place being taken by Hermon a Pelasgian.[9]

While Histiaeus was at Susa, there came to Miletus some friends of his, exiled Naxian aristocrats who had been driven out by the popular party.[10] Miletus was then being ruled by the cousin and son-in-law of Histiaeus, Aristagoras son of Molpagoras,[11] from whom the Naxians begged help so that they could return to their island. Miletus, Herodotus remarks,[12] was flourishing greatly at this time; the civil strife had ceased after the Parian arbitration; and the presence of a strong tyranny backed by Persia had insured against a recurrence of the faction fighting. Naxos however was also powerful, for she had eight thousand foot-soldiers and many long ships,[13] and Aristagoras knew that Miletus alone would not be able to capture the island.

He therefore decided to get the help of Artaphrenes in Sardis. This was readily given, the approval of Darius himself being added later, and two hundred ships were made ready, twice the number requested by Aristagoras.[14] Next Megabates, an Achaemenid Persian and a cousin of the Great King, was placed in command. The fleet sailed, feinting, to Caucasa in Chios,[15] where a dispute broke out between Aristagoras and Megabates, who had placed a Carian, Scylax, captain of a Myndian ship,[16] under arrest for disobedience. Scylax was a friend of Aristagoras, and may well be the Scylax who had helped to explore the Indus for Darius.[17]

From this point the narrative of Herodotus is not easily explained. The historian asserts that Megabates warned the Naxians of the coming attack:[18] that is doubtful, but it is true that the defenders were ready. They resisted successfully for four months, until the Ionians and Persians were forced to withdraw. All the attackers achieved was the building of forts for the exiles to occupy.[19]

What is certain is that after the Naxian debacle Aristagoras revolted from Persia. He may well have feared that Artaphrenes would depose him from the tyranny and sacrifice him to the populace. But Herodotus tells an exciting story to explain the outbreak of the revolt. After the failure at Naxos a slave arrived in Miletus from Histiaeus in Susa with a message that the hair of his head was to be shaved. When that was done, Aristagoras read, tattooed on his scalp, the single word 'Revolt'.[20] The tyrant however after the breach with Artaphrenes may well have been ready to revolt without such prompting; whereas it would have been in Histiaeus' interest to delay the trouble as long as possible, for he had nothing to gain from a revolt. When the break with Persia was inevitable, however, Histiaeus came westwards to join the Ionians, being perhaps motivated by nothing more subtle, or less virtuous, than patriotism.[21]

Evidently the idea of an uprising had been in the air for some time before it happened, the burden of tribute being a constant reminder of Ionia's humiliation. We have seen that as early as *c.* 513 BC Miltiades the Athenian had suggested a revolt, but Aristagoras would not have favoured action until his own position was threatened after the dispute with Megabates. Then it would have been obvious to him that a revolt, if well led, had a chance of success, owing to the enormous length of the Persian line of communication. But the renascent Ionian League, which Herodotus calls a *koinon* or commonwealth,[22] could not fight alone: help from Old Greece was urgently needed.

All the Milesian leaders agreed with Aristagoras' advice to revolt except Hecataeus the geographer who reminded them of the great strength of the Persians, of the vast extent of their empire, and of their resources. When he failed to persuade them, he urged them to become masters of the sea by building a navy to be paid for from the monies left at Branchidae by Croesus, before the enemy took them. This advice too was not taken.[23]

The first overt act of revolt was the capture, late in 499,[24] of the pro-Persian tyrants in the fleet, which had by then returned from Naxos and was moored at Myus.[25] When Coes of Mytilene, Aristagoras of Kyme, and many other tyrants including some Carians had been captured by trickery, Aristagoras himself laid down his tyranny in Miletus to gain popular support for the revolt, and handed over the tyrants to the populace in each of their respective cities.[26] The Mytileneans stoned Coes to death, though he had been a man of the people himself; but the Kymaians let their tyrant Aristagoras go free; Aeaces, son of Syloson escaped from Samos, and most of the other cities spared their tyrants. The Milesian Aristagoras next asked each city for a general to lead the uprising, and then sailed away to find allies outside Ionia.[27]

He went first to the Spartans, but failed to get help from them, because king Cleomenes saw that there was no strategic advantage to be gained. Not even a bribe of ten talents made him change his mind, and when the Ionian raised the sum to fifty, the king's daughter, then aged eight or nine, exclaimed, 'Father, the stranger will corrupt you if you don't get out of here.' Cleomenes seeing this to be true, broke off the conversations and left Aristagoras to find help elsewhere. Herodotus states that Aristagoras asked Cleomenes to attack the Great King in Persia and showed the Spartan a bronze map of the Persian empire.[28] If Aristagoras in fact asked Cleomenes to take his troops on a journey of three months up country along the Royal Road from Ionia to Persia, he was quite exceptionally ambitious: the most he could reasonably have hoped for was Spartan naval and infantry support in western Asia Minor.

After the rebuff at Sparta, Aristagoras came to Athens, where he appealed to Milesian kinship with the Athenians in support of his cause.[29] The Athenians readily listened to him because Artaphrenes in Sardis was now demanding, as the price of their immunity, that they should take back the tyrant Hippias, a man hateful to the young democracy. The Athenians voted to send help to the Ionians and appointed a notable citizen, Melanthius, to command an expedition of twenty ships. The ships were, wrote Herodotus (who was convinced that the entire Ionian revolt had been a foolish enterprise doomed to failure), the beginning of troubles for Greeks and barbarians;[30] and it is true that Athenian intervention did give to the Persians a good pretext, if one was needed, for conquering Athens, or at least for sending a punitive expedition.

With the Athenian force there came five Eretrian ships out of loyalty to their ancient friendship with the Milesians.[31] The ships and troops quickly gathered at Coressus near Ephesus for an assault on Sardis; but Aristagoras himself was not with them; perhaps because Miletus was already being attacked by a Persian force.[32] He had appointed his brother Charopinus[33] and another Milesian, Hermophantus, to lead his city's army against Sardis. With men of Ephesus to show them the way (the city however may have been unwilling to revolt), the Ionian troops and their allies marched inland beside the Cayster, and after crossing the ridges of Mount Tmolus attacked Sardis from the south. Having the advantage of surprise they met no opposition in the lower city, but Artaphrenes was able to hold out in the acropolis with a small force.[34] When a soldier set fire to the houses made of reeds the fire quickly spread, and the entire lower city, together with the sanctuary of the goddess Cybebe, was soon alight. The flames drove the Lydians and Persians into the market place through which the river Pactolus flowed.

Here they resisted valiantly, forcing the Ionians to retreat southwards towards Mount Tmolus, whence the timorous invaders, instead of renewing the attack, fled towards their ships, far away by the coast.[35] Signs of burning in the lower city found in the excavations at Sardis have reasonably been ascribed to the Ionian attack of 498 BC.[36]

The alarm had now been given to all the Persian troops west of the Halys, who converged on Sardis, only to find no Ionians in the city. They followed hard on the enemy towards Ephesus and there routed them, killing many of Ionian leaders, including the Eretrian general, Eualcidas.[37] The Athenians were so demoralised by the defeat that they withdrew their troops, refusing to listen to the pleas of Aristagoras, who was now compelled to carry on the war without them.[38] We are not told that the Eretrians withdrew at this time.

The Ionians, who still had the initiative, now acted boldly and with a concerted policy. Byzantium and the other Hellespontine cities were persuaded to revolt by an Ionian fleet dispatched to those waters, and soon the Carians joined when Ionian ships arrived off their coast, Caunus in Caria having already revolted when Sardis was attacked.[39] Further east all Cyprus except the men of Amathus eagerly joined the uprising during the winter of 498/7 BC. This eagerness is to be expected, since Cyprus had close ties of trade with the East Greeks at this time, and there may have been some recent Ionian settlement there.[40]

When the Ionians were asked to send a fleet to aid the Cypriotes, they debated the matter quickly, and then sent ships with orders that the crews were not to fight the Persians ashore.[41] This was a command of the common assembly of the Ionians, and had presumably been given to the generals by representatives of the cities meeting at Panionion. Herodotus does not make clear how the representatives or *probouloi* were appointed; at this time they may well have been popularly elected in each of the cities.

The fleet fought well off Cyprus against the Phoenicians, and the Samians distinguished themselves,[42] but the Persians did not have much difficulty in subduing the revolt; they were helped not only by the treachery of the tyrant of Curium, and of the Salaminian charioteers, but also by the loyalty of Amathus.[43] The city of Soli held out longest of all, for over four months, until the wall was sapped by the Persians; and doomed Paphos stoutly resisted a siege.[44] The Ionians, however, seeing that the Persians would soon recover the island sailed homewards before the fighting ceased, and the entire revolt in Cyprus lasted for a year only.[45]

The sad history of the second Persian conquest of Ionia must be briefly related. The rebellious Hellespontine cities were soon put down, and Persian arms were carried with ease through the Troad and the Aeolis.[46] When Artaphrenes and Otanes took Clazomenae and Kyme, Aristagoras turned his thoughts to finding a place of refuge for the Milesians, if they had to leave home. Should they go to Sardinia or to Histiaeus' redoubt at Myrcinus in Thrace? To neither, insisted Hecataeus, but to build a fort in Leros.[47] The majority however voted for the Thracian expedition; so, leaving a certain Pythagoras in charge of Miletus, Aristagoras took to Myrcinus every Milesian who wanted to come.[48] In Thrace he and his force were destroyed by the natives, while besieging the place called Nine Ways, a disaster dated by Thucydides about the end of 498 BC[49] that is not long after the attack on Sardis.

In Caria the Persians inflicted severe defeats on the Carians and their Ionian allies, among whom the Milesians suffered most;[50] but the Carians recovered from this, and under the leadership of Heraclides of Mylasa routed their enemies in a night ambush at Pedasa, killing three generals.[51] The life of this Heraclides was written by the Carian sea-dog Scylax, who thus became one of the earliest exponents of the art of biography in prose.[52]

Meanwhile Histaeus had subtly persuaded Darius to let him go from Susa—to bring the Ionians to order, so he said; but Artaphrenes in Sardis received him coolly, fearing that the Milesian was bringing even more trouble with him. 'You have stitched the shoe, Histiaeus' said the satrap, 'and Aristagoras has put it on.'[53] Sensing danger Histaeus left Sardis and crossed to Chios, where he was put in bonds because the Chiots thought him an agent of Darius. As soon as he had talked his way out of captivity, he wrote to some Persians in Sardis urging them to revolt, but his messenger, Hermippus of Atarneus, showed the letters to Artaphrenes. The satrap waited to read the incriminating replies of the Persians before executing them.[54]

The Chiots then took Histiaeus to Miletus at his request, for he hoped to become tyrant there again. But the Milesians, who had no wish again to lose their freedom, resisted, and when Histiaeus was wounded in a night attack, he was forced to return to Chios.[55] Failing to obtain ships from the Chiots, he left for Mytilene where he persuaded the Lesbians to give him eight triremes with their crews. From Lesbos they sailed to Byzantium, to lie in wait for shipping coming from the Black Sea,[56] and close the Propontis to the Persian navy.

The Persians decided to unite their forces in an attack on the hard core of the revolt, Miletus, knowing that once that city had been taken the others would not resist for long. They also brought their navy into the Aegean to challenge the Ionians' command of the sea. With the Phoenician fleet there came Cypriotes, now subject once again to Persia, Cilicians and Egyptians.[57] It was perhaps at this time that Darius' fleet made an unsuccessful attack on Lindos in Rhodes, on the way to Ionia.[58]

The Ionian representatives, the *probouloi*, at Panionion decided not to engage the Persians on land, but to man the walls of Miletus, to collect every one of their ships, and to assemble the fleet at Lade, an islet off Miletus.[59] The ships soon gathered from Ionia and the Aeolis, and the numbers which Herodotus records give some idea of the relative strengths of the Asiatic Greek cities at the time.[60] If Herodotus is correct in stating that all the ships were triremes, then the work of replacing penteconters had gone on quickly from the time of Polycrates onwards.

There were three hundred and fifty-three Ionian warships in all. Of them the Milesians on the east of the line had eighty. Priene provided twelve, and Myus three. There were seventeen Teian ships, and next to them one hundred from Chios, each with forty marines aboard. In the next station to the west were the Erythraeans with eight. Then the Phocaeans with three, and the Lesbians with seventy. The Samians with sixty were stationed furthest to the west and nearest to their island, a tactical defect since they were there strongly tempted to escape home-wards if defeat threatened.[61] The barbarian fleet was larger than the Ionian; it amounted to six hundred ships according to Herodotus;[62] yet the Persian leaders were frightened that the Ionians would win and keep their mastery of the sea, so that Miletus would not be taken. So they tried to secure by diplomacy what they could not be sure of gaining by arms.

The surviving Ionian tyrants friendly to Persia, who happened to be present in the Persian army, were asked to tell the men of their respec-tive cities that no harm would be done to them nor would their shrines be burned as a punishment for the revolt, provided that they abandoned the Ionian fleet. The offer was at first ignored, but later was readily heeded by each of the Ionian contingents, for they felt no confidence in their commander, Dionysius of Phocaea. This man was appointed because he was skilled in naval tactics, but he soon became very un-popular with his men; for he insisted on vigorous battle training, and kept the marines under arms all day. After manoeuvres the crews were not allowed ashore, but the ships were kept at anchor through the heat of the day. So they continued to exhaust themselves for seven days, until their discipline broke and they refused to obey their Phocaean commander, whose city, they pointed out, had provided three ships only.[63] Seeing the poor morale of the navy, the Samian generals now replied favourably to the Persian offer of immunity made to them by their former tyrant Aeaces.[64]

At once the Phoenicians struck, and the Samians withdrew, leaving only eleven ships with trierarchs loyal to the Ionian cause.[65] Seeing the Samians fleeing, the Lesbians stationed near them also fled, and most of the Ionians soon followed their example. Only the Chiots fought splendidly: they ran their ships through the enemy lines and inflicted heavy damage. But when, gravely outnumbered, they had lost most of their triremes, the undamaged survivors fled to Chios, while the limping Chiot ships were beached on Mycale.[66] The crews marched northwards towards the territory of Ephesus, which they reached at night during a festival of the Ephesian women, the Thesmophoria, but, so it was said, being mistaken for brigands the sailors were all killed in the darkness.[67] In fact, the Ephesians, whose loyalty to the Ionian cause was not strong, may have murdered them in the hope of pleasing the Persians.

When the battle was plainly lost, Dionysius the Phocaean sailed for Phoenicia in three captured ships. There he spent some time in successful piracy, but later he continued his career as a freebooter based in Sicily, whence he sailed to attack the Carthaginians and the Etruscans, the old enemies of the Phocaeans of Alalia.[68]

After their victory at Lade the Persians following their plan of campaign besieged Miletus by land and by sea. Siege engines were brought up and the sappers and miners set to work. The siege ended in the sixth year after the outbreak of the revolt, according to Herodotus, that is, about the summer of 494 BC.[69] When the place was stormed, most of the menfolk were killed, the women and children were enslaved, and the city was emptied of its inhabitants, as Delphi had predicted.[70] The oracle and temple at Didyma were also plundered and burned,[71] and objects from them were taken to Persia.[72] The Milesian captives were deported to Ampe, a place at the head of the Persian Gulf,[73] but the Medizing Branchidae later were given a home in Sogdiana.[74] The Persians themselves occupied the plain of Miletus and the land around the city, but the remoter parts of her territory beyond the hills they gave to the hardy Carians of Pedasus,[75] who had been in revolt not long before.[76] The Milesians who got away joined the enemies of Aeaces in Samos and fled with them to Sicily, where they captured the city of Zancle.[77]

The Athenians heard the news of the fall of Miletus with sorrow and alarm. Soon their tragedian Phrynichus composed a play on the sack of Miletus, which when performed caused the audience to weep in the theatre. The poet so offended the Athenians' sensibilities that he was fined one thousand drachmae for 'having reminded them of their own misfortunes'.[78] But such precipitate action could not conceal from their troubled consciences that Athens had done nothing to assist her Ionian cousins after the shameful retreat from Sardis.

The fall of Miletus marks the end of early Ionia. It is the correct point in time to end a local history of the Asiatic Greeks. Henceforth the history of the Ionians is most profitably studied as part of the history of the Persian wars and of the Athenian empire. The Ionians continued after the liberation that followed the battle of Mycale in 479 to produce great men: Anaxagoras in Clazomenae; and in the Teian colony Abdera, Protagoras and Democritus the philosophers; in Miletus, Hippodamus the city-planner and Leucippus the physicist; and in Chios the tragic poet Ion and the astronomer Oenopides. But the spring had gone from the year. At Lade the Asiatic Ionians were condemned to a precarious existence between the naval power of Athens, and later of Sparta, on one side, and the great empire of Persia on the other. Some Greeks even suggested after the Greek victory at Mycale that the Ionians should be evacuated, a proposal happily not adopted.[79]

Miletus did not lose all her people in 494 BC in spite of the deportations; after the battle of Mycale there were still some Milesians in Miletus ready to revolt from Persia.[80] The survivors, it seems, attempted to preserve the continuity of their political life, for the great list of stephanephoroi, Milesian priestly officials, which begins in 525 BC, marks no interruption between 494 and 479 BC.[81] But Miletus, though she was a moderately rich and carefully planned city under the first Athenian empire, may never have quite recovered the prosperity she had known in the great days of her Pontic colonisation.

If we knew what proportion of the population of the Ionian cities manned the triremes at Lade, then we could estimate the numbers of their citizens at that time. There were, on a fair estimate, about two hundred men in each trireme;[82] in addition the Chians had marines, forty picked men to each ship, and are not likely to have been the only contingent with them. Now if we assume that there was one man fit to fight out of every four free persons in each of the Ionian cities, then Miletus had a population of at least sixty-four thousand at the time of the battle, and probably many more, because some of the citizens had been posted at the walls. This estimate ignores any Milesian marines there may have been, and the number of slaves in the city is quite unknown. A comparison with the populations of other Greek states is perhaps helpful, however. Early in the fifth century there were about eight thousand Athenian hoplites, and, according to Herodotus, thirty thousand citizens (adult males) altogether.[83] Sparta with her ten thousand hoplites at this time had a slightly larger army, when the perioikoi were included.[84] Thus the total free population of Ionia with Lesbos was much larger than those of Sparta and Athens combined, and when Aristagoras proposed revolt from Persia his case may have seemed strong to the other Ionians and to their counsellors at Panionion. However, political cohesion was lacking,[85] the Aeolians were still unfederated with Ionia, and, apart from Miletus, the cities were not easily defended from land attack. It was a bold enterprise in which a unified league, such as Thales had proposed, might have won and kept its freedom, but in the event the naval defeat at Lade symbolised a political failure whose origins lay far back in the Ionian past.

CHAPTER XVII

Retrospect and Prospect

HOW, FINALLY, ARE WE TO JUDGE THE ACHIEVEMENTS OF THE EARLY Ionians? It is obvious that the significance of Ionian history lies in its peculiarly intellectual character; the greatest gift of the eastern Greeks to posterity was the creation of philosophy, a rational view of the origin and nature of the world and of man's place in it. This was chiefly the work of the Milesians of the sixth century, who with wonderful originality devised speculative systems out of which the natural sciences were ultimately to grow. They aimed to understand Nature, who had endowed Ionia so abundantly; they were not ambitious to exploit or to dominate her, for they revered the natural order of which they knew themselves to be a part; and their reverence sets them above many natural scientists of our own time. The Ionians' military failures and refusals to federate do not dim the brightness of the intellectual victories of Thales, Anaximander, and their colleagues, who by creating out of cosmogonical myths a rational world view, became the founding heroes of the Ionian enlightenment. They are sure of honour so long as those who contemplate the workings of Nature are not too proud or too ignorant to recognise their own indebtedness to their forerunners.

No less significant is the creation of historical enquiry, and systematic geography, out of the Greek epics; this was the work of the *logographoi*, who may be said to share the invention of history with the writers of the earliest books of the Old Testament. *Historie*, secular history as opposed to the theistic history of the Hebrews, may be claimed as the creation of a Milesian nobleman, Hecataeus, who like Thales and Anaximander before him, combined patient observation with bold thought. It was fortunate for the eastern Greeks that many of their leaders had fine minds. In the blending of Anatolian with Aegean and Hellenic elements that constituted Ionian and Aeolian life, the eastern Greeks created a civilisation in which the most important things, those of the mind, had precedence.

Lastly, Ionia can claim to be the home of much great poetry. In the islands and the coasts of the eastern Aegean, epic flourished abundantly, and a great poet of original genius, yet master of the ancient oral tradition, composed epics which set him far above his rivals. A century or so after Homer, Lesbos was graced by the lyrics of a great poetess whose like was never seen in Greece again; and on the Asiatic coast Callinus and his successors composed elegies and lyrics whose quality may be favourably compared with the best poetry of mainland Greece.

After the Persian wars the Ionians of the islands and the coast had less scope for political initiative, short of outright revolt from the naval dominion of Athens, whose interventions, however well meant, as when she helped for a time the Milesian nobility against the populace, were inevitably deadening. Ionians were no longer able in their own cities to join thought with action, philosophy with politics, as the statesmen of the sixth century had done; and many—notably in Naxos, in Thasos, and in Samos—were driven to take up arms against Athenian rule. There were still great intellects in Ionia, but the glories of Athens perhaps diminished the vigour of her subjects. It was fitting, and entirely in the Ionian spirit, however, that the potent, and nearly successful, revolt of Samos from Periclean imperialism was directed by a general, Melissus, who was also a philosopher.

Notes

ABBREVIATIONS

References to F. Jacoby's *Die Fragmente der Griechischen Historiker* (*FGrHist*) are made in the form 'Hecataeus 1 F 1'. Similarly fragments of the philosophers are given according to the numbering in Diels-Kranz, *Die Fragmente der Vorsokratiker* (9th ed., Berlin 1960): e.g. Thales 11 B 1, or 11 B 1. The following abbreviations will also be found in the notes:

AA	*Archäologischer Anzeiger.*
Abh.	*Abhandlungen.*
ABSA	*Annual of the British School at Athens.*
AC	*L'Antiquité classique.*
AE	Ἀρχαιολογικὴ Ἐφημερίς.
AJ	*The Antiquaries' Journal.*
AJA	*American Journal of Archaeology.*
AJP	*American Journal of Philology.*
AM	*Athenische Mitteilungen* (of the German Archaeological Institute).
ANET	*Ancient Near Eastern Texts Relating to the Old Testament,* ed. J. B. Pritchard (²Princeton 1955).
AR	*Archaeological Reports* (Annual Supplement to JHS).
AS	*Anatolian Studies.*
ASAtene	*Annuario delle Scuola Archeologica di Atene e delle Missioni italiane in Oriente.*
ATL	B. D. Meritt, H. T. Wade-Gery, M. F. Macgregor, *The Athenian Tribute Lists* I–IV (1939–1953).
BASOR	*Bulletin of the American Schools of Oriental Research.*
BCH	*Bulletin de Correspondance hellénique.*
BICS	*Bulletin of the Institute of Classical Studies,* London University.
Boll. d'Arte	*Bolletino d'Arte.*
CAH²	*Cambridge Ancient History* (Revised ed. of Vols I. and II).
CIG	*Corpus Inscriptionum Graecarum.*
CP	*Classical Philology.*
CQ	*Classical Quarterly.*
DG	*Doxographi Graeci,* ed. H. Diels (3rd ed. Berlin 1958).
F	Fragment.
FHG	*Fragmenta Historicorum Graecorum,* ed. C. and T. Müller and V. Langlois. Vol. I–V (1848–1870).
GGM	*Geographi Graeci Minores,* ed. C. Müller. Vol. I–II (1855–1861).
GRBS	*Greek, Roman and Byzantine Studies.*
HSCP	*Harvard Studies in Classical Philology.*
IG	*Inscriptiones Graecae.*
ILN	*Illustrated London News.*
IM	*Istanbuler Mitteilungen.*

ABBREVIATIONS USED IN NOTES

JEA	*Journal of Egyptian Archaeology.*
JHS	*Journal of Hellenic Studies.*
JNES	*Journal of Near Eastern Studies.*
JÖAI	*Jahreshefte des österreichischen archäologischen Instituts in Wien.*
JRS	*Journal of Roman Studies.*
MDOG	*Mitteilungen der deutschen Orient Gesellschaft.*
MH	*Museum Helveticum.*
NDA	*Neue Deutsche Ausgrabungen im Mittelmeergebiet und im Vorderen Orient,* ed. E. Boehringer (Berlin 1959).
OA	*Opuscula Archaeologica.*
OGIS	*Orientis Graeci Inscriptiones Selectae.* 2 Vols. (Leipzig 1903–1905).
ÖJH	See *JÖAI.*
PBA	*Proceedings of the British Academy.*
PdP	*La Parola del Passato.*
P.Oxy.	*Oxyrhyncus Papyri.*
RE	*Paulys Real-Encyclopädie der classischen Altertum wissenschaft,* ed. G. Wissowa.
REA	*Revue des Études anciennes.*
REG	*Revue des Études grecques.*
Rev. de Phil.	*Revue de Philologie.*
RM	*Rheinisches Museum für Philologie.*
SB	*Sitzungsberichte* (followed by name of academy).
SEG	*Supplementum Epigraphicum Graecum.*
SIG or *Sylloge*	*Sylloge Inscriptionum Graecarum,*[3] ed. W. Dittenberger. 4 Vols. (Leipzig 1915–1924).
TAPA	*Transactions and Proceedings of the American Philological Association.*
ZCP	*Zeitschrift für celtische Philologie.*

Works Cited by Author's Name Only

J. Boardman	*The Greeks Overseas* (Pelican Books, 1964).
F. Bilabel	*Die ionische Kolonisation* (*Philologus* Supplementband 14, 1921).
C. D. Buck	*The Greek Dialects,* 2nd ed. (Chicago 1955).
F. Cassola	*La Ionia nel Mondo miceneo* (Naples 1957).
V. R. d'A. Desborough	(1) *Protogeometric Pottery* (Oxford 1952).
V. R. d'A. Desborough	(2) *The Last Mycenaeans and their Successors* (Oxford 1964).
T. J. Dunbabin	*The Greeks and their Eastern Neighbours* (London 1957).
H. Gallet de Santerre	*Délos primitive et archaïque* (Paris 1958).
J. Garstang and O. R. Gurney	*The Geography of the Hittite Empire* (London 1959).

G. Grote	*A History of Greece* (Everyman ed. 1906).
W. K. C. Guthrie	*A History of Greek Philosophy* I (Cambridge 1962).
G. L. Huxley	*Achaeans and Hittites* (Oxford 1960).
L. H. Jeffery	*The Local Scripts of Archaic Greece* (Oxford 1961).
G. S. Kirk and J. E. Raven	*The Presocratic Philosophers* (Cambridge 1957).
W. A. Laidlaw	*A History of Delos* (Oxford 1933).
D. L. Page	*History and the Homeric Iliad* (California 1959).
H. W. Parke and D. E. W. Wormell	*The Delphic Oracle* 2 Vols. 2nd ed. (Oxford 1956).
J. Pouilloux	*Recherches sur l'histoire et les cultes de Thasos* I (Paris 1954).
C. Roebuck	*Ionian Trade and Colonization* (New York 1959).
M. Sakellariou	*La Migration grecque en Ionie* (Athens 1958).
E. Schwyzer	*Dialectorum graecarum exempla epigraphica potiora* (repr. Hildesheim 1960).
F. Sommer	*Die Aḫḫijavā-Urkunden* (Munich 1932).
F. H. Stubbings	*Mycenaean Pottery from the Levant* (Cambridge 1951).
M. N. Tod	*A Selection of Greek Historical Inscriptions to the end of the Fifth Century B.C.* I, 2nd ed. (Oxford 1946).
H. T. Wade-Gery	*Essays in Greek History* (Oxford 1958). [*Essays.*]
H. T. Wade-Gery	*The Poet of the Iliad* (Cambridge 1952). [*Poet.*]

Chapter I. THE FORERUNNERS OF THE IONIANS

1 Gallet de Santerre, 32–33, 57–58.
2 J. L. Caskey, *Hesperia* 31 (1962) 272.
3 K. Scholes, *ABSA* 51 (1956) 28–29.
4 L. Renaudin, *BCH* 46 (1922) 113–159.
5 C. Weickert, *İM* 7 (1957) 117–118 and *NDA* 181–196.
6 A. Furumark, *OA* 6 (1950) 179. R. Hope Simpson and J. F. Lazenby, *ABSA* 57 (1962) 173.
7 W. Buttler, *AM* 60/61 (1935/6) 190–196.
8 D. Levi, *ILN* 20 July, 1963, 88.
9 Thucydides 1.4.1 and 1.8.2. Cf. Herodotus 3.122.2.
10 Philochorus 328 F 17.
11 Bacchylides, 'Επ. I. 112–120, p. 4, Snell.
12 Ephorus 70 F 127.
13 Herodorus 31 F 45.
14 Ion of Chios 392 F I. Cf. Theopompus 115 F 276. For a Chiot inscription naming Ion and his followers see N. M. Kondoleon, *Rev. de Phil.* (1949) 5 ff.
15 Pausanias 7.3.7.
16 Steph. Byz. s.v. Μίνωα. For Minoa as a name of Paros see Steph. Byz. *loc. cit.*

17 Gallet de Santerre, 56.
18 K. Scholes, *ABSA* 51 (1956) 32.
19 Schol. Aeneid 3. 80–82. Schol. Lycophr. *Alex.* 570. See also Gallet de Santerre 176 and Laidlaw 18.
20 Stubbings 22. Desborough (2) 159–161.
21 Desborough (2) 158–159.
22 Desborough (2) 158.
23 Sakellariou 506.
24 M. J. Mellink, *AJA* 68 (1964) 157–158.
25 *ILN* 1 April 1961, 537.
26 G. F. Bass, *AJA* 67 (1963) 208.
27 *AM* 12 (1887) 230.
28 Desborough (2) 160.
29 Stubbings 5 ff.
30 Stubbings 21–22. Morricone, *Boll. d'Arte* 1950, 320 ff.
31 H. Goldman, *AJA* 27 (1923) 67 f. L. B. Holland, *Hesperia* 13 (1944) 91 and 94.
32 Weickert, *NDA* 181–196. Desborough 161–163. For a late Mycenaean defensive wall in Samos see *BCH* 83 (1959) 727 and 729–730.
33 Cf. J. M. Cook, *AR* 1960, 50.
34 Sommer 2–19.
35 Garstang/Gurney 78–82.
36 Huxley 12.
37 Desborough (2) 4 and 218 f. Cf. Page 15, who proposes to locate Aḫḫiyawā in Rhodes.
38 Huxley 14.
39 *Iliad* 9.69.
40 C. W. Blegen and others, *Troy* iv, 8 f.
41 Blegen, *CAH²*, *Troy* (1961) 14.
42 A. Furumark, *The Chronology of Mycenaean Pottery* (Stockholm 1941) 114.
43 Huxley 7 f. Desborough (2) 220–221.
44 Garstang/Gurney 105–107.
45 W. Leaf, *Troy. A Study in Homeric Geography* (London 1912) 397–399.
46 Aristoboulos 139 F 6.
47 *Iliad* 2.868.
48 Thucydides 1.12.1–2.
49 Herodotus 5.76. See also N. G. L. Hammond, *CAH²*, Vol. 2, Ch. 26, 46.
50 Seton Lloyd, *Early Anatolia* (Pelican Books 1956) 191.
51 Desborough (2) 237.
52 H. Otten, *MDOG* 94 (1963) 21.
53 C. W. Blegen, *AJA* 64 (1960) 159.
54 Pausanias 2.18.9.
55 *BICS* 3 (1956) 19.
56 Sir Alan Gardiner, *Ancient Egyptian Onomastica* 1 (Oxford 1947), 1.129* ff.
57 Garstang/Gurney 83–84. For the possibility that Apašaš, an important city on the Arzawan coast, is Ephesus see Garstang/Gurney 88.

58 Pausanias 7.3. 1–2.
59 Callinus of Ephesus quoted by Strabo (668).
60 H. Goldman, *Tarsus II* (Princeton 1956) 205 ff.
61 R. D. Barnett, *AS* 3 (1953) 83–84.
62 Agias, *Nosti* in *Homeri Opera* 5.108 ed. T. W. Allen.
63 [Antimachus Colophonius] F 150 ed. Wyss.
64 1.94.2–7.
65 G. A. Wainwright, *JEA* 46 (1960) 24–28.
66 Wainwright, *AS* 9 (1959) 197–213.
67 Thucydides 4.109.4.
68 J. Friedrich, *Kleinasiatische Sprachdenkmäler* (Berlin 1932) 143–145.
69 For a comprehensive treatment of the problem of Etruscan origins see F. Schachermeyr, *Etruskische Frühgeschichte* (Berlin 1929). Compare M. Pallottino, *The Etruscans* (Pelican Books 1955) 46–73.
70 *Iliad* 2.653–680.
71 Sommer 4–5.
72 Pausanias 7.3.2.
73 Leleges as allies of Priam: *Iliad* 10.429. In Pedasus: *Iliad* 21.86–87. In Tenedos: Diegesis to Callimachus F 91 Pfeiffer. In the Ephesia: Pausanias 7.2.8. In Samos: Asius 545 F 1. Lelegian slaves of the Carians: Philip of Theangela, 741 F 2. Lelegian subjects of Minos in the Cyclades: Herodotus 1.171.2. Leleges in Locris: Hesiod F 115 Rzach³. Pherecydes ap. Strab. 632–633 states that there were before the Ionian migration Carians in the neighbourhoods of Mycale and Ephesus, and north of Ephesus Leleges as far as Phocaea. There were also Leleges in Chios and Samos, where Ancaeus was king (*FGrHist* 3 F 155).
74 Pausanias 7.3.7.
75 A. Goetze, *Kleinasien²* (Munich 1957) 181. See also Huxley, *Crete and the Luwians* (Oxford 1961) 17–24.
76 Friedrich, *Kleinasiatische Sprachdenkmäler* 90–107. See also L. Robert, *Hellenica* 8 (1950) 5–21 for Carian texts in Caria.
77 Herodotus (1.171.2) considered that the continental Carians of Asia Minor were descendants of the insular peoples, formerly called Leleges, who had been subject to Minos. For discussion of Carians and Leleges in Greek legend see W. Aly, *Philologus* 68 (1909) 428–444 and F. Cassola, *PdP* 54 (1957) 192–209.

Chapter II. THE IONIAN MIGRATION

1 The Dorian movement eastwards is not within the scope of this book: for a clear account of it see J. M. Cook, *CAH²*, Vol. 2, Ch. 38, 18–24.
2 For the extent of Ionia see Strabo 632 (14.1.2).
3 Desborough (2) 162 and 254.
4 Weickert, *IM* 9–10 (1959/60) 37 f.
5 Boardman 47–48. Cf. Hanfmann, *HSCP* 61 (1953) 7–8.
6 This is the most likely position for Pygela: J. M. Cook, *AR* 1960, 40.

7 Desborough (1) 221.
8 *AJA* 68 (1964) 157–158. For a figurine of Hittite type, said to be from Ephesus see Hanfmann, *AJA* 66 (1962) 1–4.
9 *AJA* 68 (1964) 163.
10 H. L. Lorimer, *Homer and the Monuments* (London 1950) 105–107. Boardman 49.
11 J. M. Cook, *AR* 1960, 40.
12 [Apollodorus], *Epit.* 3.33 mentions an attack by Achilles during the Great Foray.
13 Sakellariou 506.
14 *JHS* 72 (1952) 105. Fig. 10.
15 Cf. J. M. Cook, *ABSA* 53–54 (1958–1959) 10–14.
16 Boardman 51.
17 Ion of Chios 392 F 1.
18 Boardman 51.
19 Technau, *AM* 54 (1929) Beil. iv: 1, 6, 7. Desborough (1) 216.
20 *AR* 1960, 41.
21 Suda s.v. Πανύασις.
22 5.66.2.
23 5.58.2.
24 8.73.3.
25 1.145.
26 Pausanias 7.1.7–8. See also E. T. Vermeule, *AJA* 64 (1960) 18–20.
27 *Iliad* 13.685.
28 F 4 Diehl.
29 Herodotus 5.65.3. Hellanicus 4 F 125. Pausanias 2.18.9.
30 Hellanicus 4 F 125.
31 Pausanias 1.19.5–6. See also Herodotus 5.76.
32 Thucydides 1.12.3. This chronology of the fifth century BC historians fits the archaeological evidence for widespread destruction in Peloponnese *c.* 1200 BC well. The earliest evidence for Dorian *settlement* in Peloponnese is however much later, being not earlier than *c.* 1075 BC in the Argolid and *c.* 1000 BC in southwestern Peloponnese (see Desborough (2) 251 ff). It is possible that the earliest evidence for Dorian occupation has not yet been found. On Thucydides' date for the Trojan war see *PdP* 54 (1957) 209 ff.
33 His account was probably published between 508/7 and 476/5 BC. See F. Jacoby, *Mnemosyne* 13³ (1947) 33.
34 Strabo 632–633 (14.1.3). See also J. P. Barron, *JHS* 82 (1962) 6 n. 40.
35 7.2.1–7.5.1.
36 Herodotus 9.97.
37 Aelian, *VH* 8.5.
38 Zenobius, *Adag.* 5.17.
39 Desborough (2) 148 ff.
40 Isocrates, *Panath.* 241 CD (Vol. 2.23 ed. Blass).
41 Herodotus 1.146.2–3.
42 Strabo 633.

43 Herodotus 9.97.
44 Pausanias 7.2.6.
45 *FGrHist* 3 F 155.
46 Pausanias 7.2.8–9.
47 Pausanias 7.4.2–3.
48 Pausanias 7.4.2. For a later Procles ruling in Samos see Aethlios 536 F 3 and the Diegesis to Callimachus F 100 Pf.
49 Strabo 633.
50 M. Schede, *AM* 44 (1919) 20.
51 Themistagoras of Ephesus ap. Etym. Magnum, s.v. ᾿Αστυπαλαία. See also Wilamowitz, *Kleine Schriften* 5.1 (1937) 160 n.2. and Bilabel 173–174.
52 Strabo 633. Cf. Pausanias 7.2.10.
53 Hellanicus 4 F 101. Schol. Dionys. Per. 823. See also Sakellariou 76–77.
54 Pausanias 7.2.10. For Κυάρητος read Κυδρῆλος.
55 Strabo 633.
56 *SEG* 4.513. Theopompos 115 F 59. Strabo 639.
57 Hecataeus (1 F 11) simply calls Melie a city of Caria.
58 Vitruvius 4.1.
59 Wade-Gery *Poet* 64.
60 Mimnermus ap. Strab. 633.
61 F 12 Diehl.
62 Pausanias 7.3.3.
63 The genos Προμήθειοι in Colophon had their name from Promethus: for them and for Ch. Picard's identification of Polyteichides read L. Robert, *Rev. de Phil.* 10³ (1936) 164.
64 Strabo 633.
65 Pausanias 2.18.8.
66 Pausanias 7.3.5.
67 Anacreon F 118 Page. Pausanias 7.3.6. Ion of Chios tried to claim Athamas as a son of Oenopion (Ion 392 F 1 with Etym. Mag., Orion λόγχας). Cf. A. von Blumenthal, *Ion von Chios* (Stuttgart–Berlin 1939) 17.
68 Strabo 633. In Paus. 7.3.6 read Ποίκης for ῎Αποικος: the name Ποίκης is Tean: *JHS* 67 (1947) 68 n. 1.
69 Pausanias 7.3.6.
70 Strabo 633. Pausanias 7.3.7. Cnopus is said to have been helped by a priestess of Enodia who was sent by the Thessalians and brought him victory: Polyaenus 8.43.
71 Pausanias 7.3.9.
72 Strabo 633 gives this name. In Pausanias 7.3.9 their leader is called Parphoros a Colophonian.
73 Their first settlement may have been at Chytrion, which lay in a plain near Urla some distance south of the Gulf. See J. M. Cook, *AR* 1953–1954 (1957) 149–150 and 156–157.
74 Strabo 633.
75 Pausanias 7.3.10.
76 Nicolas of Damascus 90 F 51.

77 Pausanias (7.3.10) has *Ἄβαρτος* for *Ἄβαρνος*: but *Ἄβαρνος* should be read. There was a tribe *Ἀβαρνεύς* of the Phocaeans: Hesych. s.v. and the name Abarnos is linked with Phocaea's colony Lampsacus. See Ephorus 70 F 46 and Jacoby's commentary on Hecataeus 1 F 220.

78 Ion 392 F 1 (F 16 Von Blumenthal). Oenopion's name may have been adopted by a Chian tribe: Forrest, *ABSA* 55 (1960) 188–189.

79 *Hom. Hymn* 3. 147 and 152.

80 3.104.4.

81 7.95.1.

82 8.46.2–3.

83 8.48.

84 Schol. Dionys. Per. 525 (*GGM* 2.451). For Ionians in Ios see Steph. Byz. s.v. *Ἴος*.

85 Read *Δήλιοι* for *Δήλων*.

86 Zenobius, *Adag.* 5.17.

87 Et. Gen. B. s.v. *Εὐξαντίδος*. See also Callimachus F 67, 7 Pf.

88 Callimachus F 75, 70–74 (from Xenomedes of Ceos).

89 1.146.1.

90 Herodotus 8.43. Pausanias 4.34.9. Strabo 373.

91 Herodotus 8.46.4.

92 Thucydides 7.57.4. Diodorus 4.37.

93 Herodotus 8.46.4.

94 Herodotus 7.90.

95 *IG* XII.9.56. See also W. P. Wallace, *The Euboian League and its Coinage* (New York 1956) 23 n. 52.

96 Pausanias 1.5.3. Ps.-Scymnus 572 (where Cerinthus is also said to be an Athenian foundation).

97 *Iliad* 2.536.

98 Strabo (446–447) held that Chalcis and Eretria were settled by Athenians before and after the Trojan war. Herodotus (8.46.2) simply calls the people of both places Ionians. Cf. Pindar, *Paean V*, 30.

99 Aeschines, *De Falsa Legatione* 116. See also A. H. J. Greenidge, *Greek Constitutional History* (London 1896) 51.

100 Apollonius Rhod. *Arg.* 1.620 ff.

101 [Apollodorus] *Bibl.* 1.9.6.

102 Heraclides, *FHG* 2.214.

103 Heraclides Ponticus ap. Steph. Byz. s.v. *Ὠλίαρος* calls the island Σιδωνίων ἀποικία.

104 Herodotus (1.171.5), quoting the Cretans, mentions the expulsion of Carians from the islands by Ionians and Dorians, but does not state when he believed them to have been driven out. On Carian naval power after the Trojan war in the Cyclades see Diodorus 5.84 and compare J. L. Myres, *JHS* 26 (1906) 108. Cycladic Carians may be archaeologically indistinguishable from Minoans, Mycenaeans or Ionians of the Cyclades: Thucydides believed (1.8.1. Cf. 3.104) that over half the burials in Delos cleared by the Athenians in 426/5 were

of Carians because, he thought, the weapons found in the tombs were Carian and the kind of burial was like that used in Caria in his time. Unfortunately his words do not show clearly what date he supposed the tombs to have been made, nor what their true date in fact was. For archaeological commentary on the remarks of Thucydides compare C. R. Long, *AJA* 62 (1958) 297–306 with R. M. Cook, *ABSA* 50 (1955) 267–270, who discuss the Rheneia deposit. Apart from one Mycenaean sherd, all the pottery in the deposit is Geometric and later: see K. A. Rhomaios, *Archaiologikon Deltion* 12 (1929) 208–210. It is reasonable to associate the deposit with the clearance of tombs in Delos in 426/5, but it provides no evidence at all for the survival of Carians in Delos. To argue from the Geometric remains in the deposit that there were Carians in Delos in Geometric times is quite unwarranted.

105 Bilabel 70. Cassola 235–236.

106 Bilabel 163. Bischoff, *RE* 10.2 (1919) 1585.

107 Bilabel 188. Boedromion is attested in Oliaros.

108 Miletus, Samos, Priene, Iasos, Amorgos, Delos, Tenos, Chalcis, Eretria, Herakleia (Latmos). Cassola 228. Bischoff, *RE* 10.2 (1919) 1597. For more detail about Ionian months see Bischoff 1582–1586.

109 1.147.2.

110 Though the Ionian month Apatourion corresponds in time to Attic Maimakterion, in Athens the festival of the Apatouria was held in Pyanepsion: L. Deubner, *Attische Feste* (Berlin 1932) 232–234.

111 The forms Ἀπατουριών, Ἀπατοριών, and Ἀπατουρεών of the month name are found. They presumably come from *Ἀπατορϝεών. *ἀπατορϝια perhaps means 'assembly of fathers', the ἀ- being copulative (Cassola 227). The Scholiast on Aristophanes, *Acharnians* 146 equates Ἀπατούρια with Ὁμοπατούρια. Cf. Eitrem, *Eranos* 20 (1921/2) 105.

112 Ephorus 70 F 22. The worship of Athena Apatouria in Troizen (Pausanias 2.33.1) is evidence rather of Athenian influence there than of the survival of an ancient cult of the Old Ionians of Peloponnese.

113 Sanscrit *bhrātryam,* Old Slavic *bratrija* 'brotherhood'. On Irish *bráthair,* 'member of a brotherhood' see D. A. Binchy, *PBA* 29 (1943) 222. For an ancient theory about phratries see Dicaearchus in Steph. Byz. s.v. πάτρα. Hesychius' φρήτηρ ἀδελφός shows that some Ionians kept the meaning 'brother' after the dialect had replaced ā by η. See A. Andrewes, *Hermes* 89 (1961) 137.

114 The names are first found, as sons of Ion in Herodotus 5.66.2 and Euripides, *Ion* 1579–1581 (where there is a lacuna and the MSS have τελέων for Γελέων; Wilamowitz retained Τελέων. Compare Pollux 8.109 where Gelontes are called Τελέοντες).

115 Plutarch, *Solon* 23.5. A similar explanation is to be found in Strabo 383. See also C. Hignett, *A History of the Athenian Constitution* (Oxford 1952) 50–55.

116 Herodotus 5.66.2 and 5.69.2.

117 J. H. Oliver, *Hesperia* 4 (1935) 5 ff. S. Dow, *Proc. of the Massa-*

chusetts Hist. Soc. 71 (1953–1957) 1–35. F. Sokolowski, *Lois sacrées des Cités grecques.* Supplement (Paris 1962) 27–31.

118 J. P. Barron, *JHS* 82 (1962) 2. Cf. A. G. Dunham, *A History of Miletus* (London 1915) 135 f.

119 *SIG³* 57, 1–3.

120 *SB Berlin* 1904, 85.

121 Bilabel 120–121.

122 Bilabel 123–124.

123 Bilabel 124.

124 L. Robert, *Rev. de Phil.* 10³ (1936) 115.

125 C. Roebuck, *TAPA* 92 (1961) 497.

126 1.147.1.

127 Hellanicus 4 F 125. Cf. Pausanias 2.18.8. See also Barron, *JHS* 82 (1962) 4 n. 24. In an inscription concerning an Aisymnetes of 67/6 BC the Neleidae are called a *patria* of the Pelagonid phratry of the deme Teichioussa, which was perhaps their traditional home in the Milesian countryside. The name Pelagon, like Borus, is Pylian: *Iliad* 4.295. For the inscription see B. Haussoullier, *Rev. de Phil.* 21 (1897) 38.

128 Chesion was a place in west Samos, the Carian part of the island: see Wilamowitz, *SB Berlin* 1904, 931 and Pfeiffer on Schol. Callim. *Hymn.* 3.228. There were two tribes in Samos in the second century BC (*SIG³* 976 line 40). Themistagoras (ap. Etym. Mag. s.v. ᾽Αστυπαλαία) gives their names as Chesia and Astypalaia, but dates them to the time of Procles and Tembrion. The Chesians would be the Carians, the Astypalaians the Greeks of Samos town, of which a name was Astypalaia (Polyaenus 1.23). It may be that Themistagoras dates the creation of the two tribes too early, for there undoubtedly were once six Ionian tribes in Samos. The six tribes became, it seems, *chiliastyes,* subdivisions of the two new tribes, but the occasion is unknown. It was presumably later than the founding of Perinthus where Ionian tribe names are known. For Oenopes as a *chiliastys* of the tribe Chesia see *SEG* 1.362 line 35 (late fourth century BC). For discussion see Roebuck, *TAPA* 92 (1961) 505 n. 22. Whether the four Old Ionian tribes in Samos were brought in by Procles and the Ionians from Epidaurus or by the Athenian immigrants (Schol. T. *Iliad* 15.341) is not clear.

129 Bilabel 176. The Boreis were numbered fifth in the order of tribes at Perinthus: L. Robert, *Rev. de Phil.* 10³ (1936) 113–115.

130 *CIG* 3078–3079.

131 J. Keil, *JÖAI* 16 (1913) 245–248.

132 Ephorus 70 F 126. See also M. Sakellariou, ῾Ελληνικά 15 (1957) 220–231.

133 A similar weakening of the Ionian element by the reduction of Ionian tribes to *chiliastyes* can be seen in Samos: see note 128 above. On the decadic arrangement of *chiliastyes* and *hekatostyes,* 'thousands' and 'hundreds' see Roebuck, *TAPA* 92 (1961) 503–505.

134 *Iliad* 2.362–363. See also A. Andrewes, *Hermes* 89 (1961) 130–132.

135 Tyrtaeus F 1, 51 Diehl.
136 L. H. Jeffery, *ABSA* 51 (1956) 157 ff. See also W. G. Forrest, *ABSA* 55 (1960) 187–189.
137 As Beloch suggested (*Gr. Gesch.* 1.2².100).
138 Sakellariou 411–412.
139 Bilabel 215.
140 Bilabel 244.
141 Schwyzer p. 337. Buck 143.
142 *Inschriften von Priene* No. 64.
143 1.142.3–4.
144 Cassola (246–256) indeed has held that the Ionian tribes originated in Asia Minor and that they were tranferred thence to Attica: but apart from conflicting with the tradition this view fails to explain the absence of the Boreis and Oenopes from Attica.
145 Cf. J. Chadwick, *CAH*², Vol. 2, Ch. 39, 12 and contrast L. R. Palmer, *The Interpretation of Mycenaean Greek Texts* (Oxford 1963) 60–64.
146 Of all Greek dialects Attic and Ionic are more closely linked than any others except Arcadian and Cypriot. The latter pair are historical survivors of a tongue spoken in Peloponnese in the Mycenaean age before the Dorian invasion (Buck 7): similarly Attic-Ionic is a descendant of a tongue (not demonstrably identical with the ancestor of Arcado-Cypriote) spoken in Peloponnese and central Greece in Mycenaean times. The Mycenaean texts may record a dialect closer to Proto-Arcado-Cypriote than to Proto-Ionic: see Palmer, *op. cit.* 64.
147 When did the change $\bar{a} > \eta$ occur? The Ionian name of the Medes $M\hat{\eta}\delta o\iota$, who called themselves Māda does not help, because we do not know when the Ionians first heard of that people. Nor can we be sure how an Ionian would have represented the ā of Māda. Ionic lost the digamma later than the shift from $\bar{a}$ to η, for original *$\kappa o\rho F a$ became *$\kappa o\rho F\eta$ before dividing into Attic $\kappa o\rho\eta$ and Ionic $\kappa o\nu\rho\eta$. Though the loss of digamma in Ionic is almost certainly post-Mycenaean, we cannot be sure that Ionians already in the Mycenaean age did not say *$\kappa o\rho F\eta$. Compare, however, E. Risch, *MH* 12 (1955) 61 ff.
148 Buck 53. In Naxos, Andros, Ceos, and Amorgos some early inscriptions distinguish between original ē (written E) and ē developed from ā (written H), but this proves nothing about the time at which ā changed to ē. The peculiar features of Naxian are well illustrated by Nicandre's dedication: Jeffery 291.
149 Buck 69–70.
150 Buck 143.
151 Note however that though Herodotus held Ionians to have lived in those parts in prehistoric times he has nothing to say about the *dialect* of the Ionians outside Asiatic Ionia: see Chadwick, *CAH*², Vol. 2, Ch. 39, 12. A survival of the Ionian name in northern Peloponnese may perhaps be seen in the name of the river Iaōn (Dionys. Perieg. 416). The Boeotian Hesiod dated by the Ionian

month Lenaion (*Opera* 504), but this may be due to Eretrian influence rather than a survival of a primitive Ionian calendar in central Greece. The original name of Ionia *'ΙαϜονια may be Asianic in form. Compare *ΛυκαϜονια, *ΚαταϜονια. See also A. Goetze, *Language* 30 (1954) 352 and cf. Cassola 292–295.

Chapter III. AEOLIAN AND MAGNESIAN SETTLEMENTS

1 Desborough (1) 81, 217–218.
2 J. M. Cook, *ABSA* 53–54 (1958/9) 10.
3 Reported by Akurgal. See J. M. Cook, *AR* 1960, 41.
4 *Odyssey* 17, 133–135.
5 Line 37. See also J. M. Cook, *CAH²*, Vol. 2, Ch. 38, 6.
6 Strabo (582) says that Orestes began the Aeolian migration. His son Penthilus brought the migrants overland as far as Thrace. Archelaus, son of Penthilus, led them over to the neighbourhood of Cyzicus and Dascylium. Under Gras, son of Archelaus, they occupied Lesbos. There is no archaeological evidence for the strange story of the migration through Thrace, but the genealogy of the descendants of Penthilus may be genuine. It is perhaps taken from the *Aeolica* of Hellanicus of Lesbos (Cf. *FGrHist* 4 F 32).
7 Strabo 402. Some of the Aeolians led by Penthilus stayed in Euboea: Strabo 447.
8 See note 6 above.
9 Strabo 402. See also Wade-Gery *Poet* 57, 66.
10 Thucydides 3.2.3.
11 Strabo 582, 621. For Locrians in Canae see Strabo 615.
12 Aristotle F 611, 37 Rose. Pollux 9.83.
13 *Homeri Vita Herodotea* p. 193, 18–19. Allen.
14 *Vita Herodotea* p. 217, 540–547. Allen.
15 1.149.1.
16 For Akurgal's soundings here see J. M. Cook, *AR* 1960, 32.
17 1.149.1.
18 Herodotus 1.149.2.
19 *FHG* 2.216.
20 Herodotus 1.151.2.
21 Pliny, *NH* 5.139. Cf. Cook, *CAH²*, Vol. 2, Ch. 38, 4–5.
22 It may have lain near Thermi on the east coast where there was a prehistoric settlement: Cook, *loc. cit.*
23 Steph. Byz. s.v. Τένεδος.
24 Diegesis to Callimachus F 91 Pf.
25 Pindar, *Nemean* 11.33 ff. Hellanicus 4 F 32.
26 e.g. Strabo 647.
27 Hesiod F 5 Rzach.
28 *Homeri Vita Herodotea* p. 193, 5. Allen.
29 Anacreon F 3 Page.
30 Cf. *FGrHist* 482 F 3, Strabo 636, and G. R. Morrow, *Plato's Cretan City* (Princeton 1960) 30–31.

31 Zenobius 3.88. O. Kern, *Die Inschriften von Magnesia am Maeander* (Berlin 1900) ix. cf. Wilamowitz, *Hermes* 30 (1895) 184 n. 3.
32 Parthenius, *Erot.* 5.
33 Buck 11 and 149 ff.
34 Herodotus 7.176.4. Thucydides 1.12.
35 Cf. Desborough (2) 137 f.
36 L. Robert, *Hellenica* I (1940) 68.
37 Attested in Kyme, Mytilene, Pergamum, Scepsis: *RE* 10.2 (1919) 1577.

Chapter IV. IONIAN EPIC POETRY

1   C. M. Bowra, *Tradition and Design in the Iliad* (Oxford 1950) 266.
2   *Iliad* 2.459–463. Perhaps he saw them on a visit to Ephesus for the festival of the Ephesia (Wade-Gery *Poet* 62). Asia proper was inland from Ephesus near Sardis, where there was a tribe Asias (Herodotus 4.45.3). Here was the centre of the old confederacy of Aššuwa. For the name Asia see Bossert, *Asia* (İstanbul 1946). Homer's simile perhaps alludes to augury: for an Ephesian sacred law of the sixth century BC shows that bird flight was interpreted there. See F. Sokolowski, *Lois sacrées de l'Asie Mineure* (Paris 1955) No. 30.
3   *Iliad* 24.614–617.
4   *Iliad* 2.145.
5   Cf. C. M. Bowra, *JHS* 80 (1960) 22–23.
6   *Iliad* 13.11–14.
7   *Iliad* 4.141–145.
8   *Iliad* 9.4–7.
9   F 279 Bowra.
10 Alcidamas ap. Aristot. *Rhet.* 2.23.(1398b).
11 Acusilaus 2 F 2.
12 Ephorus 70 F 103.
13 The name is found in Thessaly in its Aeolic form: T. W. Allen, *Homer. The Origins and the Transmission* (Oxford 1924) 49.
14 Cf. Jeffery 19–21.
15 For the date see Boardman, *JHS* 82 (1962) 197.
16 2.53.2.
17 F 265 Rzach.
18 *Opera* 654–657.
19 Plutarch, *Moralia* 153 F. On the text see G. S. Kirk, *CQ* 44 (1950) 150 n. 1.
20 Pausanias 9.9.5 (with Sylburg's Καλλῖνος for Καλαῖνος).
21 Compare Herodotus 4.32.
22 Plutarch, *Romulus* 12.
23 Schol. Aristoph. *Peace* 1270. See J. U. Powell, *Collectanea Alexandrina* (Oxford 1925) 248.
24 *PdP* 14 (1959) 282–283.
25 *FGrHist* 443 F 2.
26 *Homeri Opera*, Vol. 5, pp. 105, 107 and 126, ed. Allen.

27 Clement of Alexandria, *Strom.* 1.21 (1445). See also Allen, *Homer. The Origins and the Transmission* (Oxford 1924) 63.
28 *Homeri Opera*, Vol. 5, p. 106–107. Allen.
29 M. Ervin, Ἀρχαιολογικὸν Δελτίον 18 (1963) 37–75.
30 *Homeri Vita Herodotea c.* 15–16. Schol. Eur. *Troad.* 822.
31 *Homeri Opera*, Vol. 5, p. 128 Allen.
32 Aristotle ap. Diog. Laert. 2.46 (Vol. 1.76 Long).
33 F 186 and 190 Rzach.
34 Porphyry, *Vita Pythagorea* 1 and 10. Iamblichus, *Vit. Pyth.* 11.
35 Suda s.v. Κρεώφυλος.
36 Plutarch, *Lycurgus* 4.
37 Hom. *Hymn to Apollo*, lines 147 ff.
38 Pausanias 4.33.2. See also C. M. Bowra, *CQ* 13 (1963) 145–153.
39 *Iliad* 20.404.
40 On this lay see F. Bölte, *RM* 83 (1934) 319–347.
41 *Homeri Vita Herodotea*, lines 402 ff and 421 Allen.
42 J. B. Bury, *The Ancient Greek Historians* (Dover ed. 1958) 2–8.
43 T. W. Allen, *Homeri Opera*, Vol. 5, p. 156. The verses are from the *Margites* a poem in hexameters and iambics about a ninny. The poem is already called Homer's by Archilochus. For a new fragment of the Margites see *P.Oxy.* 2309.
44 See R. Jakobson, *Oxford Slavonic Papers* 3 (1952) 21–66 and C. Watkins, *Celtica* 6 (1963) 194–249.
45 Th. Bergk, *Opuscula Philologica* 2 (Halle 1886) 392–408, esp. 404–405.
46 *Works and Days* 694.
47 Zenobius 3.36.
48 *Odyssey* 12.70.
49 G. S. Kirk, *The Songs of Homer* (Cambridge 1962) 114.
50 The oral, formulaic, nature of the Homeric hexameter was first proved by Milman Parry. See especially *Les formules et la métrique d'Homère* (Paris 1928), *L'épithète traditionnelle dans Homère* (Paris 1928), and his articles in *HSCP* 41 (1930) 73–147 and 43 (1932) 1–50.
51 F 7 Diehl.
52 Still well worth reading is Io. Valentinii Franckii, *Callinus, sive quaestionis de origine carminis elegiaci tractatio critica* (Altonae et Lipsiae 1816). See also the evocative pages of Freya Stark, *Ionia. A Quest* (1954) 85–86.
53 Suda s.v. ἐλεγείνειν.
54 Strabo 578. For a double flute of Phrygian type and a seven-stringed lyre in a group of statues at Boğazköy see K. Bittel, *NDA* 114–118.
55 Suda s.v. ἔλεγος.
56 Herodotus 7.73.
57 Kinkel, *Epicorum Graecorum Fragmenta* I. 196–198. See also Notopoulos, *Hesperia* 29 (1960) 194.
58 *Homeri Opera*, Vol. 5, p. 108 Allen.

59 Pausanias 4.33.2.
60 Tatian, *in Graecos* 31.
61 The ancient evidence for the Pisistratean recension is collected by T. W. Allen, *Homer. The Origins and the Transmission* 226–238.

Chapter V. EARLY WARS AND FEUDS OF THE ASIATIC IONIANS

1 J. M. Cook, *ABSA* 53–54 (1958–1959) 1 ff.
2 *Iliad* 18.218–220.
3 Aelius Aristides 15.373. See also M. P. Nilsson, *RM* 60 (1905) 161 f and J. Boardman, *JHS* 78 (1958) 7.
4 Herodotus 1.150 with 1.143.3.
5 Mimnermus F 12, 6 Diehl. The poet is correctly claimed for Smyrna by J. M. Cook, *ABSA* 53–54 (1958–1959) 27–28. See also F. Jacoby, *Hermes* 53 (1918) 268 ff.
6 Pausanias 5.8.7. The Smyrnaean poet Magnes was a contemporary of Gyges (Nicolas of Damascus 90 F 62): since his name is more likely to have been given to an Aeolian than to an Ionian, there may still have been Aeolians in Smyrna about 700 BC or a little later.
7 *De Architectura* 4.1.3–5.
8 J. M. Cook, *AR* 1960, 47. G. Kleiner, *NDA* 172–180. See also *Gnomon* 31 (1959) 702–703
9 Hiller v. Gaertringen, *Inschriften von Priene* (Berlin 1906) No. 37, 55 ff, 101 ff and p. 209, No. 500.
10 *FGrHist* No. 535.
11 *Inschr. v. Priene* 37. *FGrHist* 491 F 1. Anaea had been Samian at the time of the Ionian migration: Pausanias 7.4.3. The town of Mycale itself (Steph. Byz. s.v. Μυκάλη) is not named in the exchanges. Priene once won Mycale from Miletus by appealing to Homer's Trojan Catalogue: Schol. Hom. B494 [Vol. 3, p. 137, Dindorf].
12 On the Meliac war see especially Wilamowitz, *Kleine Schriften* 5.1.128 ff, Wade-Gery *Poet* 63–64, and Roebuck, *CP* 50 (1955) 32–33.
13 Hippias of Erythrae 421 F 1.
14 Amphiclus is perhaps a descendant of the great-grandfather of King Hector: Pausanias 7.4.9. The name of Polytecnus recurs in a Chian tribal name: Forrest, *ABSA* 55 (1960) 178–179. Neleid names such as Pisistratus, Neleus, and Melanthus in Chiot inscriptions suggest the presence of Neleids in the island, as Mr W. G. Forrest points out to me.
15 Aristotle, *Politics* 1305 b 18–22.
16 Polyaenus 8.66. Plutarch, *De Mul. Virt.* 3.
17 Herodotus 1.18.3.
18 Valerius Maximus 1.5. For early Ionian sibyls see *GRBS* 2 (1959) 95.
19 Parthenius, *Erot.* 14. Antheus has the same name as, and was a descendant of, Anthes who brought over the Dymainian tribe of Dorians from Troizen to Halicarnassus (Callimachus F 703 Pf.).
20 Aristaenetus, *Epp.* 1.15.

21 Polyaenus 8.35. Diog. Laert. 1.32 and Diodorus 9.3.2 mention a war between Cos and Miletus: this too cannot be dated closely.
22 Polybius 16.12. See also E. L. Hicks, *JHS* 8 (1887) 83–84.
23 Tod 25.
24 26 F 1, xliv.
25 90 F 52–53.
26 With this *Archon* in Assessus compare the *Archos* in Teichioussa, Chares (Jeffery 334). The Milesians evidently had regular officials stationed in outlying parts of their territory.
27 Tottes perhaps went on to Chios, where there was a clan called Totteidae: W. G. Forrest, *ABSA* 55 (1960) 174 f.
28 90 F 53.
29 For the (re-)expulsion of the Neleidae in the fifth century see Barron, *JHS* 82 (1962) 3. Cf. Glotz, *Comptes Rendus de l'Acad. des Inscr.* 1906, 511 ff. There seems to be no special reason to think that the name Epimenes has anything to do with the Milesian officials called Epimēnioi, on whom see Tod 35.
30 For the date see Forrest, *Historia* 6 (1957) 160 ff. For a different view: E. Will, *Korinthiaka* (Paris 1955) 391 ff and cf. F. Geyer, *Topographie und Geschichte der Insel Euboia* I (Berlin 1903) 24–27.
31 Thucydides 1.15.3. For an early war of Chalkis against most of Boeotia see Theopompus 115 F 212. It is not clear that this is part of the Lelantine war, however.
32 5.99.
33 Herodotus 3.47.
34 Thucydides 1.13.3.
35 Herodotus 1.18. Erythrae's early naval interests are recalled by the story that biremes were invented there: Damastes 5 F 6.
36 For the overland route from Urarṭu through central Anatolia via Bogazköy, Ancyra, Gordion, and the Hermus valley to the Aegean coast see J. M. Birmingham, *AS* 11 (1961) 183–195. The route was much travelled during the flourishing of Phrygian power in the half century before the Cimmerian invasion of Phrygia, *c.* 740–696. After that it became less important. See also *GRBS* 2 (1959) 94–95. R. S. Young (*Proceedings of the American Philosophical Society* 107 (1963) 362–364) suggests that the Phrygians may have transmitted the Phoenician alphabet to the Greeks and created the vowels. An eighth century emigrant from Kyme was Hesiod's father, who was driven out by poverty to Ascra in Boeotia: *Opera* 633–640. Cf. Ephorus 70 F 100.
37 Aristotle F 611, 37 Rose. Pollux 9.83. For a tradition of Homer's stay in Kyme with the parents-in-law of Midas see *Homeri Vita Herodotea*, lines 130–140 Allen.
38 Birmingham, *AS* 11 (1961) 168–190 gives a good bibliography. Add now Boardman, *Anatolia* 6 (1961) 179–189 for Ionian adaptation of Phrygian bronze belts.
39 Nicolas of Damascus 90 F 44.
40 G. M. A. Hanfmann, *BASOR* 154 (1959) 29–30.

41 Nicolas of Damascus 90 F 47. Cf. Herodotus 1.12.2.
42 Nicolas 90 F 47 (10). Herodotus 1.13.
43 Plutarch, *Greek Questions* 45.
44 Cf. Bilabel 209–210. L. Robert, *Rev. de Phil.* 10³ (1936) 163.
45 Nicolas of Damascus 90 F 62.
46 Herodotus 1.14.4. See also notes 54 and 55 below.
47 F 13 Diehl. See also Pausanias 9.29.4. J. M. Cook, *ABSA* 53–54 (1958–1959) 28.
48 Hence the proverb τὸν Κολοφῶν' ἐπέθηκεν, said of putting an end to any business: Strabo 643.
49 Strabo 264. Dunbabin, *Western Greeks* 34.
50 F 3 Diehl. See also C. M. Bowra, *CQ* 35 (1941) 119–126. One person who may have incurred the censure of Xenophanes was the poet Theodorus. He wrote luxurious songs which were still sung by the women at Colophon in Aristotle's time, and he met a violent death (Athenaeus 618EF. Pollux 4.55).
51 Plutarch, *De Musica* 29.
52 Pausanias 1.14.4. Plut. *De Musica* 5–6.
53 Alcman F 145 Page.
54 The use of ἐς in Herodotus 1.14.4. suggests that Gyges may have *entered* Smyrna and Miletus. See F. Jacoby, *Hermes* 53 (1918) 296.
55 For destruction at Miletus about this time see G. Kleiner ap. Hanfmann, *BASOR* 162 (1961) 12 n. 8 and J. M. Cook, *AR* 1960, 49 for a destruction of the same period at Smyrna. These destructions are more likely to have been the work of Gyges than of the Cimmerians, for Herodotus says that the Ionian cities were raided but not ruined by the Cimmerians (1.12). Kalabaktepe was originally unfortified, but became a walled place of refuge about 650. The wall was perhaps renewed after 546 BC. Cf. A. von Gerkan, *Milet* 1.8 (Berlin 1925) 116–117.
56 Strabo 590. See also W. Leaf, *Strabo on the Troad* (Cambridge 1923) 125–126.
57 Boardman 249.
58 Steph. Byz. s.v. Τρῆρος. Arrian 156 F 27.
59 Herodotus 4.11–12.
60 Strabo 61. Kobos is perhaps the subject of Callinus F 4 Diehl.
61 Callisthenes 124 F 29.
62 Herodotus 4.12.3.
63 Lehmann-Haupt, *RE* 11.1 (1921) 410–411. Kaletsch, *Historia* 7 (1958) 31. The name of their leader in the battle with the Assyrians, Teušpa, looks Iranian. Cf. Teispes, Herodotus 7.11.2.
64 Herodotus 4.12.2. Ps.-Scymnus 947 ff. Bilabel 33. Herodotus' words suggest that there were no Greeks in Sinope when the Cimmerians settled on the Chersonese. Habrondes therefore may have found the barbarians already in occupation when he arrived with his settlers. Cf. Grote, 4.43.
65 Arrian 156 F 60 and 76.
66 Strabo 61. This happened in 696 BC according to Jerome, in 676

according to Africanus. The earlier date is preferred by the excavators at Gordion (R. S. Young, *AJA* 64 (1960) 243), the later by A. Akurgal, *Phrygische Kunst* (Ankara 1955) 123–125.

67 Steph. Byz. s.v. Συασσός.

68 L. Hartman, *JNES* 21 (1962) 25. Kaletsch, *Historia* 7 (1958) 29 on Herodotus 2.152. See also Diodorus 1.66.12. Hanfmann, *BASOR* 166 (1962) 10–11 for evidence of Carians in Sardis–two graffiti.

69 Callisthenes 124 F 29. Herodotus 1.15. For signs of destruction in Sardis in the mid-seventh century see Hanfmann, *BASOR* 162 (1961) 12–13. For the chronology of the reigns of Gyges and Ardys see H. Kaletsch, *Historia* 7 (1958) 25–30.

70 Lygdamis may be a Greek rendering of a barbarian name: or Dugdamme may be an Assyrian rendering of a Greek or Anatolian name. A Lygdamis is found in Caria (Tod 25). Wilamowitz thought that Lygdamis the leader of the Cimmerians was a Carian (*Kleine Schriften* V.1, 134 n.2.).

71 1.6.3.

72 Callimachus, *Hymn* 3.251–258.

73 Rescript of Lysimachus, *Inschriften von Priene* p. 209, No. 500.

74 F 19 Diehl (Strabo 647).

75 Theognis 603. In 1103–1104 the poet perhaps follows Callinus, who had seen Gyges attack Colophon, Smyrna and Magnesia ad Sipylum: Jacoby, *CQ* 35 (1941) 106 n. 3.

76 F 3 Diehl.

77 F 2 Diehl.

78 Athenaeus (525 C) states that the Magnesians were taken by the Ephesians, Strabo (647) that Magnesia was occupied by the Milesians [Cf. J. M. Cook, *JHS* 79 (1959) 25 n. 25] 'in the following year'. It is impossible to choose between these versions.

79 R. C. Thompson, *Liverpool Annals* 20 (1933) 107 ff. Šandakšatra: Lehmann-Haupt, *RE* 11.1 (1921) 417 f.

80 Aristotle F 478 Rose (Steph. Byz. s.v. Ἄντανδρος). Cf. Pliny, *NH* 5.123.

81 Herodotus 1.16.2. Kaletsch, *Historia* (1958) 37.

Chapter VI. THE FIRST IONIAN COLONIES

1 Note however that Smyrna was not allowed to contribute to the Panionion (Herodotus 1.143.3) and some places, such as Hairai, were not large enough to qualify for membership or were subordinated to larger neighbours who were members. Hairai at one time autonomous: cf. Thucydides 8.19. The process of subordinating smaller cities to larger had begun by 700 as the provisions of the treaty at the end of the Meliac War show (*Inschriften von Priene* 37).

2 Strabo 448.

3 Cf. Boardman 66.

4 Strabo 448.

5   Boardman 67.
6   Jeffery 11–12. Dunbabin 59–61.
7   Jeffery 68.
8   Boardman 63 ff.
9   Strabo 247. Livy 8.22.
10 Strabo 243. Ps.-Scymnus 238–239. Dunbabin, *The Western Greeks* (Oxford 1948) 6–7.
11 Strabo 247.
12 Plutarch, *Greek Questions* 11.
13 Thucydides 6.3.1–2. Strabo 267. Ps.-Scymnus 273–274.
14 Hellanicus 4 F 82.
15 Boardman 183.
16 Thucydides 6.3.3.
17 Thucydides 6.4.5.
18 Antiochus 555 F 9.
19 Dunbabin, *Western Greeks* 13.
20 Ps.-Scylax 111. Bilabel 246.
21 Steph. Byz. s.v. Κύβος [Hecataeus 1 F 343]. See also H. Treidler, *Historia* 7 (1958) 263.
22 Steph. Byz. s.v. Ἀμοργός.
23 G. M. A. Richter, *Archaic Greek Art* (New York 1949) 26–28.
24 Boardman 217.
25 Aristotle ap. Plut. *Mor.* 761a.
26 Thucydides 4.110.1. Diodorus 12.68.
27 Aristotle, *Politics* 1303 b2, 1306 a2.
28 Thucydides 4.123.1.
29 Plutarch, *Greek Questions* 11. Others of the Corcyrean Eretrians settled at Oricus on the mainland opposite the island. See Beaumont, *JHS* 56 (1936) 165. Cf. Callimachus F 12 Pf.
30 Gallet de Santerre 33–35.
31 4.35.4.
32 4.33.4.
33 4.33.1–2. The offerings were ears of wheat according to Callimachus, *In Delum* 283–284.
34 Paus. 1.31.2.
35 Athenaeus 234 EF. See also Gallet de Santerre 286.
36 4.33.3. Περφερέτας [*Liverpool Annals* 3, 155] a title of Zeus in Thessaly and Ὑπερβερεταῖος a Macedonian month suggest that there were ties between the Perpherees, the Hyperborean maidens and northern Greece. Cf. Laidlaw 42.
37 Paus. 9.27.2.
38 4.35.3.
39 Wilamowitz, *Apollo* (Oxford 1908) 31. W. H. Buckler, *JHS* 55 (1935) 78.
40 *Odyssey* 6.162.
41 Theog. 1.5–10.
42 Himerius, *Or.* 18.1.
43 Lines 81–82 and 87. Laidlaw 18–19. Aristotle knew of an oracle of

Glaucus in Delos: *FHG* 2.154. For the oracle of the marine goddess
Brizo see Semus of Delos 396 F 4.

44 Of the Ionian tribes only Argadeis are attested in the island:
Szanto, *SBWien* 144 (1901) 47. Cassola 249.

45 F 78 Bowra.

46 Plutarch, *Greek Questions* 30.

47 Clinton, *Fasti Hellenici* 1.196.

48 Thucydides 4.88.2.

49 Thucydides 4.103.3. Steph. Byz. s.v. Ἄργιλος says that the name
means 'mouse' in Thracian, a mouse having been seen when the
foundations of the city were being laid. On Andros and her colonies
Th. Sauciuc, *Andros, Sonderschriften des Österr. arch. Inst.* (1914)
may be read with profit.

50 L. Ghali-Kahil, *Études thasiennes* 7, *La Céramique grecque* (Paris
1960) 18 and 140. For pottery of the first half of the seventh century
BC in Thasos see P. Bernard, *BCH* 88 (1964) 77–146.

51 Oenomaus of Gadara ap. Euseb. *P.E.* 6.7. Steph. Byz. s.v. Θάσος
(No. 230 Parke/Wormell).

52 Antimachus F 67. Wyss. Cf. Archilochus F 119 Diehl.

53 Pausanias 10.28.3.

54 Aelian, *VH* 10.13.

55 Parke/Wormell No. 231. See also *SEG* 15.517, A Col. 2. 50–52.

56 F 22 Diehl. Another possible mention of tyranny by Archilochus:
P.Oxy. 2310 F 1.i.20.

57 F 19 Diehl.

58 Arist. *Rhet.* 3.17 1418b28 (Archilochus F 74 Diehl). See also
P.Oxy. 2313.F 1(a).

59 Cf. F. Jacoby, *CQ* 35 (1941) 97 ff.

60 Oppolzer, *Canon of Eclipses* No. 1304. Others prefer to identify the
so-called 'eclipse of Archilochus' with that of 6 April 648 (Oppolzer
No. 1328).

61 *SEG* 15.517, A Col. 2. 22–43. For the excavation of the inscription
see the fine article of Kontoleon, *AE* 1952, 32–95.

62 F 53 Diehl.

63 Plutarch, *aud. poet.* 12.33ab. [Archilochus F 10 Diehl].

64 *SEG* 15.517, A Col. 3. H. W. Parke, *CQ* 8 (1958) 90–94.

65 *FGrHist* No. 502. Archilochus F 51 Diehl. Hiller v. Gaertringen,
IG XII.5. (1902) p. 445, and *ibid* part 2 (1909) p. 315.

66 e.g. Leophilus. F 70 Diehl. Cf. Pouilloux 32.

67 See also F 117 Diehl.

68 F 24 Diehl. Cf. *P.Oxy.* 2312 F 4(a), 3 and S. Luria, *Philologus* 105
(1961) 180.

69 F 95 Diehl.

70 F 88 Diehl.

71 F 71 Diehl.

72 Oenomaus ap. Euseb. *P.E.* 5.31 (Parke/Wormell No. 232).

73 F 6 Diehl.

74 F 51, 1A, 46 and 58–59.

75 F 51, 1A, 46–51. See also *GRBS* 5 (1964) 24.
76 F. Gschnitzer, *Abhängige Orte im Griechische Altertum* (Munich 1958) 27–31.
77 Herodotus 6.46.2 and 6.47.2. He states (6.47.1) that he had seen mines in Thasos worked by the Phoenicians long before. There is no evidence in Archilochus for Phoenicians in Thasos. Semitic names are found in the island by the fifth century BC, however: Pouilloux 20.
78 Philochorus 328 F 43. Cf. Archilochus F 2 Diehl for the Ismaric wine of Maroneia he had to drink on active service. Callimachus F 104 also alludes to a battle of the Parians against the Thracians.
79 Plutarch, *Inst.Lac.* 34, 239b.
80 F 15 Diehl.
81 F 18 Diehl (Athenaeus 523 D).
82 F 40 Diehl.
83 F 3 Diehl.
84 F 1 Diehl.
85 Galen, *Protr.* 23. Plutarch, *Mor.* 560D. Parke/Wormell, Nos. 4 and 5.
86 Heraclides, *Pol.* 8, states that Calondas said to Apollo in his defence ἀλλὰ καθαρός εἰμι, ἄναξ. ἐν χειρῶν γὰρ νόμῳ ἔκτεινα. 'I killed him in action.'
87 Jeffery 300–301.
88 Boardman 239. Cf. G. M. A. Richter, *Archaic Greek Art* (New York 1949) 26.
89 *ABSA* 46 (1951) 201 line 7. For the date of the colony see Boardman 239.
90 Dionysius Byz. *Anaplus Bosp. Thracii* F 30. *GGM* 2.37.
91 Strabo 331, F 52.
92 Strabo 319. See also A. R. Burn, *The Lyric Age of Greece* (London 1960) 97.
93 Herodotus 1.168. Delphi is said to have predicted the failure: Parke/Wormell No. 48.
94 Boardman, *CR* 14 (1962) 82.
95 Ps.-Scymnus 709. Roebuck 109.
96 Eustathius ad. Dion. Per. 513.
97 Ps.-Scymnus 706. Some Aeolians from Alopeconnesus also went to Aenus: Strabo 331, F 52.
98 Herodotus 5.122.2. For the coast of the Troad see J. M. Cook, *The Greeks in Ionia and the East* (London 1962) 27–28.
99 *Homeri Vita Herodotea*, lines 281–287 (Allen).
100 W. Leaf, *Anatolian Studies Ramsay* (Manchester 1923) 267–281.
101 *Iliad* 20. 307–308. See also Strabo 608 and F. Jacoby, *Hermes* 68 (1933) 42.
102 Strabo 607 and 635. Bilabel 51–53.
103 Boardman, *JHS* 82 (1962) 197. To the Aeolians at Troy the Locrians sent an annual tribute of two maidens to atone for the impiety to Athena Ilias of Locrian Ajax during the sack of Troy:

this strange custom had begun by the time of the foundation of
Epizephyrian Locri in Italy (*c.* 673 BC): Aristotle ap. Polybius 12.5.
See also W. Leaf, *Troy* (London 1912) 134.

104 Hellanicus 4 F 160. Myrsilus 477 F 17.

105 W. Leaf, *Strabo on the Troad* (Cambridge 1923) 289–300. L. Robert,
Hellenica 4 (1948) 70 and n. 8.

Chapter VII. COLONIES OF THE EASTERN IONIANS

1 Herodotus 6.20. See also J. M. Cook, *ABSA* 56 (1961) 90–101.

2 Anaximenes of Lampsacus 72 F 26. See also B. Haussoullier, *Rev.
de Phil.* 26 (1902) 125–143. J. L. Benson, *Ancient Leros* (Durham,
N.C. 1963).

3 L. Robert, *Hellenica* 1.114–115.

4 Suda s.v. Σιμωνίδης. Steph. Byz. s.v. 'Αμοργός.

5 F 7 Diehl. Cf. Phocylides F 2.

6 *FGrHist* 534 T 1.

7 Mela 1.77.

8 Boardman 89.

9 Berosus 680 F 7c (31). Abydenus 685 F 5. See also A. R. Burn, *The
Lyric Age of Greece* 51. Roebuck 64–65. The Assyrians at this period
called Greeks, including those in Tarsus, Iamani or Iadna 'Ionians'
[H. Bengston, *Philologus* 92 (1937) 148–155], a tradition which has
continued to this day. Thus Turks now call Greece Yunanistan. For
Greek imports to Tarsus before the Assyrian attack in 698 see
Hanfmann in Goldman, *Tarsus* III (Princeton 1963) esp. 129–130.
For synchronisms of Tarsus and Al Mina see Boardman 69–70.

10 Strabo 667.

11 J. Garstang, *Prehistoric Mersin* (Oxford 1953) 253–259.

12 K. Lehmann, *Samothrace*² (New York 1960) 13.

13 Herodotus 8.90.

14 Apollodorus 244 F 178a, who however dates the Samian settlement
in 976/5 BC. The discovery of an Aeolian inscription in the island
[P. M. Fraser, *Samothrace. The Inscriptions on Stone* (New York
1960) 21] does not invalidate the tradition that the Greek colonists
were Samians.

15 F 63 Rzach, *Theogony* 340.

16 *Homeri Opera* 5 p. 106, 14–15 Allen.

17 F 8 and 17 Kinkel. See also C. M. Bowra, *Hermes* 73 (1938) 216–217
and A. J. Graham, *BICS* 5 (1958) 35–36.

18 Boardman, *AR* 1963, 37 n. 11.

19 339.

20 Boardman 247. Y. Boysal, *AA* 1959, 8–20.

21 See J. M. Cook, *AR* 1960, 34. A. Akurgal, *Anatolia* 1 (1956) 15 ff.

22 Cf. J. D. P. Bolton, *Aristeas of Proconnesus* (Oxford 1962) 131–132.

23 Strabo 635. Ps.-Scymnus 705.

24 Strabo 331 F 52. Ps.-Scymnus 698 f. For an amusing incident in a

war between the Greeks of Cardia and the Thracian Bisaltae see Charon of Lampsacus 262 F 1.

25 Pausanias 9.27.1. Strabo 588 mentions Parians here but their presence is doubtful: Forrest, *Historia* 6 (1957) 170 n. 1. Steph. Byz. s.v. Γραικός mentions an Aeolian settlement here.

26 Roebuck 113–114. For tunny fishing at Parium see L. Robert, *Hellenica* 8 (1950) 80–97 and 10 (1955) 272–274. Abydos won Sestos from the *Athenians*, in an obscure struggle, after appealing to Homer: Schol. Hom. B494 [Vol. 3, p. 137, Dindorf].

27 Etym. Mag. p. 436, 40. Bilabel 155.

28 Mela 2.24. Steph. Byz. s.v. Βισάνθη.

29 Strabo 331, F 56. Ps.-Scymnus 714–715.

30 Dei(l)ochus 471 F 3.

31 Charon of Lampsacus 262 F 7. (For Carian names with root *Mandr*- see A. Laumonier, *Les Cultes indigenes en Carie* (Paris 1958) 524–525. Many Ionians had them too: e.g. Anaximandros, the Samian engineer Mandrocles, Mandrolytus of Priene, a pupil of Thales [Crusius, *Philologus* 49 (1890) 677], and the clan in Paros οἱ ἀπὸ M[αν]δροθέμιος [*IG* XII.5.1027].) Polyaenus 6.42.

32 Ps.-Scymnus 949–950.

33 The inhabitants of this district were called Syrians or White Syrians by the Greeks, not Phrygians. The chief city was Pteria, which may be the same as Ḥattušaš [Herodotus 1.76.1. Steph. Byz. s.v. Πτέριον].

34 E.-M. Bossert, *MDOG* 94 (1963) 53–71.

35 Boardman, *AR* 1963, 51.

36 Ps.-Scymnus 947–948.

37 W. Leaf, *JHS* 36 (1916) 1–15.

38 Theopompus 115 F 389.

39 Boardman 109 f and 266–267.

40 Strabo 549.

41 Arrian, *Periplus* 14 (*GGM* 1.378).

42 Mela 1.108.

43 Strabo 497–498.

44 Boardman, *AR* 1963, 50.

45 4.13–16. See the delightful book of Bolton, note 22 *supra*.

46 Cf. Roebuck 112.

47 Bolton, *op. cit.* 131.

48 Herodotus 4.16.

49 Herodotus 4.13.

50 Bolton, *op. cit.* 180.

51 C. M. Bowra, *Greek Lyric Poetry*[2] 18 and 27. Alcman called them Ἀσσηδόνες or Ἐσσηδόνες: Steph. Byz. s.v. Ἰσσηδόνες.

52 Boardman 252.

53 Herodotus 4.17.1.

54 Boardman, *AR* 1963, 42–43.

55 E. H. Minns, *Scythians and Greeks* (1913) 563–566.

56 Boardman, *AR* 1963, 45.

57 *ATL* 1.496 f for discussion of the identification of Cercinitis.
58 Herodotus 2.33.4. Strabo 319 (perhaps from Demetrius of Callatis, *FGrHist* No. 85).
59 Ps.-Scymnus 765 f.
60 E. Condurachi, in *Griechische Stadte und Einheimische Volker des Schwarzmeergebiets* (Berlin 1961) 3. Boardman, *AR* 1963, 37.
61 Boardman 259.
62 Arrian, *Periplus* 31.
63 Ps.-Scymnus 730–733. Boardman, *AR* 1963, 34.
64 Boardman 256.
65 Ps.-Scymnus 748 f. Bilabel 15.
66 *FGrHist* 496 F 5.
67 Herodotus 6.21.1.
68 Herodotus 6.22.2–6.23.
69 Strabo 264.
70 Jeffery 286–287.
71 Strabo 264.
72 Strabo 654. See also Dunbabin, *Western Greeks* 34.
73 Athenaeus 523 C.
74 Mela 1.99. Steph. Byz. s.v. Μύρλεια.
75 Herodotus 4.152.
76 Pausanias 6.19.2.
77 Bilabel 240–243.
78 Boardman 224.
79 Athenaeus 576 A. See also Justin 43.3 and Plutarch, *Solon* 2. On the date of the founding of Massilia see L. Woodbury, *Phoenix* 15 (1961) 144 n. 34 on Thucydides 1.13.6.
80 Strabo 179.
81 Justin 43.4.1.
82 Strabo 182. See also M. R. Bloch, *Scientific American* 209.1 (1963) 93.
83 R. Joffroy, *Le Trésor de Vix* (Paris 1954).
84 F. Villard, *La Céramique grecque de Marseille* (Paris 1960) 154 ff.
85 Strabo 179. For survivals of Greek speech in S. France see W. von Wartburg, *Zeitschrift für Romanische Philologie* 68 (1953) 1–48.
86 Strabo 159–160. Boardman 225–226. Roebuck 95. Bilabel 243.
87 Ps.-Scymnus 205–207. Villard, *op. cit.* 72–73.
88 E. MacWhite, *ZCP* 25 (1956) 24–27 and T. F. O'Rahilly, *Early Irish History and Mythology* (Dublin 1946) 83–84.
89 Stesichorus F 7, Page.
90 Herodotus 1.163.
91 Though Tarshish may also mean Tarsus in the O.T.
92 Herodotus 1.165.2.
93 1.163.1. Herodotus also says that the Phocaeans explored Τυρσηνίη: but the pioneers in exploring the Etruscan coast were Euboeans. Perhaps the Etruscan settlements at the head of the Adriatic are meant here.
94 F. Jacoby, *RE* 6.1 (1907) 1509–1511. *FHG* 4.408–409.
95 Herodotus 2.154.

96 Strabo 801.
97 Boardman 138. Cf. R. M. Cook, *JHS* 57 (1937) 228.
98 2.178.2. See also C. Roebuck, *CP* 46 (1951) 212–220.
99 2.178.3.
100 Herodotus' words suggest that he–mistakenly–supposed the emporium to have been founded by Amasis, but this is not certain: he may only mean that there was some kind of reorganisation of Naucratis and some adjustment of relations between Greeks and Egyptians in the time of Amasis. The archaeological evidence does not show what reorganisation there may have been, if indeed there was any. Cf. Boardman 134.
101 Herodotus 2.159.3.
102 Jeffery 355.
103 Boardman 133.
104 Herodotus 2.163.1. 2.169.1.
105 Herodotus 2.154.3.
106 Herodotus 2.181.1.
107 Herodotus 2.182.1.
108 Herodotus 2.180.2.
109 Herodotus 2.182.1–2.
110 Herodotus 3.47.
111 Herodotus 2.182.2.
112 3.26.1. The Αἰσχριωνίη φυλή is not attested in Samos: possibly it was a γένος, not a tribe (Bilabel 176). The name Aeschrion is found in Samos: Athenaeus 335 C mentions an iambic poet of that name from the island.

Chapter VIII. IONIA IN THE TIME OF ALYATTES

1   Herodotus 1.15.
2   H. Kaletsch, *Historia* 7 (1958) 34–39 and 46–47.
3   Herodotus 1.17.1.
4   Nicolas of Damascus 90 F 63.
5   Pollux 9.83.
6   1.94.1.
7   See the fundamental articles of P. Jacobstahl, *JHS* 71 (1951) 85–95 and E. S. G. Robinson, *JHS* 71 (1951) 156–167. For a detailed discussion of some early Lydian and Ionian coins see E. S. G. Robinson, *Centennial Publication of the American Numismatic Society* (New York 1958) 585–594.
8   Herodotus 1.17.
9   Herodotus 1.18.1.
10 Herodotus 1.18.3.
11 Herodotus 1.19–22. On his recovery Alyattes also sent to Delphi a silver bowl with a stand made of welded iron, the work of Glaucus of Chios, who discovered the technique of welding: Herodotus 1.25.2. Pausanias 10.16.1–2.
12 Herodotus 3.48–49.

13 Herodotus 1.16.2. Nicolas of Damascus 90 F 64. For an incident in the war see [Dositheus] 290 F 5.
14 J. M. Cook, *ABSA* 53–54 (1958–1959) 23–27 and J. K. Anderson, *ibid.* 148.
15 Herodotus 1.93.2. For the pottery see v. Olfers, *Abh. Berl. Akad.* 1858, 539 ff. On the tomb: G. M. A. Hanfmann, *BASOR* 170 (1963) 52–57.
16 Eusebius dates the accession of Alyattes in 609, the Parian Marble (*FGrHist* 239 A 35) perhaps in 604. Herodotus with his long chronology dated it 71 years before the fall of Sardis to Cyrus, and so perhaps in 617 BC (1.25.1 with 1.86.1). Compare H. Strasburger, *Historia* 5 (1956) 139–140.
17 F 2 Diehl.
18 F 1 Diehl.
19 F 4 Diehl.
20 Athenaeus 597 A.
21 Hermesianax F 7, 35–37 (Powell).
22 Herodotus 1.16.2.
23 See R. M. Cook, 'Dogs in Battle', *Festschrift Rumpf* (Krefeld 1952) 38–42. Alyattes is said to have used dogs in his battles against the Cimmerians: Polyaenus 7.2.1 cf. 4.2.16, and L. W. Hunter, *Aeneas on Siegecraft* (Oxford 1927) 175.
24 Polyaenus 7.2. See also Heraclides, *FHG* 2.218 F 22. On the Colophonian ἱπποτρόφοι see L. Robert, *Rev. de Phil.* 10³ (1936) 164.
25 Herodotus 1.74.1.
26 Oppolzer, *Canon of Eclipses* No. 1489, which was total late in the day on the Halys frontier of Lydia.
27 Herodotus 1.74.3–4. Correct the Λαβύνητος of the MSS to Ναβύνη-τος (Nabun'aid). The Babylonian king at this time was in fact Nebuchadrezzar II. For the possibility that Nabun'aid or Nabonidus acted as emissary of Nebuchadrezzar II in the making of the treaty see R. P. Dougherty, *Nabonidus and Balshazzar* (New Haven 1929), and for Cilician interest in the affair D. J. Wiseman, *Chronicles of Chaldaean Kings* (British Museum 1961) 39. For a brief mention of war between Alyattes and Astyages see *P.Oxy.* 2506 F 98. Astyages may have become king before the time of the Halys treaty. Cicero (*De Div.* 1.49) indeed distinctly implies that the eclipse battle was fought in the reign of Astyages. See also the valuable discussion of Grote, Vol. 4, pp. 28–29 n. 2. E. Meyer, however [*RE* 2.2.1865] proposed to date the accession of Astyages in 584 BC. Cf. *GRBS* Vol. 6.
28 Aelian, *VH* 3.26. Polyaenus 6.50.
29 Baton of Sinope 268 F 3.
30 Herodotus 1.92.3.
31 Nicolas of Damascus 90 F 65.1.
32 For the payment of Lydian mercenaries see R. M. Cook, *Historia* 7 (1958) 261.
33 Nicolas 90 F 65.4 with Jacoby's commentary. Aelian, *VH* 4.27.

Pamphaes perhaps belonged to the pro-Lydian party of Priene in exile in Ephesus. Another member of the opposition in Priene was Salaros, said to have been a rival of Bias: Diog. Laert. 2.46.

34 Cf. Herodotus 1.92.2–4.

35 Diogenes Laertius 1.83.

36 *Politics* 1305 a 18.

37 Cf. Diogenes Laertius 1.100.

38 Frontinus, *Stratagems* 3.9.7.

39 *Greek Questions* 32. Cf. Dunham, *History of Miletus* 128–129.

40 Aeinautai are also found at Chalcis and Eretria: B. Petrakos, *BCH* 87 (1963) 545–547.

41 F 1 Diehl.

42 Gergithai, barbarians in the Troad: Herodotus 5.122.2 and 7.43.2 cf. Strabo 616. In the Aeolis: Strabo 616. Possibly Gergithai formed part of the suppressed native Anatolian population at Miletus, who had moved to the city from the countryside. Compare the Pedieis in the Magnesian and Prienian domain, who were still causing trouble to Priene in Hellenistic times: C. B. Welles, *Royal Correspondence in the Hellenistic Period* (New Haven 1934) 8 B 2–3 and p. 43.

43 Heraclides Ponticus ap. Athen. 524 A. This could perhaps refer to faction fighting of the mid-fifth century BC: but if so we miss a reference to Athenian intervention.

44 Herodotus 5.28.

45 F 7 Diehl.

46 F 12 Diehl.

47 Plutarch, *Greek Questions* 57.

48 Thucydides 8.21.

49 76 F 60.

50 The poet's date is uncertain. C. M. Bowra (*Hermes* 85 (1957) 391–401) places him in the fifth century BC. W. G. Forrest (*BCH* 80 (1956) 43 n. 3) argues for a connexion with Cleisthenes of Sicyon early in the sixth century [cf. F 11 Kinkel] and with the Sacred War against Cirrha [cf. F 5]. I incline to an earlier date than Bowra's because the formulaic character of the genealogical fragments suggests that Asius was working within the still vigorous oral tradition of epic [see F 1, 2, 8 and 10] and the atticisms of the fragment quoted by Douris may be due not to the poet but to faults in transmission of the text. See also F. Jacoby, *FGrHist.* III B Komm. Noten. p. 269 n. 8.

51 *Dithyrambs* 18, 2 (p. 65 Snell).

52 1.6.3.

53 Athenaeus 553 E.

54 Athenaeus 512 BC. See also Aristophanes, *Knights* 1321–1334.

55 E. Buschor, *Altsamische Standbilder* 1 (Berlin 1934) Plate 160.

56 *Hymn* 3.147.

57 Eratosthenes 241 F 11.

58 Buschor, *Altsamische Standbilder* 25 f. and Plates 86–89, 107. For

another such Samian *Kore*, dedicated by Mandrios to the nymphs
see *AA* 1964, 87–91.

59 L. H. Jeffery, *ABSA* 51 (1956) 157–167. Cf. J. H. Oliver, *AJP* 80
(1959) 296–301. S. Mazzarino, *Fra Oriente e Occidente* (Florence
1947) 233–241.

60 115 F 122 a.

61 M. I. Finley, *Historia* 8 (1959) 163–164.

62 By the Milesians according to Strabo 647. See J. M. Cook, *JHS* 79
(1959) 25 n. 25.

63 Zenobius 3.88.

64 Diogenes Laertius 1.117–118.

65 Diogenes Laertius 1.118.

66 Apollodorus 244 F 338 a (Ol. 59). See also Jacoby, *Abhandlungen zur
Griechischen Geschichtschreibung* (Leiden 1956) 108.

67 Phanodicus 397 F 4 b.

68 Demodocus F 6 Diehl. Hipponax F 73 Diehl.

69 Diogenes Laertius 1.83.

70 *Greek Questions* 20. *OGIS* 13 lines 22 f. See also W. R. Halliday, *The
Greek Questions of Plutarch* (Oxford 1928) 108. Valerius Maximus
7.2.3 implies that Bias and the Prienians were forced to abandon
their city on one occasion, perhaps after the Samian victory.

71 *Inschriften von Priene* No. 37, lines 105–107.

72 Phanodicus 397 F 4 b.

73 Diogenes Laertius 1.85.

74 1.170.

75 Diogenes Laertius 1.84 and 88.

76 22 B 39.

Chapter IX. AEOLIAN POETS AND STATESMEN

1 Hellanicus 4 F 85 ab.

2 C. M. Bowra, *Greek Lyric Poetry*[2] 9–10.

3 Compare Terpander F 5 Bergk.

4 *HSCP* 61 (1953) 16.

5 F 110 Bowra.

6 See F. Jacoby, *CQ* 35 (1941) 100 n. 1.

7 F 106 Lobel-Page.

8 F 76 Diehl.

9 Plutarch, *De Musica* 6.

10 Plutarch, *De Musica* 28.

11 F 1 Bergk.

12 1.23.

13 Herodotus 1.23–24. See also C. M. Bowra, *MH* 20 (1963) 121–134
on dolphin-dances, which, he suggests, may have been performed in
honour of Poseidon. Such dances would also have been appropriate
to Apollo Delphinius.

14 Suda s.v. Ἀρίων.

15 Herodotus 1.23. See also A. W. Pickard-Cambridge, *Dithyramb, Tragedy and Comedy* (²Oxford 1962) 97–101.

16 F 77 Diehl.

17 Compare Pickard-Cambridge, *Dithyramb Tragedy and Comedy*² 7-8

18 F 8 Bergk.

19 *Politics* 1311 b 26–30.

20 Diogenes Laertius 1.81.

21 617.

22 Diogenes Laertius 1.74. See also D. L. Page, *Sappho and Alcaeus* (Oxford 1955) 151–2. Cf. M. Treu, *Alkaios* (1952) 145.

23 Suda s.v. Πιττακός.

24 5.94–95. Apollodorus 244 F 27.

25 It had been fortified by Archaeanax of Mytilene: Strabo 599.

26 Herodotus 5.94.1.

27 Strabo 599–600. Diogenes Laertius 1.74.

28 Alcaeus Z 105 ab. Lobel-Page.

29 Eusebius. Armenian Version. p. 186 Karst. (607/6) Vers. Jerom. p. 173 Fotheringham (607/6–604/3). Phrynon may also have been the founder of the Athenian settlement at Elaious on Cape Helles in the Thracian Chersonese: Ps.-Scymnus 707–708. See also Wade-Gery, *Essays* 166 n. 2.

30 Jeffery 416, Nos. 43–44.

31 Alcaeus Z2.

32 Heraclitus, *Quaest. Hom.* 5 on Alcaeus Z2. Cf. Page, *Sappho and Alcaeus* 188.

33 Alcaeus V.1 i Lobel-Page.

34 Scholiast on Alcaeus E 3.

35 Scholiast on Alcaeus D 2 (a).

36 Alcaeus G 2.

37 L. Robert, *REA* 62 (1960) 285–315. Cf. M. Paraskeuaidis, *RE* 47 (1963) 1403–1420.

38 Alcaeus G 1.

39 A. Andrewes, *The Greek Tyrants* (1956) 93.

40 Alcaeus Z 8.

41 Alcaeus Z 27. Alcaeus also mentioned his brother Antimenidas in connexion with a 'Second Exile' and 'Action at the Bridge' [*P.Oxy.* 2506 F 98]; but we are not told where the bridge was, and the whole context of the fragment is very obscure. From *P.Oxy.* 2506 F 98 it appears that Alcaeus was once accused of bloodshed but protested that he was innocent.

42 Strabo 37.

43 *FGrHist.* 239 A 36.

44 Alcaeus D 11.

45 For his proposal, later abandoned, to subdue the islanders see Herodotus 1.27.

46 76 F 75.

47 Thucydides 4.107.3.

48 Herodian 2.858.28 Lenz. See also Mazzarino, *Fra Oriente e Occidente* 192. Pittacus perhaps inherited the title βασιλεύς: 'Grind, mill, grind, for Pittacus grinds too, who reigns as king over great Mytilene' said a song sung in the mill at Eresus (Carmina Popularia 23 Page).

49 Alcaeus Z 24.

50 *Politics* 1285 a 29 ff.

51 617.

52 Diogenes Laertius 1.76.

53 Diogenes Laertius 1.76. Cf. Aristotle, *Politics* 1274 b 19–23.

54 Diogenes Laertius 1.76.

55 Alcaeus G 2, 20.

56 Diogenes Laertius 1.75.

57 Diogenes Laertius 1.75. *P.Oxy.* 2506 F 102 mentions Pittacus and Croesus together, but the context is obscure.

58 Diogenes Laertius 1.76.

59 Diogenes Laertius 1.75.

60 Sappho F 98 Lobel-Page.

61 Strabo 617.

62 Sappho F 71.

63 Alcaeus Z 61.

64 Herodotus 2.135.1.

65 F 203. Sappho's relations with her three brothers Larichus, Charaxus, and Erigyios are discussed in the very fragmentary text *P.Oxy.* 2506 F 48.

66 Herodotus 2.134. Strabo 808.

67 Herodotus 2.134.3. See also Sappho F 202.

68 Herodotus 2.134.1.

69 Sappho F 15 with F 5.

70 Herodotus 2.135.6.

71 Sappho F 132.

72 F 16.

73 F 98a.

74 F 16. Anactoria is Milesian Anagora of the Suda s.v. Σαπφώ. Anactoria was a name of Miletus: Steph. Byz. s.v. Μίλητος.

75 Suda s.v. Σαπφώ. Sappho F 95.

76 F 96.

77 F 131. See D. L. Page, *Sappho and Alcaeus* 133–136. Of Sappho's friends Telesippa and Megara (Suda s.v. Σαπφώ) nothing is known.

78 617.

79 F 48.

80 F 49.1.

81 F 130.

82 V. Scully, *Architectural Review* 135 (1964) 129–134.

83 Hellanicus 4 F 35a. Strabo 426. For the oracle see Schol. Aristoph. *Clouds* 144.

84 *FHG* 2.163.

85 Plutarch, *Greek Questions* 2.

86 Plutarch, *Greek Questions* 2. For punishment of adultery in Tenedos see Steph. Byz. s.v. *Τένεδος*.
87 Aristotle, *Politics* 1269 a 1–3.
88 *FHG* 2.217.
89 Aristotle, *Politics* 1306 a 35–36.
90 *FHG* 2.217.
91 Strabo 622. For a description of the haven of Kyme see *AA* 1962, 40 ff.

Chapter X. THE BIRTH OF NATURAL PHILOSOPHY*

1 Philodemus ap. *Hermes* 55 (1920) 254.
2 7 A 2 [Suda s.v.].
3 There is some uncertainty about the book's title, which is in any case an Alexandrian invention. See M. L. West, *CQ* 13 (1963) 157.
4 Aristoxenus ap. Diod. 10.3.4.
5 Ion F 30 Von Blumenthal.
6 7 B 1.
7 7 A 8. See note 3 above.
8 7 B 4. See also West, *CQ* 13 (1963) 162.
9 H. G. Güterbock, *AJA* 52 (1948) 131.
10 7 A 2. 7 B 4.
11 7 B 2.
12 West, *CQ* 13 (1963) 172.
13 Isidorus ap. Clement. *Strom.* 6.53.5 states that the cloth was placed upon the oak, but the text may be confused here or Isidorus may have misunderstood Pherecydes.
14 *Metaphysics* 1091 b 8.
15 Diog. Laert. 2.46.
16 *Politics* 1259 a 9 ff.
17 174 A. The ingenious suggestion has however been made that Thales went down into a well in order to observe stars culminating during daylight: see M. Landmann and J. O. Fleckenstein, *Vierteljahrschrift der Naturforschenden Gesellschaft in Zurich* 88 (1943) 98–112.
18 1.170.3.
19 We may perhaps think of him as a Cadmean from Thebes on Mycale in the Milesian domain.
20 Diog. Laert. 1.22. No need to read *Νηλιδῶν* for *Θηλιδῶν* with Bywater.
21 Herodotus 1.170.3.
22 Diog. Laert. 1.27. Thales 11 A 11.
23 *DG* 384, 20–25.
24 2.20.2.
25 11 A 11.

* Of the vast and ever-growing literature on the Presocratics I have read much, but not more than is good for me. Some helpful modern discussions are cited here and there in the notes, but my aim has been to recover thoughts of the Ionian philosophers from the fragments whose meanings are least disputed.

26 Herodotus 2.109.3.
27 Diog. Laert. 1.27.
28 *Moralia* 147 A.
29 Thales 11 A 20.
30 21 B 19.
31 1.74.2.
32 Guthrie 48 points out that Assyrian astrologers made observations when they expected an eclipse of the sun to be visible, to see if the eclipse in fact occurred. But that was not the same as regularly to predict the time and place of solar eclipses.
33 Oppolzer, *Canon of Eclipses* No. 1489. Pliny, *NH* 2.12.53 gives the date 585/4 BC. See also Chapter 8, note 26 above and O. Neugebauer, *The Exact Sciences in Antiquity* (²Providence 1957) 142–143.
34 Callimachus F 191, 55 Pfeiffer. See also Kirk-Raven 82.
35 *Odyssey* 5.273.
36 11 A 17.
37 11 A 8 (but the Chronicles here cited date Thales' death in the tenth Olympiad!). A fragment of Alcaeus (Z125) suggests that Thales was known in Lesbos also, but proves nothing.
38 11 B 4.
39 11 A 1 (23) and 11 B 1.
40 *De Caelo* 294 a 28 (Thales 11 A 14). Aristotle objects that Thales did not explain how the water was supported that supported the earth. Thales may have believed that the water was self-supporting or that it extended downwards without limit.
41 *Metaphysics* 983 b 6 ff. (Thales 11 A 12). M. L. West, *CQ* 13 (1963) 175 ingeniously suggests that Thales had a doctrine of vortices: but no extant source explicitly ascribes the concept of δίνη to him.
42 Kirk-Raven 12–14 and 90–91. *ANET* 61–72.
43 *ANET* 3–4.
44 *Genesis* 49.25.
45 Psalm 136.6. See also U. Hölscher, *Hermes* 81 (1953) 385–391.
46 Herodotus 4.8.2.
47 Hesiod, *Theogony* 726–728.
48 Seneca, *Qu.Nat.* 3.14.
49 Aristotle, *De Anima* 411 a 7.
50 Diogenes Laertius 1.24.
51 *De Anima* 405 a 19.
52 Burnet, indeed, held that 'to say the magnet and amber are alive is to imply, if anything, that other things are not' (*Early Greek Philosophy*⁴ 50).
53 Anaximander 12 B 2.
54 Aristotle, *Physics* 203 b 7.
55 Hippolytus, *Ref.* 1.6.1–2 (12 A 11). Kirk-Raven 105–107.
56 Ps.-Plutarch, *Strom.* 2 (12 A 10).
57 Hippolytus, *Ref.* 1.6.4–5 (12 A 11).
58 Aetius 2.21.1.
59 Aetius 2.20.1 (12 A 21).

60 Hippolytus, *Ref.* 1.6.5.
61 Hippolytus, *Ref.* 1.6.3. Ps.-Plut. *Strom.* 2.
62 Aristotle, *De Caelo* 295 b 10.
63 *Phys.* 24.13. (Anaximander 12 B 1). *DG* p. 476.
64 s.v. 'Αναξίμανδρος.
65 *Phys.* 24.13. See also C. H. Kahn, *Anaximander and the Origins of Greek Cosmology* (New York 1960) 166 ff and compare G. S. Kirk, *CQ* 5 (1955) 32–37.
66 12 A 27.
67 12 A 23.
68 Hippolytus, *Ref.* 1.6.7.
69 Aetius 5.19.4.
70 12 A 30 (Plut. *Symp.* 730 E).
71 244 F 28 and 29.
72 There is no need to regard these words as interpolated: see below p. 194 for the possibility of there having been a second Polycrates.
73 Anaximander 12 A 1.
74 Herodotus 2.109.3.
75 12 A 4.
76 Cleostratus 6 A 1. *GRBS* 4 (1963) 97–99.
77 ap. Strab. 7.
78 4.36.2.
79 Hecataeus 1 T 11 b.
80 Anaximander 12 A 6.
81 Herodotus 5.49.1.
82 Suda s.v. 'Αναξίμανδρος.
83 Aelian, *VH* 3.17.
84 Jeffery 332 and 334.
85 Anaximander 12 A 5 a.
86 12 A 1.
87 *Nat.Hist.* 2.31.
88 Pliny, *Nat.Hist.* 18.213.
89 Suda s.v. 'Αναξίμανδρος.
90 Diog. Laert. 2.2.
91 Diog. Laert. 2.3. Suda s.v. 'Αναξιμένης. cf. Kerferd, *MH* 11 (1954) 117–121.
92 13 A 5. 13 B 1.
93 13 A 10.
94 13 A 6.
95 13 A 20.
96 13 A 7, 4. 13 A 14. 13 B 2 a. For a discussion of what Anaximenes may have meant by saying that the stars are 'fixed like nails in the crystalline' see Guthrie 135 ff. Burnet, however (*Early Greek Philosophy*[4] 77 n. 4), denied that the simile represents genuine doctrine of Anaximenes.
97 13 A 7, 6.
98 13 A 7, 6 discussed by Kirk-Raven 157.
99 13 A 17.

100   13 A 21.
101   13 B 2.
102   Diog. Laert. 2.3.
103   Diog. Laert. 5.42.
104   13 B 2 (Aetius 1.3.4).
105   This point is well made by E. Schrödinger, *Nature and the Greeks*
       (Cambridge 1954) 53.
106   4.95.2.
107   F 6 Diehl³.
108   22 B 40.
109   Diog. Laert. 8.6.
110   244 F 339 and F 29. Diels rejected the reference to Polycrates, need-
       lessly. See p. 194 n. 22 below.
111   Strabo 638 with Porphyry, *Vit.Pyth.* 9. See also J. S. Morrison,
       CQ 6 (1956) 142.
112   Diog. Laert. 8.3.
113   Iamblichus, *Vit.Pyth.* 249.
114   Diogenes Laertius 8.3.
115   Pythagoras DK 14, 8 p. 100 lines 1–5.
116   O. Neugebauer, *The Exact Sciences in Antiquity*², 36.
117   Cf. Diog. Laert. 8.12.
118   58 B 15.
119   58 C 6.
120   Diog. Laert. 1.12.
121   F 7 Diehl.
122   F 18 Diehl.
123   566 F 133.
124   Diog. Laert. 9.18.
125   Aristotle, *Rhet.* 1400 b 5.
126   *FGrHist* 450 T 1.
127   Diog. Laert. 8.36.
128   Diog. Laert. 9.1.
129   Hippolytus, *Ref.* 1.14.5. For plant fossils in Paros see Guthrie 387 n. 4.
130   21 B 37.
131   21 A 48.
132   21 B 29 and 33.
133   21 B 30.
134   21 B 28.
135   21 A 33, 3. (Hippolytus, *Ref.* 1.14.3.)
136   21 A 40 and 38.
137   21 B 32.
138   21 A 41 a. (Aetius 2.24.9.)
139   21 A 41 a and 21 A 33. See also Guthrie 393–394.
140   21 B 11.
141   21 B 14.
142   21 B 16.
143   21 B 15.
144   21 B 23.

145 21 B 24.
146 21 B 25–26.
147 *Metaphysics* 986 b 21 ff.
148 21 B 34.
149 21 B 18.
150 21 B 38.
151 Varro ap. Aug. *Civ. Dei* 7.17.
152 21 B 1.
153 21 B 2.

Chapter XI. CROESUS AND THE IONIANS

1 Herodotus 1.92.3–4.
2 Nicolas of Damascus 90 F 65.
3 Aelian, *VH* 4.27. See also Burn, *The Lyric Age of Greece* 213.
4 Herodotus 1.26.1. Cf. H. Kaletsch, *Historia* 7 (1958) 47.
5 Herodotus 1.92.4.
6 Herodotus 1.92.1. Tod 6.
7 Herodotus 1.92.1–2. The Parian Marble (239 A 41) dates *c.* 555 an embassy or the arrival of an offering from Croesus at Delphi.
8 Herodotus 1.69.3–4. For the gold mines of the Mermnadae near Pergamum see Strabo 680.
9 Herodotus 1.26.2. Aelian, *VH* 3.26. Polyaenus 6.50.
10 Callimachus F 102 Pfeiffer with Diegesis.
11 J. Stroux, *Philologus* 89 (1934) 310 ff. on Ovid, *Ibis* 623 f.
12 Suda s.v. ʼΑρίσταρχος.
13 Herodotus 1.27.
14 601.
15 Diog. Laert. 1.25.
16 Cilicia lay for a time within the Babylonian domain, having been subjected by Neriglissar in 557/6 BC (Wiseman, *Chronicles of Chaldaean Kings* 40–42).
17 1.28.
18 Herodotus 1.74.4.
19 Herodotus 1.77.1–2.
20 Herodotus 1.34–45.
21 Herodotus 1.46.1.
22 Herodotus 6.125.2–5. Cf. W. G. Forrest, *BCH* 80 (1958) 51.
23 L. H. Jeffery, *ABSA* 57 (1962) 144.
24 6.37.1–2.
25 Charon 262 F 7 a.
26 Herodotus 6.38.1.
27 Herodotus 6.35.3.
28 *FGrHist.* 239 A 42.
29 F 104, 23 ed. Masson.
30 Suda s.v. Ἱππῶναξ. Compare F 1 Masson.
31 Ps.-Acron ad. Horat. *Epod.* 6.14.
32 F 191 Pfeiffer.

33 Compare F 14–17.
34 Pliny, *NH* 36.5.11.
35 F 3.
36 F 40.
37 F 92.
38 F 42.
39 F 50.
40 F 127.
41 F 125. See also *GRBS* 4 (1963) 7–8.
42 F 27.
43 F 127 and 72.
44 F 26, 3.
45 F 12.
46 F 123.
47 F 105. Cf. Callimachus F 194, 28–31 Pfeiffer.
48 F 28 and F 143.
49 F 5–10.
50 Harpokration s.v. φαρμακός.
51 Tzetzes, *Hist.* 23.726–756. See also J. E. Harrison, *Prolegomena to the Study of Greek Religion* (Cambridge 1903) 99.
52 Athenaeus 282 A–C (Ananius F 5 Diehl).
53 F 3 Diehl.
54 Ananius F 4.
55 F 2.
56 F 32 Masson.
57 Ananius F 1.
58 Anaximenes of Lampsacus 72 F 19. For the date see the Nabonidus Chronicle ii in S. Smith, *Babylonian Historical Texts* (London 1924) 115 (*ANET* 305 f) and Burn, *Persia and the Greeks* 38.
59 Herodotus 1.53.3. Aristotle, *Rhet.* 1407 a 38.
60 Herodotus 1.70 and 3.47.1.
61 Herodotus 1.75–76.1. The connexion of Thales with this battle (1.75.3), which Herodotus doubted, is perhaps a confusion with the eclipse battle between Alyattes and the Medes. If Thales was present at the eclipse battle, it is easier to see why his name was so closely linked with the eclipse. Perhaps he also helped Alyattes to get his troops over the Halys.
62 Herodotus 1.76.3–1.77.4. Herodotus gives what seems to be a Lydian version of the battle near Pteria: in fact Croesus may have been forced to withdraw after a defeat by Cyrus' army, which was said to be larger than the Lydian (Herodotus 1.77.1). Polyaenus (8.2) suggests that the Persians pursued the Lydians westward much more rapidly than is implied by the Herodotean account of the fall of Sardis.
63 Ephorus 70 F 58.
64 Herodotus 1.77.4 and 1.79.1.
65 Herodotus 1.79.2–1.80.6.
66 Herodotus 1.82–83.

67 Herodotus 1.84.
68 Nicolas of Damascus 90 F 67.
69 Herodotus 1.84.3. On King Meles see Nicolas of Damascus 90 F 16. Nanis daughter of Croesus betrayed the citadel according to a romantic tale in Parthenius (*Love Stories* 22).
70 This oracle also predicted the capture of Sardis shortly before it happened (Herodotus 1.78.3).
71 Burn, *Persia and the Greeks* 42.
72 A. H. Smith, *JHS* 18 (1898) 267 f.
73 *Epinicians* 3.23 ff. In Herodotus (1.86.2) Cyrus has Croesus placed on the pyre, but saves him at the last moment. Compare also Nicolas of Damascus 90 F 68.
74 Kaletsch, *Historia* 7 (1958) 43. S. Smith, *Isaiah Chapters XL–LV* (London 1944) 36.
75 244 F 29 with Clinton, *Fasti Hellenici* 2 (1841) 8–9 under 546 BC. The supplement in the Parian Marble (239 A 42) giving 541 BC for the fall of Sardis is questionable. By Herodotus a date for the fall of Sardis is implied, for he placed the restoration to power of Pisistratus at the battle of Pallene (in 546/5) 36 years before the expulsion of Hippias (1.62 with 5.65.3), and his narrative suggests that the battle was earlier than the fall of Sardis. See Wade-Gery, *Essays* 166 n. 3. C. Hignett, *A History of the Athenian Constitution* (Oxford 1952) 328 and Busolt, *Griechische Geschichte* 2 (Gotha 1895) 459–460 note. On Herodotus' chronology of the Athenian tyranny see F. Jacoby, *Atthis* (Oxford 1949) 188–196.
76 Ctesias of Cnidus 688 F 9 (5) with Steph. Byz. s.v. Βαρήνη. Compare A. T. Olmstead, *History of the Persian Empire* (Chicago 1959) 40.

Chapter XII. THE PERSIAN CONQUEST OF IONIA

1 Herodotus 1.141.1–4.
2 Herodotus 1.152.1–153.1.
3 Xenophon, *Inst. Cyri* 7.1.45. J. M. Cook, *The Greeks in Ionia and the East* (London 1962) 110.
4 Herodotus 1.153.3–4.
5 Herodotus 1.154.
6 Herodotus 1.156.2.
7 Herodotus 1.157.1–3.
8 Strabo 622. See also G. E. Bean, *JHS* 74 (1954) 85–87. Cf. *JHS* 75, 155.
9 Herodotus 1.158–159.
10 Tod 10, a κοινή version of an earlier Ionic translation of a letter of Darius, who also favoured Milesian Apollo (Tacitus, *Annals* 3.63).
11 Herodotus 1.160.1–3.
12 Herodotus 1.161. Not all the Prienians were enslaved, for the city provided twelve ships at the battle of Lade (Herodotus 6.8.1). Bias too survived the attack of Mazares for he was active later during the assault of Harpagus on Ionia (Herodotus 1.169.2–1.170.1) and is said to have died of old age in Priene (Diog. Laert. 1.84).

13　Herodotus 1.162 and 1.163.3–4.
14　Herodotus 1.164.1–3.
15　Herodotus 1.164.3. It was perhaps at this time that the Persians burned the temple of Athena in the city (Pausanias 7.5.4).
16　Herodotus 1.165.1.
17　Antiochus 555 F 8.
18　Herodotus 1.165.1–2.
19　Herodotus 1.165.3.
20　Herodotus 1.166.1.
21　Pausanias 10.8.6. Cf. Antiochus 555 F 8 and Thucydides 1.13.6.
22　Herodotus 1.166.2–3 and 167.3–4.
23　Herodotus 1.167.1–2.
24　Herodotus 1.168.
25　Jeffery 355. Tean food: Athenaeus 160 A.
26　F 46 Page.
27　C. M. Bowra, *Greek Lyric Poetry*² 269.
28　Strabo 644. Teos provided ships at the battle of Lade (Herodotus 6.8.1).
29　Pindar [F 36, 17–18 Bowra] describes the riches of the Abderite land.
30　Ps.-Scymnus 886 f.
31　Herodotus 1.169.1–2.
32　Herodotus 1.170.1–2.
33　Herodotus 1.171.1.
34　Herodotus 1.174.2–6.
35　Herodotus 1.175–176.
36　R. N. Frye, *The Heritage of Persia* (London 1962) 74.
37　Agathocles 472 F 6.
38　Herodotus 3.90.1–2. Cf. Darius' Behistun inscription 1.6 [R. G. Kent, *Old Persian* (New Haven 1950) 119]. Burn, *Persia and the Greeks* 59.
39　Herodotus 3.120.1–2.
40　Herodotus 3.122.1. Tod 10.
41　G. M. A. Richter, *AJA* 50 (1946) 17. E. Erdmann, *Forschungen und Fortschritte* 26 (1950) 150–153.
42　Thucydides 1.13.6. Compare Malalas, *Chron.* p. 158 ed. Dindorf (Bonn 1831) and Cedrenus, *Synops.* 243 who both mention a war between the Ionians and Cyrus. For the possibility that there was a Persian attack on Samos in the time of Cyrus see Boardman, *AJ* 39 (1959) 200–202. Cf. Pausanias 7.5.4 for Persian burning of the Samian Heraeum.
43　1.169.2.
44　1.151.2.

Chapter XIII. THE ISLANDERS IN THE AGE OF POLYCRATES

1　Gallet de Santerre 290–296.
2　P. Amandry, *Fouilles de Delphes* 2 (Paris 1953) 31.

3 Andriscus 500 F 1. Plutarch, *De Mul. Virt.* 17.
4 Aristotle ap. Athen. 348 A. *Politics* 1305 a 41.
5 Herodotus 5.30.1.
6 Pausanias 7.3.3. Προμήθειοι were a γένος in Colophon also: L. Robert, *Rev. de Phil.* 10³ (1936) 162–164. See also *GRBS* 5 (1964) 22.
7 F 75 Pfeiffer (Xenomedes of Ceos 442 F 1).
8 Jeffery 411 and Plate 55.
9 [τ]ο αϝυτο λιθο εμι ανδριας και το σφελας (Note the digamma, unusual in Ionic). The interpretation given in the text is Miss E. Harrison's. M. Guarducci, however (*Epigraphica* 4 (1942) 155 ff) thinks that the inscription means that the statue is monolithic, not jointed, the base also being a monolith. Cf. Jeffery 292.
10 Paus. 5.10.3.
11 [Aristotle], *Oec.* 2.3.
12 Herodotus 1.61.4.
13 Herodotus 1.64.1–2.
14 Herodotus 1.64.2.
15 3.104.3.
16 Polyaenus 1.23.
17 Plutarch, *De Mal. Herod.* 22. See also Plut. *Laconian Apopthegms* 67 with D. M. Leahy, *JHS* 77 (1957) 272–275.
18 Cf. J. L. Myres, *JHS* 26 (1906) 99–101.
19 5.31.2.
20 Herodotus 5.30.1.
21 Herodotus 3.39.3.
22 It is possible that Herodotus has combined two persons called Polycrates, a father and son, for the Suda s.v. Ἴβυκος imply that the tyrant Polycrates had a father of the same name (compare J. Labarbe, *AC* 31 (1962) 181): but if there were two persons called Polycrates, it is not clear whether the elder or the younger is to be considered the brother of Pantagnotus and Syloson. When Apollodorus (*FGrHist* 244 F 29) stated that Polycrates was at the height of his power in 547/6, he was perhaps referring to the elder Polycrates: if he was, then the Samian tyranny may be supposed to have begun at least as early as the middle of the sixth century B C (compare also M. White, *JHS* 74 (1954) 36–43. J. P. Barron, *CQ* 14 (1964) 210 f).
23 Herodotus 3.120.3. Polyaenus 1.23.
24 Herodotus 3.39.2.
25 Theod. Metoch. p. 668 ap. *Aristotelis Opera* ed. I. Bekker 10 (Oxford 1837) 313.
26 Polyaenus 6.45.
27 *Orat.* 29.22 ff ed. Colonna. See also C. M. Bowra, *Greek Lyric Poetry*² 249. The father is perhaps Polycrates I, the viceroy Polycrates II.
28 F 4 Page.
29 3.121.1.
30 F 1 (a) 47, 48 Page. J. P. Barron, *CR* 11 (1961) 185–187.
31 Thucydides 3.104.2.

32 Suda s.v. ταῦτά σοι Πύθια καὶ Δήλια. See also H. W. Parke, *CQ* 40 (1946) 105–108.

33 Compare J. A. Davison, *CQ* 41 (1947) 18–24.

34 1.14.2. Biremes had been invented much earlier by the Erythraeans: Damastes 5 F 6.

35 Herodotus 3.39.4.

36 Herodotus 3.60.1–3.

37 E. Fabricius, *AM* 9 (1884) 163–197. Cf. J. Goodfield, *Scientific American* 210 (1964) 104–112.

38 F. R. Bichowsky, *Compressed Air Magazine* 48–49 (1943–1944) 7086–7090 quoted by M. White, *JHS* 74 (1954) 41.

39 3.60.4. See also E. Buschor, *AM* 55 (1930) 49 ff.

40 Such as that made on the temple of Athena in Phocaea by Harpagus: Pausanias 7.5.4. Cf. Boardman, *AJ* 39 (1959) 200.

41 Pliny, *NH* 36.90.

42 Herodotus 1.51.2–3.

43 Herodotus 3.41.

44 Pausanias 8.14.8 and 10.38.6.

45 Pausanias 3.12.10. Another eastern Greek working at Sparta about this time was Bathycles the Magnesian, maker of the Amyclaean throne, with the help of some fellow citizens of his: Pausanias 3.18.9 and 14.

46 Paus. 10.38.6.

47 H. Hoffmann, *AJA* 57 (1953) 195.

48 Jeffery 328.

49 Aristotle, *Politics* 1313 b 24.

50 Anacreon F 8 Page. See also C. M. Bowra, *Greek Lyric Poetry*² 274–275.

51 Herodotus 3.47.1.

52 Herodotus 3.39.2.

53 Herodotus 3.44.2.

54 3.45.1.

55 3.45.4.

56 3.46.1–2.

57 A. Lane, *ABSA* 34 (1933/1934) 178–179.

58 Herodotus 3.47.

59 Herodotus 3.48.1.

60 3.54.1.

61 3.55.

62 3.56.1.

63 3.57.1.

64 3.58.4.

65 3.59.4.

66 3.122.3–4.

67 3.122.1.

68 3.125.2.

69 R. A. Parker and W. H. Dubberstein, *Babylonian Chronology 626 BC–AD 75* (Providence 1956) 14.

70 Herodotus 3.125.3.
71 3.120.2–3.
72 3.126.2.
73 3.127.1.
74 3.128.
75 3.139–141.
76 3.142–143.
77 3.144–146.2.
78 Strabo 638. Herodotus 3.149.
79 3.148.
80 5.27.1. Wade-Gery *Essays* 163.
81 3.149. 6.13.2. The Aeaces son of Brychon (Tod 7. Jeffery p. 330–331) who dedicated booty (σύλη) to Hera while holding the office of ἐπιστάτης may well be a kinsman of the Samian tyrants, though the date of the dedication is uncertain – any time between 540 and 494 is possible. For Samian σύλη see *FGrHist* 544 F 3.
82 Plutarch, *Solon* 14. On Euboean ties with the mainland see Wilamowitz, *Hermes* 21 (1886) 91–115.
83 Aristotle, *Politics* 1316 a 32.
84 Aristotle, *Politics* 1304 a 29.
85 Aristotle, *Politics* 1306 a 36.
86 Heraclides ap. *FHG* 2.217.
87 Theognis 891–894.
88 Herodotus 5.77.2. See also R. Burrows and P. N. Ure, *ABSA* 14 (1907/1908) 237–240.
89 W. Wallace, *Hesperia* 5 (1936) 278.
90 F 38, 20–24 Bowra.
91 Simonides F 77.6 Diehl. See also Bowra, *Greek Lyric Poetry*² 309 n. 7.
92 Strabo 487.
93 Theophrastus, *De Lapid.* 52.
94 Herodotus 4.35.4. This was presumably a joint venture of the cities of Ceos, though the island was still not federated as late as 450 BC: see D. M. Lewis, *ABSA* 57 (1962) 2.
95 F 75, 32–34 with F 67, 7.
96 B. V. Head, *Historia Numorum*² (Oxford 1911) 483–484 (Staters of Carthaea and Iulis).
97 Strabo 448. Cf. A. Pridik, *De Cei Insulae Rebus* (Berlin 1892) 23.
98 *IG* XII 5, 1.593. See also C. D. Buck, *The Greek Dialects*² (Chicago 1955) 191–192.
99 Strabo 486.
100 Jeffery 297.
101 *AM* 76 (1961) 67 ff.
102 Michel, *Receuil d'Inscriptions Gr.* 834.
103 Epigram 1 p. 105 Snell⁶. Read Καρθαίων in line 2.
104 Suda s.v. Βακχυλίδης with Strabo 486 and Etym. Mag. 582, 20.
105 Callimachus F 222, 2 Pfeiffer.
106 *IG* XII 5.1.609, 102 ff and 637.

107 *IG* XII 5.1.609, 1; 141; and 175.
108 For the date see Suda s.v. Γλαῦκος Καρύστιος with C. M. Bowra, *Greek Lyric Poetry*² 311 n. 3.
109 F 4 Page.
110 F 25 Page.
111 F 25 Page. For the topography of the Eretrian hinterland see W. P. Wallace, *Hesperia* 16 (1947) 114–146.
112 Herodotus 5.102.3. The name recurs at Styra [Wallace, *Hesperia* 16 (1947) 142 n. 79] which by this time may have been part of the Eretrian domain. Styrians and Eretrians paraded together at Plataea: Herodotus 9.28.5.
113 F 89 Bergk.
114 O. Rubensohn, *RE* 36 (1949) 1809–1810. *Idem, Das Delion von Paros* (Wiesbaden 1962).
115 Pouilloux 269 f and 53.
116 Iamblichus, *Vit. Pyth.* 267.
117 Sir Thomas Heath, *A History of Greek Mathematics* I (Oxford 1921) 69.
118 Cf. *RE* 36 (1949) 1811–1812.
119 Jeffery 296, No. 39.
120 *IG* XII 5.292.
121 *RE* 4² (1923) 1730.
122 *IG* XII 5.872, 66. Herakles is said to have killed the sons of Boreas in Tenos: Acusilaus 2 F 31.
123 Eparchides 437 F 1.
124 Theopompus 115 F 111. (But the occasion of the anecdote is uncertain. Killikon the Syrian traitor was already proverbial by 421, when he was mentioned in Aristophanes' *Peace* (line 363). Other versions mention a betrayal of Samos or Miletus to the Prienians by Killikon.) See also Callimachus F 607 Pfeiffer.

Chapter XIV. THE FIRST IONIAN HISTORIANS

1 *FGrHist* 534 T 1. 545 F 1.
2 *FGrHist* 450 T 1. See also F. Jacoby, *Atthis* 364.
3 *FGrHist* 450 T 1 (Diog. Laert. 9.20).
4 *FGrHist* No. 489.
5 Suda, s.v. Φερεκύδης Βάβυος Σύριος. I leave aside his namesake Pherecydes the Lerian historian who may have lived in Hellenistic times, though the Suda date him early in the fifth century BC. *FGrHist* No. 475. See also F. Jacoby, *Mnemosyne*³ 13 (1947) 13–64.
6 J. B. Bury, *The Ancient Greek Historians* (New York repr. 1958) 14–15.
7 Ch. 5.
8 1 F 1a.
9 1 F 27.
10 1 F 26.
11 1 F 30.

12 1 F 18a.
13 Diels, *DG* 385. Cf. W. Aly, *Hermes* 62 (1927) 305–307.
14 He may have discussed the subject with the Egyptian priests; for his dealings with whom see W. A. Heidel, *Memoirs of the American Academy of Arts and Sciences* 18 (1935) 53–134.
15 R. L. Beaumont, *JRS* 29 (1939) 74–86.
16 1 F 38.
17 1 F 55.
18 *FGrHist*, Vol. I. Komm. p. 371. L. Pearson, *Early Ionian Historians* 90.
19 1 F 140–141. The Oenussae and Corseae islands were also treated as being in Europe: F 142–143.
20 F 292–299.
21 Herodotus 4.44.1–2.
22 Hecataeus 1 F 284.
23 1 F 287.
24 1 F 292.
25 1 F 291.
26 1 F 299.
27 G. M. A. Richter, *AJA* 50 (1946) 15–30.
28 Pliny, *NH* 34.68.
29 1 F 301.
30 2.143.1.
31 1 F 234; 236; 229; 230.
32 1 F 239.
33 1 F 240.

Chapter XV. HERACLITUS

1 Diogenes Laertius 9.6. Cf. Pherecydes 3 F 155.
2 Heraclitus 22 A 3.
3 Antisthenes ap. Diog. Laert. 9.6.
4 Diog. Laert. 9.3.
5 Diog. Laert. 9.12.
6 22 B 121.
7 Diog. Laert. 9.6. Heraclitus may as βασιλεύς of the Ephesians have been a priest of Artemis. For the king of Ephesus was called Ἐσσήν, which was also a title in use at the Artemisium, meaning 'chief bee' (Etym. Mag. 383.30. Cf. Pausanias 8.13.1).
8 Cicero, *De Finibus* 2.5.15. Suda s.v. Ἡράκλειτος.
9 22 B 93.
10 Compare 22 B 92.
11 22 B 1 and 2.
12 22 B 50.
13 22 B 107.
14 22 B 55.
15 22 B 60.
16 22 B 61.

17 22 B 67.
18 22 B 18 and 123.
19 22 B 80.
20 22 B 53.
21 *Eudemian Ethics* 1235a 25.
22 Note however that these examples may be given by Aristotle, not by Heraclitus: see Kirk, *Heraclitus* 17 and 168–169.
23 Plato, *Cratylus* 402 A. See Kirk and Raven, *Presocratic Philosophers* 197 and compare G. Vlastos, *AJP* 76 (1955) 338–344.
24 22 B 12 with 22 B 91.
25 Aristotle, *Metaphysics* 1010 a 13.
26 22 B 6 (sun) and R. Walzer, *Oriens* 6 (1953) 133 (stars).
27 22 B 30 and 31.
28 22 B 64.
29 22 B 36.
30 22 B 136 (from a metrical paraphrase of Heraclitean doctrine).
31 22 B 117.
32 Diog. Laert. 9.10.
33 F 6, 1–2 Diehl.
34 Diog. Laert. 9.10.
35 22 B 94.
36 The statement that 'strife is justice' in Heraclitus 22 B 80 may well be a criticism of Anaximander. See Kirk, *Heraclitus* 401.
37 22 A 13.
38 Kirk, *Heraclitus* 301.
39 22 B 120.
40 22 B 32.
41 22 B 14.
42 22 B 93.
43 22 B 92.
44 22 B 14.
45 22 B 5.
46 22 B 44.
47 22 B 29.

Chapter XVI. IONIAN TYRANTS AND THE IONIAN REVOLT

1 For a full account of Darius' campaign see Burn, *Persia and the Greeks* Ch. 7. The bridge may have been built by Mandrocles of Samos, the engineer who made a pontoon bridge over the Bosporus for Darius in the same campaign. Later Mandrocles dedicated in the Samian Heraeum with an elegant epigram a picture of the army crossing to Europe: Herodotus 4.87–88. For another Ionian bridge builder of this period, Harpalus, see Diels, *Vorsokratiker* I⁹ p. 42.
2 4. 137–138.
3 On the date see G. G. Cameron, *JNES* 2 (1943) 313 with n. 32. See also H. T. Wade-Gery *Essays* 159.

---

4 For this man see also Thucydides 6.59.3. Hippoclus' son Aiantides married Archedice daughter of Hippias, the former tyrant of Athens. The name Hippocles or Hippoclus is Neleid: see Zenobius, *Adag.* 5.17.
5 Herodotus 4.97.6 with 5.11 and 5.37.1.
6 Herodotus 5.11.2 and 5.23.1.
7 Herodotus 5.23.2.
8 Herodotus 5.26.
9 Diodorus 10.19.3 with Zenobius 3.85 and Charax of Pergamum 103 F 18. Herodotus 5.27.
10 Herodotus 5.30.1.
11 Herodotus 5.30.2. The name Molpagoras suggests that he or his father took part in the debates of the αἰσύμνηται μολπῶν, the priestly officials later called *stephanephoroi*, one of whom presided over the religious life of the city each year. A list (*Milet* 1.3 No. 122) of these annual priesthoods may well begin in 525/4 BC (F. Jacoby, *Atthis* (Oxford 1949) 180). A Molpagoras is found in the fortieth place in the list. Three sons of an Anaximander are found in the seventh, thirteenth, and nineteenth places in the list. If they are brothers, they may be listed six places apart because there were six tribes in Miletus and their tribe's turn to provide an αἰσυμνήτης came every seventh year. For a cult law of the Molpoi see F. Sokolowski, *Lois Sacrées de l'Asie Mineure* (Paris 1955) No. 50 and S. Luria, *Philologus* 83 (1928) 113–136. With the Onitadai, a family named in the law, compare the Naxian hero 'Ονίτης (*AE* 1914, 133).
12 5.28.
13 Herodotus 5.30.4.
14 Herodotus 5.31.3–4.
15 Herodotus 5.33.1.
16 Herodotus 5.33.
17 *A.T.L.* 1.498.
18 Herodotus 5.33.4.
19 Herodotus 5.34.2–3.
20 Herodotus 5.35.2–3.
21 Cf. A. Blamire, *CQ* 9 (1959) 148.
22 Herodotus 5.109.3.
23 Herodotus 5.36.2–4.
24 For this probable date, four years before the end of the revolt, see Burn, *Persia and the Greeks* 198.
25 Herodotus 5.37.1.
26 Herodotus 5.37.2.
27 Herodotus 5.38.2.
28 Herodotus 5.49.5.
29 5.97.2.
30 Artaphrenes and Hippias: Herodotus 5.96.2. Melanthios: 5.97.3.
31 An Eretrian fleet is also said to have defeated the Cypriotes off Pamphylia before the attack on Sardis: Lysanias of Mallos 426 F 1.

32 Lysanias 426 F 1 mentions a siege of Miletus, to relieve which the Ionians, he claims, attacked Sardis.

33 The name Charopinus is also found amongst the Milesian αἰσύμνη- ται μολπῶν, e.g. *Milet* 1.3 No. 122, Χαροπῖνος Μανδρωνακτίδεω (479/8).

34 Herodotus 5.100.

35 5.101.1–3.

36 G. M. A. Hanfmann, *BASOR* 166 (1962) 5–9.

37 Herodotus 5.102.2–3.

38 Herodotus 5.103.1.

39 5.103.2.

40 Revolt of Cyprus: Herodotus 5.104.1. Ionian settlement: cf. Boardman 122.

41 Herodotus 5.109.3.

42 Herodotus 5.112.1.

43 5.113.1 and 5.114.1.

44 Soli: 5.115.2. Siege mound at Paphos: Burn, *Persia and the Greeks* 203–205.

45 Herodotus 5.116.

46 5.117 and 123.

47 Herodotus 5.125. See also J. L. Benson, *Ancient Leros* (Durham N.C. 1963) 46–47.

48 Herodotus 5.126.1.

49 Thucydides 4.102.2. On the date see Busolt, *Griechische Geschichte* 2² p. 538 note and 548.

50 Herodotus 5.119–120.

51 5.121.

52 Suda s.v. Σκύλαξ Καρυανδεύς. Bury, *The Ancient Greek Historians* 24.

53 Herodotus 6.1.2. See also A. Andrewes, *The Greek Tyrants* 126.

54 Herodotus 6.4.

55 Herodotus 6.5.1–2.

56 6.5.3.

57 6.6.

58 *FGrHist* 532 F 43. Jacoby however prefers to date the attack in 490.

59 Herodotus 6.7.

60 Cf. Roebuck, 21–23.

61 Herodotus 6.8.2.

62 6.9.1.

63 6.12.3.

64 6.13.1.

65 6.14.2. For the course of the battle see also J. L. Myres, *Greece and Rome*² 1 (1954) 50–55.

66 6.15–16.1.

67 6.16.2.

68 6.17.

69 6.18.

70 6.19.2.

71 6.19.3.
72 A bronze Apollo was taken from the temple to Ecbatana: Pausanias 1.16.3, where 'Xerxes' is a mistake for 'Darius'. For a Milesian inscription on a bronze knuckle bone-weight found at Susa see Jeffery 334.
73 Herodotus 6.20.
74 Curtius Rufus 7.5.28–35.
75 Herodotus 6.20.
76 5.121.
77 6.22.2–23.6.
78 6.21.2. The title of the play is not known, but the Suda s.v. Φρύνιχος mention a play called *Just Men* or *Persians* or *Men in Council*, who were perhaps a chorus of Persian elders: see A. W. Pickard–Cambridge, *Dithyramb, Tragedy, and Comedy*[2] (Oxford 1962) 63 n. 3.
79 Herodotus 9.106.2–3.
80 Herodotus 9.104.
81 Cf. Jacoby, *Atthis* 357 n. 25. For the known names of the Milesian phratries see L. Robert, *Gnomon* 31 (1959) 673. Of them the Tylonii were perhaps descendants of the pre-Mermnad dynasts of Lydia, who were also called Heraclidae. The Lydian royal name Sadyattes is also found at Miletus in the list of Stephanephoroi (*Milet* 3 (Berlin 1914) No. 122 lines 55 and 108). Compare the Lydian Heraclidae in Colophon and Clarus [*ÖJH* 15 (1912) 46 No. 2 with *BCH* 18 (1894) 216 No. 3. See also L. Robert, *Rev. de Phil.* 10 (1936) 163 n. 6.].
82 Roebuck, *CP* 48 (1953) 10–12.
83 Herodotus 9.28.6 with 5.97.2. See also R. Meiggs, *CR* 14 (1964) 2–3.
84 Herodotus 9.28.2.
85 An attempt to create political unity in the revolt may perhaps be seen in the 'Panionian' coins of the early fifth century. These are staters with reverses having an incuse square divided into four squares. P. Gardner, *A History of Ancient Coinage* (Oxford 1918) 99, conjectured that each stater represents a month's pay of a sailor or marine. The coins for the revolt may all have been struck in one place, those having a Sphinx representing Chios, the foreparts of a winged horse Lampsacus, and the winged boar Clazomenae. [(Cf. C. Seltman, *Greek Coins* (London 1955) 87–89.) For the flying boar who once ravaged the land of the Clazomenians see Artemon 443 F 1.] However, Gardner's theory has not found wide acceptance amongst numismatists and the 'Panionian' coins may in fact all be Chian.

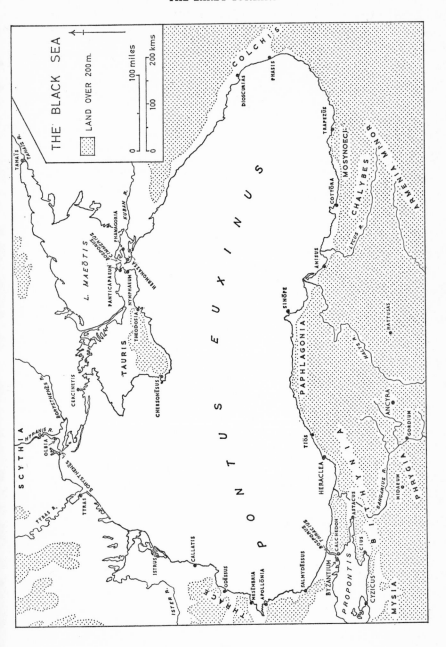

THE BLACK SEA

LAND OVER 200 m.

0   100   200 kms
0   100 miles

COLCHIS

PHASIS

DIOSCURIAS

TANAÏS
TANAÏS R.

KUBAN R.

CIMMERIUM
CORŌCONDAMĒ
PHANAGORIA

L. MAEŌTIS

PANTICAPAEUM
NYMPHAEUM

CHERSONĒSUS

THEODOSIA

TAURIS

CHERSONĒSUS

CERCINETIS

SCYTHIA

HYPANIS R.
OLBIA
BORYSTHENES R.

TYRAS R.
TYRAS

ISTER R.

ISTRUS

CALLATIS

ODĒSSUS
MESEMBRIA
APOLLŌNIA

SALMYDĒSSUS

THRACIA

BYZANTIUM
THRACIUS
BOSPORUS
CALCHEDON

PROPONTIS

CYZICUS

MYSIA

ASTACUS

CIUS

BITHYNIA

TIŌS

HERACLEA

SANGARIUS R.

PHRYGIA

GORDIUM

HIDAEUM

ANCYRA

HATTUSAS

HALYS R.

PAPHLAGONIA

SINŌPE

AMISUS

LYCUS R.

COTYŌRA

TRAPEZŪS

MOSYNOECI

CHALYBES

ARMENIA MINOR

ASIA MINOR

PONTUS EUXINUS

203

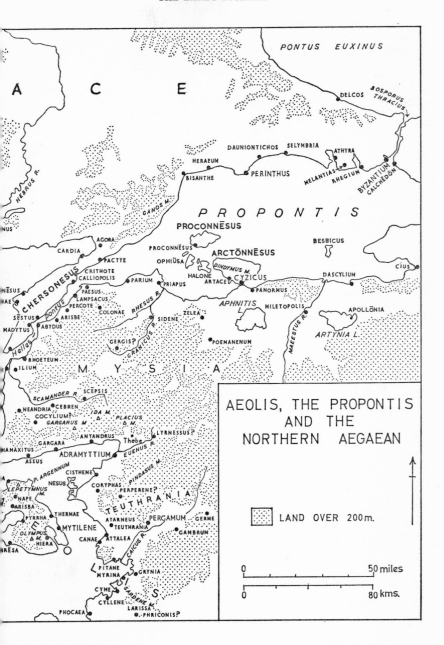

PONTUS   EUXINUS

A   C   E

BOSPORUS
THRACIUS
DELCOS

DAUNIONTICHOS   SELYMBRIA
HERAEUM   ATHYRA
BISANTHE   PERINTHUS   MELANTIAS   BYZANTIUM
                                        RHEGIUM   CALCHEDON

GANOS M.

P R O P O N T I S
PROCONNĒSUS

AGORA   BESBICUS
CARDIA   PROCONNĒSUS   ARCTŌNNĒSUS
        PACTYE   OPHIŪSA   DINDYMUS M.   CIUS
CRITHOTE   HALONE   DASCYLIUM
NĒSUS   CALLIOPOLIS   PARIUM   ARTACE CYZICUS
NAE   PAESUS   PRIAPUS   PANORMUS
LAMPSACUS   APHNITIS   MILETOPOLIS   APOLLŌNIA
PERCOTE   L.
SESTUS   ARISBE   COLONAE RHESUS R. SIDENE   ZELEA   ARTYNIA L.
MADYTUS   ABYDUS   MAESTUS R.
                 GERGIS   POEMANENUM
RHOETEUM   GRANICUS
ILIUM   M   Y   S   I   A

SCAMANDER R.   SCEPSIS
NEANDRIA   CEBREN   IDA M.   PLACIUS
COCYLIUM?   GARGARUS M.   D M.
GANGARA   ANTANDRUS   Thebe   LYRNESSUS?
HAMAXITUS   ADRAMYTTIUM   EUENUS R.
ASSUS
P. ARGENNUM   CISTHENE   PINDASUS M.
NESUS   CORYPHAS   PERPERENE?
LEPETYMNUS   M.
NAPE   TEUTHRANIA
ARISBA   THERMAE   ATARNEUS   PERGAMUM   GERME
PYRRHA   TEUTHRANIA
OLYMPUS   MYTILENE   CANAE   ATTALEA   CAICUS R.   GAMBRUM
HIERA
RESA   PITANE
MYRINA   GRYNIA
CYME
CYLLENE   LARISSA
PHOCAEA   PHRICONIS?

AEOLIS, THE PROPONTIS
AND THE
NORTHERN AEGAEAN

[dotted box] LAND OVER 200 m.

0   50 miles
0   80 kms.

IONIA AND THE

LAND OVER 200 m.

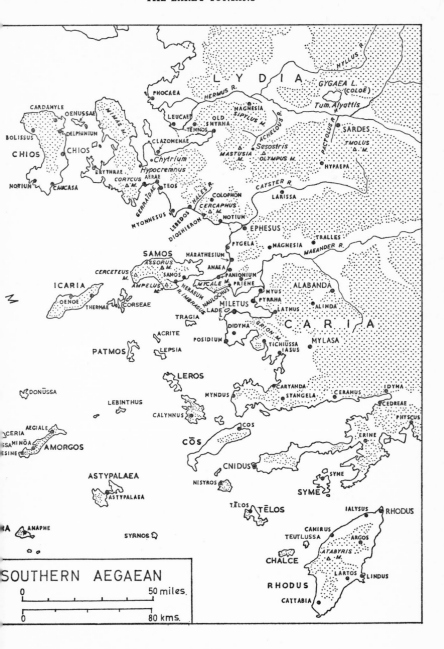

SOUTHERN AEGAEAN

0 ———————— 50 miles.

0 ———————— 80 kms.

Supplementary Notes

p. 18 A debate on the causes and date of the Trojan war will be found in *JHS* vol. 84, where J. L. Caskey clearly restates the arguments in favour of dating the fall of Troy VIIA in the middle of the thirteenth century BC.

p. 28 The diverse origins of the settlers at Teos are well illustrated by the titles of some of the pyrgoi or demesnes in the Tean countryside, which preserve the names of early colonists. Some of the names are Mycenaean, others heroic and Homeric, others again are Anatolian. See D. W. S. Hunt, *JHS* 67 (1947) 76 and T. B. L. Webster, *From Mycenae to Homer* (London 1958) 151.

p. 38 For the suggestion that there were Laconians amongst the settlers at Magnesia by the Maeander see F. Kiechle, *Lakonien und Sparta* (Munich 1963) 78 note 14.

p. 41 If by dating Homer and Hesiod four hundred years before his own day Herodotus (2.53.2) meant that they lived ten generations of 40 years before his time, then the poets may perhaps be dated about ten generations before *c.* 440 BC, i.e. in the second half of the eighth century BC: but the matter remains very problematical. Cf. Wade-Gery, *Poet* 89. Those who believe that the Lelantine war cannot be dated must ignore the argument from the war to Hesiod and Homer as presented here.

p. 48 I have deliberately avoided speculating upon the origin of the Ionian League and content myself with the observation that the southern Ionian cities are likely to have been founding members. Two northern members Phocaea and Chios joined relatively late, and the canonical number of twelve had been reached before Smyrna applied for admission. A good general account of the League is given by M. O. B. Caspari in *JHS* 35 (1915) 173–188.

p. 52 Phrygian dealings with the Greeks are well discussed by T. J. Dunbabin in *The Greeks and their Eastern Neighbours* (London 1957) chapter vi.

p. 55 The position of Old Eretria is uncertain; it may have been at Xeropolis or Levkandi between Chalcis and New Eretria. The settlement at Levkandi, which is being excavated by the British School at Athens, appears to have been abandoned towards the end of the eighth century BC, perhaps during the Lelantine war. *AR* 1965, Euboea and *ILN*, June 5, 1965, with Strabo 403 and 448.

p. 57 The earliest Chalcidian colonies may have been the closest to home: Ps.-Scymnus mentions Chalcidian occupation of Scyrus,

SUPPLEMENTARY NOTES

Sciathus, Icus and Preparethus. Bradeen in *AJP* 73 (1952) 356–380 usefully discusses early settlements in the Chalcidice.

p. 61 The historical background to Archilochus is examined by J. Pouilloux, N.-M. Kontoleon, D. Page and K. J. Dover in *Archiloque* (Fondation Hardt. Entretiens, Tome X. Geneva 1964).

p. 68 The placing of Cercinetis/Carcinitis assumed here is more likely than Kiepert's location, p. 203. See also Boardman *AR* 1963, 44

p. 79 The name *aeinautae* may well reflect the maritime interests of Miletus: Graham, *Colony and Mother City* (1964) 98.

p. 115 Professor H. T. Wade-Gery, with whom I have had a pleasant and profitable correspondence, tells me that he questions the alleged reading *Lu* — in the Nabun'aid — Cyrus chronicle. He also points out that the self-immolation of Boges on a pyre (Herodotus 7.107) tells against the theory that in Iranian religion fire was defiled when living humans were burnt upon it.

p. 124 The Naxian colossus in Delos is elegantly described by R. Pfeiffer in his *Ausgewählte Schriften* (ed. W. Bühler, Munich 1960) 55 ff.

p. 132 For some Eretrian laws of the sixth century BC see E. Vanderpool and W. P. Wallace, *Hesperia* 33 (1964) 381–391.

p. 151 An account of the architectural remains of the new Didymaion built in the early years of Persian control of Ionia is given by G. Gruben in *Jahrbuch d.d. Arch. Instit.* 78 (1963) 78–177. Like Quintus Curtius, the Suda s.v. Βραγχίδαι ascribe the destruction of the temple to 'Xerxes', but that seems to be a mistake for 'Darius'.

pp. 163–4 Thucydides' remarks about Carians in Delos are well discussed by A. M. Snodgrass in *JHS* 84 (1964) 113 ff.

p. 201 n. 33. S. Luria has looked for prehistoric forerunners of *molpoi* and *aisymnetai*: *Acta Antiqua* (Budapest 1963) 31–36.

I am grateful to my colleague Dr David Gooding for help in reading the proofs.

Naucratis, foundation, 72; Herodotus, 73; and Thales, 95
Navigation, 96
Naxos, colonies, 56; Aristagoras, 145; and Delos, 123; in Ionian migration, 26–27; Milesians and Erythraeans attack, 123; populism in, 125; quarries, 124; and Thasos, 61; tyranny in, 123 ff; and Ionian revolt, 145
Naxos in Sicily, 56
Neandria, 62
Neapolis in Thrace, 62
Neco, 73
Neleidae, flee from Pylos to Athens, 26; and Ionian tribes, 32; and civil strife in Miletus, 49 ff; in Iliad, 43; the Codrid branch in northern Ionia, 28–29; expelled from Miletus, 171
Neleus (or Neileos), founder of Ionian Miletus, 26; in Naxos, 26; his descendants, 50–51
Neriglissar, 190
Neuboule, 60
Nicandre, 124, 166
Nile, and Thales, 95; and Hecataeus, 136; battle on, 21; Greeks upstream, 73
Nostoi, 21, 42, 46

Oak, Battle at the, 84
Oasis, 74
Odessus, 69
Oenopion, 16
Ogenos, 94
Olen, Lycian poet, 58
Olympus, poet, 85
Onnes, 50–51
Ophioneus, 93
Oroetes, 130
Orestes, and Aeolian migration, 167
Otanes, 149; in Samos, 131

Pactyes, 117–118
Pallene, Battle of, 124
Pamphaes of Priene, 79
Panionion, and Melie, 48; Smyrna excluded from League, 47; and Ionian revolt, 148. See also Ionian League
Pantaleon, son of Alyattes, 78, 109
Panyassis, 25

Parium, 65–66
Paroemiac metre, 44–45
Paros, and Acanthus dispute, 59; archons in, 60; Archilochus on life in, 60; arbitration in Miletus, 80; trade, 134; and Thasos, 59 ff; and Ionian migration, 29
Patmos, 64
Pausanias, on Hyperboreans, 57; on Ionian migration, 26
Pazarlı, 66
Pedasa, 121
Pedieis, 182
Pelagon, hero, 165
Penthelidae, 86; and Aeolian migration, 36; and Sappho, 89
Perception, according to Xenophanes, 107; in Heraclitus, 141
Periander, and Arion, 86; and Sigeum, 87; and Miletus, 76
Perinthus, 65, 80
Perpherees, 58
Persians, rise of, 113; conquer Lydia, 114 f; conquer Ionia, 117 ff; imperial administration, 121 f; and Ionian revolt, 144 ff
Phanagoreia, 120
Phasis, 67
Pheidon of Kyme, 92
Pherecydes of Syros, cosmogony, 93–94; and Magnesians, 83; and Pythagoras, 93
Pherecydes of Athens, on Ionian migration, 26
Philistines, 20
Phitres (or Amphitres), 50–51
Phobius, 49
Phocaea, Adriatic exploration, 72; and Alalia, 119; originally Aeolian district, 25; her colonies, 70–72; navigators, 72, 179; and Ionian League, 29; and Naucratis, 73; Protogeometric pottery at, 25; tribes in, 34
Phocais, poem, 42
Phocians, in Phocaea, 28
Phocylides, 80
Phoebias of Samos, 126
Phoenicians, alleged secret books, 94; script, 41, 44; fleet at Lade, 150; navigation, 96; alleged presence in Thasos, 176. See also Carthaginians

Phratries, 30, 164; in the Aeolis, 38
Phrygians, invade Asia Minor, 19–20; their bronzework, 52; poetry and music, 45; dealings with Kyme, 52
Phrynichus, Athenian poet, 152
Phrynon, 87, 184
Phylai, Ionian, 31–33; in Lampsacus, 163; in Samos, 165
Phylaktes, in Kyme, 91
Pindar, on Ceos, 132; on Homer, 40; on Abdera, 193
Pindarus, Ephesian, 109
Pisander, settles Tenedos, 37
Pisistratus of Athens, and Delos, 124; and Homer, 46
Pittacus, title, 185; and Alcaeus, 86–87; legislation, 89
Pithecusae, 55
Piyamaraduš, 17
Ploutis, Milesian faction, 79
Poltymbria, 62
Polycrates, and Amasis, 128; two persons of the name ?, 194; rise of Samian tyranny, 125; navy, 127; Himerius on, 126; death, 130
Polymnestus of Colophon, 53
Poseidon of Helicon, 27–28; Homer mentions, 43
Poseidon Hippios, 60
Priam, 18
Priene, war with Lydians, 78; pro-Lydian party in, 182; position, 24; war with Samos, 83–84; Ionian founder, 27
Probouloi, 148
Procles, in Samos, 27
Proconnesus, 65–67
Prometheus of Kyme, 92
Promethii, 28, 123
Propontis, 65
Prostatai, at Naucratis, 73
Prytanis, in Miletus, 79
Psammetichus I, 72; II, 73
Pteria, 113; Battle of, 191
Pygela, 27, 38
Pylians, in Homer, 43; and Ionian migration, 26 ff
Pyramids, 90, 96
Pyrrha in Lesbos, 37, 42
Pytharchus of Cyzicus, 121

Pythagoras, boxer, 82
Pythagoras of Ephesus, 33, 78
Pythagoras of Samos, and Polycrates, 104; in Italy, 103; and Pherecydes Syrius, 93; his doctrines, 104–105
Pythermus of Phocaea, 117
Pythermus of Teos, 113

Rainbow, 106
Rameses III, 20
Red dye, 66, 132
Rhode, 71
Rhodes, 16
Rhodians, exploration by, 71–72; and Siris, 70
Rhodopis, 90
Rhoecus, 127–128

Sadyattes, Lydian notable, 79
Sadyattes, Lydian king, 75
Saioi, 61
Samos, and Minoan Crete, 15–16; Ionian settlement, 27; tribes in, 33, 165; trade with Levant, 64; and Lelantine war, 51; colonies, 64; war with Megarians, 80; settlers in Egypt, 73–74; war with Priene, 84; Protogeometric pottery in, 25; Samians in Crete, 129. See also Polycrates
Šandakšatra, 54
Sappho, her poetry, 89; and Rhodopis, 90; on poetry in Lesbos, 85; exile, 88; emotions of, 91
Sardis, falls to Cyrus, 114–115, 192; Ionians attack, 147; Protogeometric pottery in, 52; satrap at, 121; Greek architects at, 127–128
Sardinia, 84
Sarcophagi, 77
Sarpedon, 16
Satrapies, 121
Scepsis, 62
Scylax of Caryanda (or Myndus), 137, 145
Scyppium, 28
Scythians, 53, 67
Sestos, 62
Sibyls, 49, 143
Side, 64
Sigeum, 87

Volcanoes, 106

Welding, 180
Wine trade, 71, 73. See also Maroneia

Xenophanes, on coinage, 75; on Colophonians, 53; as historian,

135; theism,

Zancle, 56, 70
Zas, 93–94
Zeus the Liberator, 130